Pro PayPal E-Commerce

Damon Williams

Apress®

Pro PayPal E-Commerce

Copyright © 2007 by Damon Williams

ISBN-13 (pbk): 978-1-59059-750-7

ISBN-10 (pbk): 1-59059-750-8

Printed and bound in the United States of America 9 8 7 6 5 4 3 2 1

Lead Editor: Matthew Moodie
Technical Reviewer: Michael Blanton
Editorial Board: Steve Anglin, Ewan Buckingham, Gary Cornell, Jason Gilmore, Jonathan Gennick, Jonathan Hassell, James Huddleston, Chris Mills, Matthew Moodie, Dominic Shakeshaft, Jim Sumser, Matt Wade
Project Manager: Richard Dal Porto
Copy Edit Manager: Nicole Flores
Assistant Production Director: Kari Brooks-Copony
Production Editor: Laura Esterman
Compositor: Linda Weidemann, Wolf Creek Press
Proofreader: Lori Bring
Indexer: Michael Brinkman
Artist: April Milne
Cover Designer: Kurt Krames
Author Photo: George Lin
Manufacturing Director: Tom Debolski

Distributed to the book trade worldwide by Springer-Verlag New York, Inc., 233 Spring Street, 6th Floor, New York, NY 10013. Phone 1-800-SPRINGER, fax 201-348-4505, e-mail orders-ny@springer-sbm.com, or visit http://www.springeronline.com.

For information on translations, please contact Apress directly at 2560 Ninth Street, Suite 219, Berkeley, CA 94710. Phone 510-549-5930, fax 510-549-5939, e-mail info@apress.com, or visit http://www.apress.com.

The source code for this book is available to readers at http://www.apress.com in the Source Code/ Download section.

To Mom, Dad, and Nana

Contents at a Glance

Contents

Foreword

This is an exciting time for PayPal. Our business has grown exponentially over the past few years, and we see a tremendous future ahead. PayPal's developer community is an important part of our future and will be instrumental in helping PayPal be the global leader in online payments.

When you build PayPal into a website, you get much more than a payment processing service. Our commitment to providing the most secure payments platform in the world is why we employ a team of experts whose responsibility it is to stay one step ahead of fraudsters. And when problems do arise with a transaction, our dispute resolution tools and our customer support representatives help both buyers and sellers resolve issues in a professional manner.

With thousands of businesses turning to PayPal every week to meet their payment needs, the demand for developers with PayPal expertise grows greater each day. Resources such as *Pro PayPal E-Commerce* will help you make informed decisions when choosing the right payment solution for your or your client's business.

It is developers like you who will have the next brilliant idea for new, creative uses of the PayPal platform. We look forward to partnering with you on innovative, cutting-edge technologies that provide the best user experience for our customers around the world.

Rajiv Dutta
President, PayPal

About the Author

DAMON WILLIAMS has worked at PayPal since 2004, where he has specialized in making life easier for people trying to integrate PayPal into websites and applications. His background includes experience in software engineering, information architecture, community building, and publishing. Before working at PayPal, Damon spent five years as the publisher of *Feedback Magazine* in Austin, Texas, where he also moonlighted as a DJ and promoter. He currently manages PayPal's developer program, where he is building a global community for innovation and support on the PayPal platform. Damon holds a bachelor's degree in electrical engineering from the University of Texas at Austin.

About the Technical Reviewer

■**MICHAEL BLANTON** is the Senior Manager of Merchant Integration for PayPal Merchant Services and has been with the Merchant Services team for three years. During that time, he's provided technical consulting to partners such as Dell, Apple iTunes, Napster, and Chase Paymentech. He has also presented PayPal integration information at conferences and contributed to numerous open source projects based on Java technology. He has over eight years of experience in e-commerce consulting and over ten years of experience with online payments processing.

Acknowledgments

I would like to thank all of the people I have worked with during my first two years at PayPal. I wish I could list all the names, but the list would be too long and I would still probably leave some people out. Working at PayPal has been a tremendous learning experience, both personally and professionally.

Thank you to the following people for contributing to this book in the form of code, advice, images, support, or guidance: Yannick Bercy, Michael Blanton, Patrick Breitenbach, Dave Burchell, Paulam Chang, Jason Chow, Erin Curran, Matthew Dennison, Chris Hogben, Rachel Kumar, Tom Kutter, Alex Lange, Aaron Lee, Matt Lerner, George Lin, Michael Metzger, Margaret Morris, Laurie Redding, Colin Rule, Todd Sieber, Clarice Soloway, Brian Sparr, Mayumi Stroy, Karen Sweetland, Winston Toy, Vicki Vance, Tim Villanueva, Sam Wu, Harry Xue, and Gray Watson.

Thanks to the PayPal Merchant Technical Support team for your contributions to and continued support of the PayPal Developer Community.

Finally, thanks to everyone out there building websites, applications, and services that work with PayPal. Without you, there would be no need for this book in the first place.

Introduction

Who This Book Is For

This book is primarily for software developers. I assume you have a basic understanding of Internet technologies and programming techniques. Code samples are scattered throughout the text and are provided in numerous languages, so fluency in languages such as Java and PHP will help you get the most value from the book. All the code samples in this book, as well as additional code that isn't included in the text, are provided in the Source Code/Download section of the Apress website at `www.apress.com`.

If you are a business owner or entrepreneur with little to no programming experience, however, there is still a significant amount of information you can glean from these pages. While a good portion may be too technical for your interest, this book provides details on almost all PayPal technologies, and as such can give you a better sense of the type of work that would need to be done in order to integrate PayPal into your grand schemes, even if you ultimately won't be the one hacking out the code.

How This Book Is Structured

This book consists of nine chapters and an appendix. The sections that follow offer a general overview of the content.

Chapter 1: Introduction to PayPal

Chapter 1 provides background information about PayPal and introduces the notion of PayPal as a platform. Pre-integrated solutions are presented, as well as guidelines for how to choose the best PayPal solution to meet your needs. The context for the rest of the book is set in this introductory chapter.

Chapter 2: The PayPal Account

Chapter 2 takes a look at the PayPal account, a distinction that lies at the core of the PayPal system. It's what makes the connection between your email address and your bank account, and it allows you to configure the payment technologies that PayPal makes available. It's also through your PayPal account that you are able to generate reports that detail the success of your business.

Chapter 3: Basic Website Payments

Chapter 3 begins the inquiry into how PayPal can be used to accept online payments. PayPal's success can largely be attributed to its ease of use, and the options covered in this chapter are the source of that reputation. Later chapters cover more advanced technologies, almost all of which are not as simple to set up and manage as those covered in this chapter.

Chapter 4: Encrypted Website Payments

Chapter 4 takes the notions presented in Chapter 3 and extends them by adding an optional layer of security via public key cryptography. By using the techniques presented in this chapter, you can offer payment options on your website that are impenetrable by hackers and fraudsters.

Chapter 5: Postpayment Processing

Chapter 5 takes a look at what takes place after the transaction is complete. This chapter covers the popular Instant Payment Notification (IPN) and Payment Data Transfer (PDT) technologies, which you can leverage to improve the buyer experience and automate many aspects of your business.

Chapter 6: The PayPal API

Chapter 6 covers the publicly available functionality that PayPal exposes via its API interface. Both the traditional SOAP and the new Name-Value Pair (NVP) interface are covered. The API can be used to accept payments, send payments, and perform administrative duties such as issuing refunds and searching transaction history.

Chapter 7: Payflow Gateway

Chapter 7 covers the Payflow Pro and Payflow Link payment solutions that PayPal acquired with its purchase of the VeriSign Payment Services business in 2005. These gateway services can optionally work with an external processor (other than PayPal), to establish the Internet Merchant Account (IMA) necessary to process credit card transactions.

Chapter 8: Reporting

Chapter 8 presents the array of reporting functionality that PayPal offers. These primarily include the reports provided in the business-reporting portal; for Payflow merchants, this includes the reports provided in PayPal Manager.

Chapter 9: Managing Online Disputes

Chapter 9 discusses best practices for reducing your risk of becoming a victim to fraudulent transactions. This chapter also covers the PayPal Resolution Center, an area on the PayPal website where buyers and sellers can communicate and attempt to resolve disputes amicably.

Appendix: PayPal Reference

The appendix contains reference material that can be used during development to quickly look up the meaning of a particular variable or error code, for instance.

■ ■ ■

## CHAPTER 1

Introduction to PayPal

Since its launch in 1998, PayPal has grown faster than almost any other company in history in terms of both customer base and revenue. Over 100,000 people sign up for PayPal's service every day, more than $1,000 goes through the PayPal financial engine every second, and thousands of individuals and businesses from across the globe come to PayPal looking for a solution to meet their online payment needs. PayPal is now available in over 100 countries and 17 currencies, with even broader expansion planned for the future. PayPal is the world's fastest growing global currency exchange, and it is clear that PayPal is creating the new standard in online payments.

Yet despite these huge numbers, many people still think of PayPal primarily as the service they use to pay for items they buy on eBay. Awareness of PayPal as a robust, feature-rich payment service is surprisingly low, which can be partially attributed to the fact that many of PayPal's most powerful options are relatively new. This book is intended to not only provide technical integration assistance to developers, but also raise awareness of the full spectrum of the PayPal platform in the global community that PayPal serves.

Inside these pages, I have pulled together a look at the various PayPal options available. PayPal's system has experienced rapid growth over the years, with new acronyms, protocols, and features cropping up on a fairly regular basis. As a result, it can be difficult for someone working with PayPal for the first time to select the solution that will best solve the problem he or she is addressing. Indeed, there is often more than one approach to take that will solve the problem at hand.

In this introductory chapter, we'll take a broad view at the options that PayPal offers, and how to select the right solution for your needs. We'll also take a look at the variety of resources available for developers who wish to integrate PayPal, as well as some third-party products and services that can help you complete your project on time and under budget. But before we get there, we'll start things off by taking a look at some of PayPal's core benefits to merchants and consumers.

The PayPal Advantage

For the thousands of businesses opening an online storefront, PayPal is becoming less of a nice-to-have payment option and more of a must-have. The reasons described in the sections that follow are a few examples of why PayPal's value proposition to merchants is so compelling, and why both small and large businesses are turning to PayPal not only as a payment option, but also as a stand-alone payment solution.

Increased Sales

PayPal research shows that the more payment options you provide to customers, the more sales you will make. In fact, online merchants that add PayPal as a payment option see an average sales increase of 14%. The reason is simple: buyers love to use PayPal. With over 130 million accounts, there is a massive core group of loyal consumers that like to spend money online. PayPal users spent over $30 billion online in 2006, which represents more than 10% of all U.S. e-commerce.

Credibility

PayPal lends credibility to small businesses. By offering a payment service where customers don't have to submit their credit card number over the Internet, merchants can instill confidence in users who are hesitant to buy from a site that they may have never visited or even heard of before. The strength of the PayPal brand has made a difference in helping many new businesses get off the ground and establish themselves in a massive global online marketplace.

Security

PayPal offers a high level of security, which is increasingly important in a world where, in the United States alone, over 20 million identities will be stolen this year. Approximately 70% of all spoof email in the world is related to eBay or PayPal, most with the intention of stealing your personal information. This is why PayPal is committed to combating the legions of online criminals who constantly invent new strategies to steal credit cards, Social Security Numbers, and passwords. Online fraud and identity theft is itself a growing industry, which is why PayPal's security and fraud protection techniques—widely regarded as the best in the world—continue to be one of the most valued cornerstones of the company and a key value for merchants.

The Checkout Experience

Let's face it, the checkout process on many e-commerce sites is painful. Every new site you buy something from, it's the same procedure over and over again: Create an account. Create a new password. Enter billing information. Enter shipping information. Confirm everything, and then hope you can remember the password if you ever need to visit the site again. I'm amazed at how many high-volume websites completely drop the ball when it comes to the checkout process, and as a result suffer from reduced buyer conversion and lost sales.

With PayPal, the process is simplified. It's as simple as remembering your email address and password, something that people are used to doing on a daily basis on numerous websites across the Internet. With a few clicks, buyers can complete a transaction using the information stored in their PayPal account. Buyers get to skip the "wallet grab"—the physical reach for the wallet (or purse) to retrieve the physical payment card is actually a significant barrier that prevents many casual web shoppers from actually following through with a purchase.

Digital Money Platform

Many people are familiar with using PayPal to send money to a buddy or complete an eBay transaction, but the notion of PayPal as a digital money *platform* is likely not as clear to the average person. However, this is precisely what PayPal makes available. Through the use of the technologies described in this book, you can build just about any application that involves moving money, including sending, receiving, authorizing, refunding, searching, and more. While I imagine you are primarily interested in creating basic e-commerce store-fronts, there is a whole new realm of applications you can develop based on the unique functionality that the PayPal platform offers.

QUICK CASE STUDIES

MyStoreRewards and StubHub are two examples of applications that leverage the PayPal platform in creative ways. Since PayPal's platform allows for both the sending and receiving of money (including many administrative capabilities), these two companies were able to build business models that have led them both to great success. Perhaps reading about their strategies might spark some creative insights for your own website.

MyStoreRewards

MyStoreRewards offers a simple way for merchants to set up a rewards program on their website that will encourage repeat business in buyers by sending them cash back on purchases made with PayPal. For a small monthly fee, MyStoreRewards will give you a little snippet of HTML to place on your website that allows your buyers to sign up for your rewards program. Buyers then have incentive to return to your website in the future, because they will save money on repeat sales. MyStoreRewards handles the program registration and payouts, and allows merchants to customize several aspects of their rewards program, including the percentage of cash back they wish to award to buyers. Create your own rewards program today at www.mystorerewards.com.

StubHub

StubHub is an online marketplace where people can buy and sell tickets to concerts, sports games, and other events. By using PayPal's API, StubHub automates the payout of tickets sold by sellers, so that they can be instantly credited once the sale has been made. StubHub adds additional value by guaranteeing delivery of the tickets to buyers in time for the event, and even offers a few "last-minute ticket" physical pickup locations around the country. Powered by a passionate community of users, StubHub quickly rose to become the premier place to buy and sell tickets online. eBay thought highly enough of the StubHub marketplace to acquire the company for $310 million in January 2007. For more information (or to search for some concert tickets), check out www.stubhub.com.

Online commerce is still in its infancy. Companies such as eBay, Yahoo!, Skype, Amazon, and Google have staked out big chunks of real estate in the Internet landscape, but the truth is that many of the great innovations that will have an impact on the way we live our lives have yet to occur. Regardless of what these innovations accomplish, one thing that many are likely to have in common is the need to move money from one place to another. Money is the backbone of business, and even the flashiest web service mashups are likely not going to last long without a viable business model to back them up.

The days of relying solely on advertising revenue are behind us as well. Unless they attract huge volumes of focused traffic, companies that want to win in today's attention economy have to go beyond just attracting eyeballs—they must provide value to end users in the form of saving them time or money, or by providing a service that they cannot get elsewhere. Simplicity and convenience will also continue to play a crucial role in reaching broad adoption and rapid growth. Fortunately, PayPal offers both in spades.

When developers and entrepreneurs together have a broader understanding of PayPal's full capabilities, including its strengths as well as its limitations, we will see an exciting evolution of the types of applications and websites released with PayPal functionality built in. As long as PayPal stays true to remaining convenient and secure for the consumer, there will be a viable payments solution to serve that evolution for years to come.

PayPal and eBay

Many people's first encounter with PayPal comes via eBay, and it's widely known that the eBay marketplace provided fuel for the rapid growth of both PayPal accounts and payment volume. Upwards of 80% of U.S. eBay listings prefer PayPal as the payment method, and in most countries over half of PayPal payment volume is from eBay transactions. When PayPal enters a new country, it often leverages the headway that eBay has made there to rapidly register new accounts and grow in popularity. eBay and PayPal will forever be tightly coupled, and with good reason.

PayPal was acquired by eBay in October 2002. This was after eBay attempted to launch its own competing payments service called BillPoint. BillPoint ultimately was not well received by the eBay community, which much preferred to use PayPal. BillPoint soon fizzled out completely, joining the dozens of other services that have attempted to play in the online payments game and have since been left in PayPal's dust.

This section is the last time eBay will be mentioned in this book. There are dozens of other books available that can show you how to use eBay and PayPal together—that's just not what this book is about. My focus is on PayPal's merchant services solutions and how web developers can make sense of them. In other words, this book covers solutions for all of the off-eBay businesses that are turning to PayPal to meet the payment needs of their businesses.

Choosing the Right Solution

With all the features that PayPal offers, how do you know which is the right solution for you and your business? It's not always obvious, and in fact there is usually more than one way to meet your requirements. Some issues you should take into consideration are the complexity level you're willing to take on, whether you want the customer to pay on your website or PayPal's, and how much of a fee you are willing to pay.

Business owners have a lot on their minds, and they often rely on developers as knowledgeable experts in the area of online payment processing solutions. In a recent PayPal survey, 89% of developers polled responded that they were either the sole decision maker or highly influential in the process of selecting a payments provider. What does that mean for you if you're a developer? Essentially, you're often counted on for more than just your coding expertise. The more you know about the various PayPal payment options available to you, the better you will be able to serve your client or employer in recommending and implementing the right solution.

This section addresses the high-level options and presents some considerations you should be aware of before making your final selections.

Website Payments Standard

Website Payments Standard is the simplest of PayPal's solutions. Through the use of some basic HTML code, you can set up Buy Now payment buttons, donation buttons, recurring subscriptions, and even a simple shopping cart. If you're on a shoestring budget for a small business, then Website Payments Standard is the way to go. When a payment button is clicked by a buyer, your code directs the user to PayPal with an HTTP form post that contains the transaction details PayPal needs to complete the purchase. The buyer logs in at PayPal, approves the transaction, and voila!—money is moved. The user is then returned to a URL you specify in the button parameters (or the PayPal homepage if no URL is specified). For more information on Website Payments Standard, see Chapter 3.

Instant Payment Notification

If you want to step it up a notch, Instant Payment Notification (IPN) is useful if you know how to write code that creates HTTP requests and parses HTTP responses. With IPN, PayPal sends an HTTP post to a URL you specify every time a new transaction occurs or the status of a previous transaction is updated. This allows you to automatically update a database with the transaction details, send a customized order confirmation email message to the buyer, or perform other similar automated processes. The notification usually happens within a split second of the transaction completing, but on rare occasions IPN messages can be delayed for up to a few minutes. For more information on IPN, see Chapter 5.

Payment Data Transfer

When customers check out with their PayPal account, they can return to the seller's website when the transaction is completed (the exception to this is Express Checkout, as explained shortly). Payment Data Transfer (PDT) gives you the ability, through a series of secure HTTP posts, to immediately retrieve details about the transaction from PayPal so that you can display them to the customer when he or she returns to your website. It is a fairly simple feature that offers an incrementally improved user experience that can add that extra bit of professionalism to the finished product. For more information on PDT, see Chapter 5.

PayPal API

PayPal opened up some basic platform functionality to developers in 2004 with the release of the first version of the PayPal API. The API operates in a request/response format over a Secure Sockets Layer (SSL) connection. The first version of the API was based on SOAP web services, required client-side SSL certificates for authentication, and did not provide much in the way of development tools. This approach quickly proved to be too difficult for the average web developer. Over the past few years, though, software development kits (SDKs) for major development platforms have been released, the client certificates have been made optional, and a second interface based solely on HTTP has been developed. These improvements have lowered the barrier to entry for developing with the API, which in turn has opened the doors to innovation and integration to a much wider audience. For more information on the PayPal API, see Chapter 6. Two payment solutions offered by the API are discussed in the sections that follow.

Express Checkout

Express Checkout is PayPal's most powerful and flexible checkout option. It uses the PayPal API to offer the buyer a customized checkout experience that is an improvement over the Website Payments Standard process. Instead of checking out on the PayPal website, the buyer only visits the PayPal website to authenticate, confirm a shipping address, and choose a payment instrument. Then, the buyer is *sent back* to the seller's website to complete the transaction. The buyer actually clicks the final pay button on the merchant's website, not PayPal's. This is useful for merchants who want to offer upsells such as rush shipping and gift wrapping. With Express Checkout, the buying experience becomes a simple three-click process for the customer.

Website Payments Pro

Website Payments Pro is PayPal's most complete payment solution. Also based on the PayPal API, Website Payments Pro takes the power of Express Checkout and adds a second feature: the ability to process credit cards directly on the merchant website. This feature, known as Direct Payment, is currently offered in the United States and the United Kingdom. The customer enters his or her credit card details, gets an instant response, and doesn't even know that PayPal is involved in the transaction. Website Payments Pro opens up sellers to a higher level of risk, and it is up to sellers to secure their website to make sure they are not allowing customers' credit card data to be compromised. PayPal's Seller Protection Policy (SPP) doesn't cover these credit card transactions; rather, it covers only transactions where buyers pay with their PayPal accounts. There's also a monthly fee associated with Website Payments Pro, which is currently $20 (USD) per month.

Payflow Gateway

Similar to Website Payments Pro, the Payflow Gateway also processes credit cards directly on the seller's website. However, with the Payflow Gateway, you do not actually have to use PayPal to process the credit card. You can establish an Internet Merchant Account (IMA) with a bank and configure the Payflow Gateway to work with that account. Alternatively, you can choose PayPal to process these transactions instead of establishing a relationship with an external bank. From a developer's perspective, the integration is unique from other solutions, and different APIs and client toolkits are used. The gateway also comes with a separate suite of reports and fraud prevention tools that are not available with the other PayPal solutions. For more information on the Payflow Gateway, see Chapter 7.

Virtual Terminal

Virtual Terminal is a unique solution in that it doesn't require any development at all. It's essentially just a credit-card processing service you sign up for and then use to process credit cards via the Virtual Terminal web page, shown in Figure 1-1.

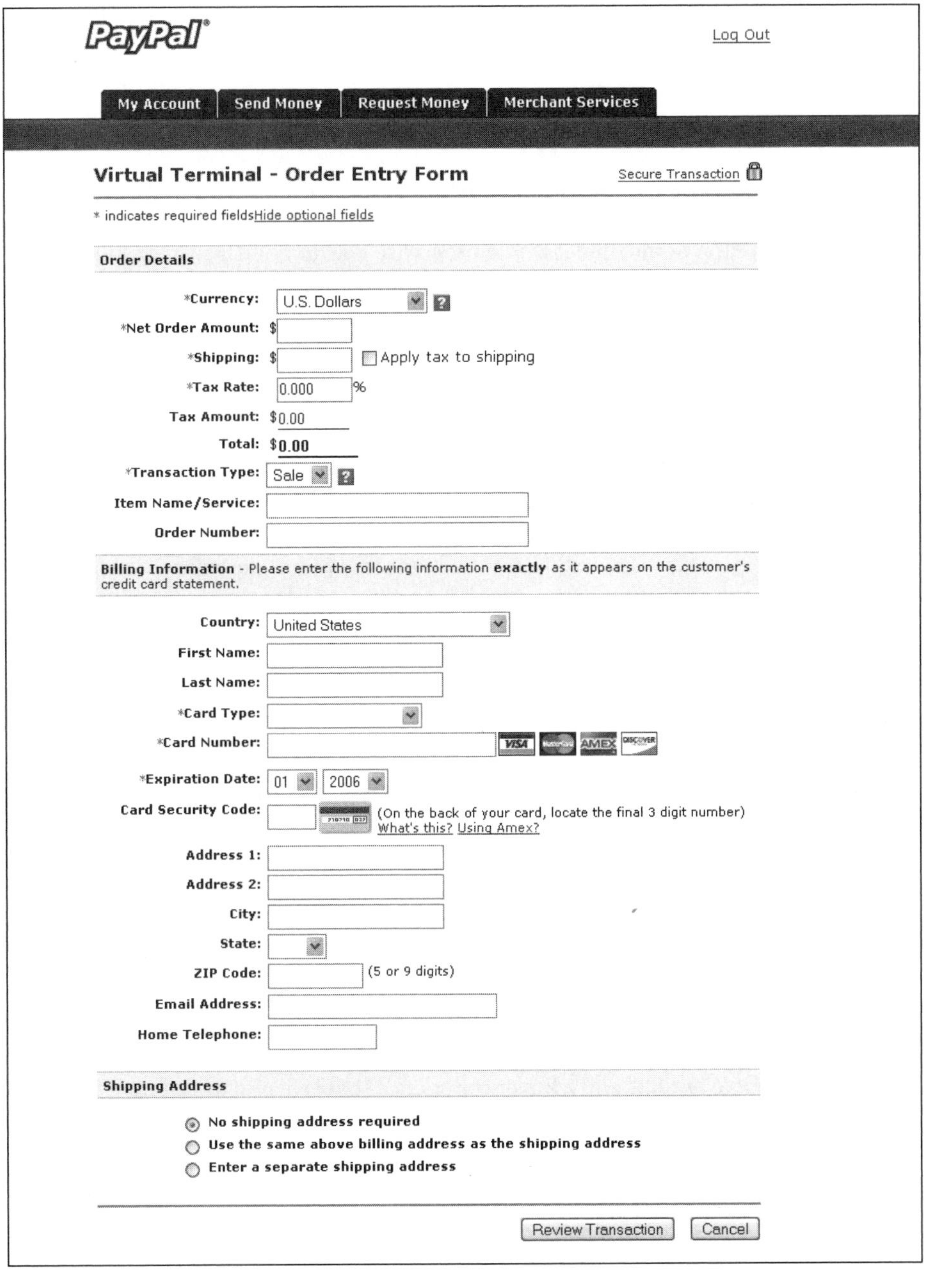

Figure 1-1. *PayPal Virtual Terminal*

Virtual Terminal is useful if you want to process credit card orders over the phone, by mail, or in person. The customer does not need a PayPal account; you just enter the credit card details into the web form and process it with the click of a button. The funds are deposited into your PayPal account, and the transaction is stored in your PayPal history for later use. I don't discuss Virtual Terminal anywhere else in the book, since this book is primarily for developers and there is no development involved with this feature. You just turn it on and use it. There is a monthly fee to use Virtual Terminal, which is currently $20 per month. For more information on Virtual Terminal, go to `www.paypal.com/vt`.

Pre-Integrated Solutions

The problem you're trying to solve as a merchant or as a developer has likely already been addressed before. In some cases, there's an out-of-the-box product or service that can get you up and running in a fraction of the time it would otherwise take to build a custom solution from scratch. The PayPal Solutions Directory, located at `https://solutions.paypal.com`, contains a lengthy directory of such services. I will highlight a few of the more popular and reliable solutions here.

Shopping Carts and Storefronts

Just want to sell some stuff? Don't have the budget or expertise to build a custom e-commerce website? A shopping cart service that is already pre-integrated to accept PayPal payments may meet your needs. For a monthly fee, many will even host your website as well, so you don't have to maintain a separate ISP relationship. The sections that follow describe some popular solutions you may want to consider.

eBay ProStores

eBay ProStores is a hosted service, meaning you don't have to download any software to get it running. You just sign up for the service and begin entering the items that you have for sale. You can customize the look and feel of your storefront, and your entire inventory is made available on the eBay website, so you tap into the massive eBay customer base. With solutions starting as low as $29.95 per month, this is a budget-conscious solution for businesses without a full-time developer on staff. For more information, visit `www.prostores.com`.

Yahoo! Merchant Solutions

Yahoo! provides a similar storefront solution to ProStores. For a monthly fee, you can have a custom website hosted on the Yahoo! servers that allows you to sell your items and make them available for shoppers searching on Yahoo!. The Yahoo! Merchant Solutions service has a different set of administrative options and a buyer experience that is distinctly different from that of ProStores, so if a hosted storefront solution is something you're interested in, I suggest taking a look at both ProStores and Yahoo! Merchant Solutions to see which one appeals to you more. For more information, visit `smallbusiness.yahoo.com/ecommerce`.

Mal's E-Commerce

Mal's e-commerce is a very popular and cost-effective shopping cart that is used by hundreds of websites across the globe. The basic service is free to use and is integrated with PayPal's standard checkout. The premium service (currently $8 per month) is integrated with Website Payments Pro and offers advanced shipping calculations that are fully integrated with UPS and USPS. It also allows for advanced graphical customization of checkout pages. Among the masses of shopping cart services available today, Mal's stands out as a leader. For more information, visit www.mals-e.com.

osCommerce

osCommerce is the most popular shopping cart software in the world. The fact that it's open source and free probably has something to do with that. It requires some technical skill on the part of the person implementing the site to set up and integrate it, and there are many plug-ins that can be added to the basic package to enhance the basic functionality of the cart. Several PayPal plug-ins are floating around out there, but I recommend using the official Website Payments Pro PayPal plug-in available for download on PayPal's Developer Central site at www.paypal.com/developer. For a simple way to customize the look of your osCommerce site, you can acquire a template from PixelMill (www.pixelmill.com) that can give a unique, professional look to your osCommerce-based website. For more information, visit www.oscommerce.org.

Digital Goods Delivery

Selling digital files such as e-books, software installers, or MP3s is a booming business, but there are many issues surrounding security and digital rights management that merchants must face in order to reduce their fraud losses. Services such as the two described in the sections that follow help merchants prevent their files from being stolen by malicious end users. They are both pre-integrated with PayPal and easy to set up and use. If you need to sell digital content on your website, consider one of these services.

E-Junkie

E-junkie is based on PayPal's IPN technology, which is discussed in detail in Chapter 5. You can either upload the files you are selling to E-junkie's servers or have E-junkie manage a remote download from your servers. You can specify the number of allowable downloads and an expiration date for the files, and you can brand your product download page to look similar to your website. E-junkie is also free for nonprofit organizations. For more information, visit www.e-junkie.com.

PayLoadz

PayLoadz is a well-established service that provides a simple method to sell downloads. Also based on IPN, it is a similar service to E-junkie with some key differences. PayLoadz offers bulk upload and FTP upload, as well as an API to access the service. Additionally, PayLoadz has a feature called AffiliateBuilder that will allow other sites to sell your digital content for a configurable commission rate. PayLoadz also has an entire storefront of digital files offered by its users where you can list your downloadable product for sale. For more information, visit www.payloadz.com.

Accounting and Invoicing

While some businesses use PayPal as their sole solution for both payment processing and order tracking, many use PayPal as just one piece of the bigger business management puzzle. Tools such as those described in the following sections may solve a particular need for you.

Blinksale

Blinksale offers a very user-friendly way to send invoices to customers that allow them to pay you via PayPal. Depending on the service level you subscribe to, you are limited to how many invoices you can send. Blinksale offers a slick way to customize the look of your invoice templates, and it can be automatically configured to send payment reminders and thank-you notes. For more information, visit www.blinksale.com.

Microsoft Office Accounting

Microsoft Office Accounting is a financial management program designed for companies with a couple dozen employees or fewer. It includes features such as payroll, invoicing, job tracking, and banking, plus full integration with Microsoft Office programs.

Two components of the package are integrated with PayPal. First, the invoices you send clients can include a link for them to submit payment directly to your PayPal account. Obviously, this allows your customers to pay you with a few clicks the instant they receive their invoice. Second, you can register to be able to process credit cards directly through the Microsoft Office Accounting application using PayPal's Website Payments Pro solution, without having to go through the trouble of configuring your API access or doing any other type of messy integration. In addition, you can download your completed payments data directly into the Microsoft Office Accounting tools, for a seamless merger with the rest of your accounting data. For more information, visit http://sba.microsoft.com.

PayPal to QuickBooks Link

Big Red Consulting has developed a tool that allows you to import your PayPal transactions into QuickBooks. If you use QuickBooks to manage your business, this product will generate a QuickBooks-compatible Interchange File Format (IIF) file from a comma-separated values (CVS) file of your PayPal account history that you can download from the PayPal website. The IIF file this product generates is much more robust than the IIF file you can have PayPal generate for you. For more information, visit www.bigredconsulting.com/aboutebaylink.htm.

Developer Resources

This book goes into a good level of detail on the options available to PayPal developers. Additionally, there are a number of online resources, described in the following sections, where you can get specific PayPal information, the latest versions of SDK downloads, recent news and announcements, and technical support for helping find an answer to a particular question.

Developer Central

Developer Central is the portal from which you can access all PayPal developer resources. It's the starting point for developers on the PayPal website. You can create an account on Developer Central if you want to use the PayPal Sandbox to test out your applications. I definitely recommend checking into Developer Central and creating an account today. For more information, visit `https://developer.paypal.com`.

Integration Center

PayPal's Integration Center contains technical documentation, reference materials, and resources that you should consult when looking online for information. The Integration Center's knowledge base contains answers to several hundred common questions and offers a useful search function. The site provides overviews of PayPal's different technologies, downloads for the various PayPal SDKs, and the latest versions of all PayPal PDF documentation. And if you have a question that you just can't find the answer to, you can file a ticket on the Integration Center that will be answered by one of PayPal's Merchant Technical Support staff. For more information, visit `https://www.paypal.com/integration`.

PayPal Developer Community

The PayPal Developer Community is a hub of activity that is visited by hundreds of developers every day. The discussion forums are an extremely popular destination where developers communicate with fellow developers about common interests and questions. The site is regularly visited by PayPal experts who can help you find answers to your questions. Additionally, this site contains the PayPal Developer Blog, where I or other PayPal folks post news, announcements, events, and some other random thoughts. Status on the PayPal live and testing systems is also available on the community homepage, so if you start receiving errors all of a sudden, you can check this page to see if a temporary site outage has occurred. For more information, visit `http://paypal.lithium.com`.

Solutions Directory

The Solutions Directory lists third-party products and services that work with PayPal. Primary among the listings are the numerous shopping cart services available that are pre-integrated with PayPal payments. For many merchants, simply choosing a shopping cart that already works with PayPal is easier than hiring a developer to build a custom solution. Additionally, there are several other categories where you may find a solution that can help you meet your business needs. These include digital goods delivery, IPN tools, affiliate program services, and membership systems. For more information, visit `https://solutions.paypal.com`.

PayPalTech

PayPalTech contains useful example code and scripts that can generate code that is customized for your website. This is a good site to find solutions to common tasks such as finding Perl code to make an API call or writing a basic IPN script. The site is maintained by PayPal employees. For more information, visit `http://paypaltech.com`.

PayPalDev.org

Before the PayPal Developer Community was launched, this site was the main place to go to get community support for PayPal issues. These forums have been up for a long time and have archived information on just about any PayPal topic you can think of. Many PayPalDev.org members have been contributing and supporting developers for many years. For more information, visit `www.paypaldev.org`.

Summary

As mentioned previously, PayPal has grown faster than almost any other business in history and continues to expand at a breakneck pace. With a vision to become the global standard in online payments, PayPal is taking on the dirty work of integrating its service with local banking establishments, currencies, and standards from countries around the world. It's clear that millions of buyers prefer the simplicity and security that PayPal offers. While eBay remains very important to the continued growth of PayPal, it's from eBay where a great deal of exciting progress is being made. That's also the segment of PayPal's business that this book addresses.

PayPal does much more than just process payments. Improvements in areas such as reporting, fraud prevention tools, seller protection policies, dispute resolution processes, and API functionality continue to push the envelope in terms of offering a complete, end-to-end digital money platform. Once you get beyond the basics, though, things can get confusing in a hurry. Depending on what you're trying to accomplish, there is likely more than one way to approach the solution. This book will help you make sense of the various options and enable you make solid decisions when designing your website or application.

PayPal has the potential to both shake up and galvanize the commerce industry and enable new possibilities for global payments. The ability to send money to anyone or buy something from someone anywhere on the planet at any time is a powerful concept. We're still a few years away from being there, but the infrastructure is being put in place to allow for this level of scalability.

The next chapter is where we start digging into the details. We'll start by taking a look at the heart of the PayPal system: the PayPal account.

CHAPTER 2

■■■

The PayPal Account

At the core of the PayPal system lies the notion of a *PayPal account*. With a PayPal account, you can store money; send and receive money; link to your bank accounts, credit cards, and mobile devices; and do many other things. Anyone with an email address can freely create a PayPal account, and there are over 120 million PayPal accounts in existence today. That's more accounts than American Express and Discover combined! PayPal accounts are growing at a tremendous pace, as Figure 2-1 illustrates.

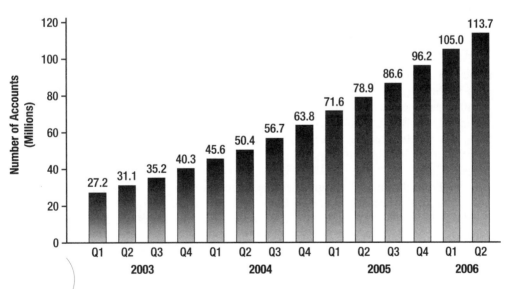

Figure 2-1. *Growth of PayPal accounts*

This chapter discusses everything related to a PayPal account. While at first glance a Pay-Pal account can appear fairly simple and straightforward, under the hood there are dozens of options that alter the way your PayPal account behaves. Understanding what all the options are and how to set them can save you headaches down the road. This chapter covers the following account-related topics:

- Account types

- Sandbox testing accounts

- Transaction fees

- Account status

- Countries where PayPal is allowed

- Currencies that PayPal works with

- Account profile settings

Account Types

PayPal offers three types of accounts to meet the needs of the different types of users: Personal, Premier, and Business. It's free to sign up for any of the three account types, but the fees and features associated with each are different. This section describes the basic differences among the account types.

Additionally, PayPal offers developers a testing environment known as the Sandbox. You can create a Sandbox account that is a Personal, Premier, or Business account, and it behaves just like a regular PayPal account except that no real money is used. For the purposes of this book, Sandbox accounts will be used throughout for all example code provided.

Personal Account

The most common type of account is a *Personal account*. A Personal account is useful for people who don't sell a lot of things online, and who use their PayPal account mainly for buying stuff or sending and receiving money between friends and family. One advantage of a Personal account is that, when you do need to accept money, it is free to do so, whereas the other types of PayPal accounts charge you a transaction fee to accept money. To open a Personal account, you need to provide only your name, address, phone number, and email address.

PayPal limits the amount of money you can receive with a Personal account. For example, the limit for U.S. accounts is $500 per month at the time of this writing. This limit is reset monthly on the anniversary of your account creation date. If you receive payments in excess of the monthly limit, you must upgrade to a Premier or Business account before accepting the payment. If you wish to maintain your Personal account status, you must deny any payment that pushes you over the limit.

Premier Account

The next step up from the Personal account is the *Premier account*. This type of account is useful if you use your PayPal account to sell things or otherwise accept money, because with a Premier account, other PayPal account holders can pay you with a credit card. With a Personal account, other PayPal account holders can only pay you with an eCheck or from funds in their PayPal account balance. Premier accounts also have access to PayPal's customer service department, seven days a week, and Premier accounts can use the PayPal Shopping Cart to sell products and services on their website. Finally, with a Premier account, you gain access to the PayPal application programming interface (API), which allows developers to create applications that programmatically interact with PayPal's financial platform within external code. Chapter 6 discusses the PayPal API in great detail.

Business Account

The *Business account* has all the features of the Premier account, and it includes other benefits, including the ability to operate under your business's name (with a Premier account, you do business under your personal name), access PayPal's business reporting tools, and configure your account so that other employees can access the account and perform a limited set of operations (see the "Multi-User Access" section later in this chapter for more information). Finally, you must have a Business account in order to apply for PayPal's Website Payments Pro payment solution. For serious businesses, the Business account is the way to go.

Sandbox Account

A *Sandbox account* is a Personal, Premier, or Business account that is created within PayPal's testing environment, known as the Sandbox. A Sandbox account is used for testing purposes. It is a fully functional PayPal account, with one major distinction: all the money is fake. You can safely test your code in Sandbox accounts without having to worry about using real money.

The sections that follow describe how to create and use Sandbox accounts. All of the examples in this book use the Sandbox, and it's a good practice to test your code without risking any actual funds. As you read through this section, you should create your own Sandbox accounts to test your PayPal code. You will need two Sandbox accounts: a Business account and a Personal account. Before you can create Sandbox accounts, though, you must first create a Developer Central account.

Creating a Developer Central Account

Sandbox accounts are created on PayPal's Developer Central website, located at `https://developer.paypal.com`. Before you can create a Sandbox account, you must create a Developer Central account. Then you can create as many Sandbox accounts as you like. Take the time now to create a Developer Central account, if you have not done so already.

■**Tip** Developer Central uses cookies to remember returning client sessions. If you ever have trouble logging in to your Developer Central account, clear all of your browser cookies. This fixes a majority of Developer Central login problems.

Once you have logged in to your Developer Central account, you can create your first Sandbox account by clicking the Sandbox tab on the Developer Central homepage, and then clicking the Create Account link located on the Sandbox page. You are encouraged to use a fictitious email address when you create Sandbox accounts, to avoid confusion between your

Sandbox accounts and your live accounts. A sample Developer Central account with a Business Sandbox account and a Personal Sandbox account is shown in Figure 2-2.

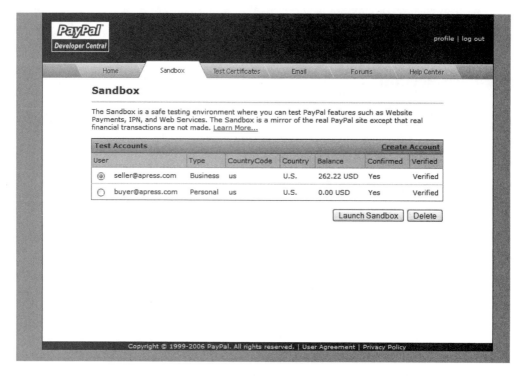

Figure 2-2. *A Developer Central account with two Sandbox accounts*

When creating your Sandbox accounts, you can use fake contact information. Once you verify your Sandbox account (see the next section for instructions), PayPal will prompt you to add a bank account to your Sandbox account. PayPal will generate a fake bank account number for you to use. Just accept the number and continue, and then make sure to confirm the bank account by clicking the Confirm Bank Account link on your Account Overview page. The usual random deposit is skipped for Sandbox accounts, and you can confirm your bank accounts automatically. You can also add credit cards to your Sandbox accounts in this manner. PayPal will generate fake credit card numbers for you to use, and they are automatically confirmed.

Accessing Sandbox Email

All email messages sent to Sandbox accounts can be accessed only in the Email section of Developer Central. Sandbox account emails are never sent to an actual email address. Even if you use a real email address to create a Sandbox account, you will never receive an actual email from the Sandbox. This is meant to reduce confusion, so that you never mistake your real PayPal account emails with your Sandbox account emails. All Sandbox email is accessed by clicking the Email tab in Developer Central. A sample Developer Central account with Sandbox email messages is shown in Figure 2-3.

■Note The location of Sandbox email is one of the most commonly overlooked features of the Sandbox. Remember that you will never receive an actual email for a Sandbox account. All email messages for Sandbox accounts are accessed in the Email section of Developer Central.

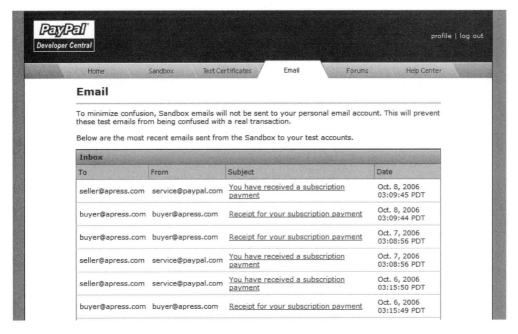

Figure 2-3. *A Developer Central account with Sandbox email messages*

The first time you deal with the Email tab in Developer Central will be to access the email message to confirm your new Sandbox account. This email contains a URL in the body of the message that you need to copy and paste into a web browser in order to complete the confirmation process. You'll be prompted for your password, and then taken into your Sandbox account. Since I recommend using a Sandbox account to test all of the features discussed in this book, it's a good idea to take a few moments now to confirm your Sandbox accounts before moving forward.

Creating Test Credit Card Numbers

One question that pops up regularly is how to get a test credit card number to use in the Sandbox. Unfortunately, PayPal does not offer a standard set of test credit card numbers to make testing easy. The only way to do this is to create a second Sandbox account, go through all the steps of verifying your email address and confirming your bank account, and then add a credit card to that Sandbox account.

When you click to add a new credit card to the account, PayPal generates a sample credit card number for you. Write down this credit card number, along with the expiration date and card verification value (CVV) code. Another inconvenience that you have to deal with is that once you've added this credit card, you can't go back later and get the credit card number. PayPal will hide all but the last four digits. So, be sure to write down the credit card number, expiration date, and CVV code from the page where PayPal initially generates the number for you—it's the only shot you'll get.

Finally, be aware that PayPal generates only Visa numbers. You can't test MasterCard, Discover, American Express, and so forth in the Sandbox.

Other Developer Central Features

Developer Central has other tabs besides the Sandbox and Email tabs.

The Test Certificates tab is used to access API certificates for your Sandbox accounts. You'll use this section only if you're developing with the PayPal API (see Chapter 6 for more information).

There is also a Forums tab to access the PayPal Developer Community website, www.pdncommunity.com. This site provides the latest announcements from PayPal that are relevant for developers, and there are always hearty discussions going on in the discussion forums, which are regularly monitored by PayPal staff to help developers get their questions answered.

Finally, the Help Center tab contains a number of useful links, including access to PayPal's PDF documentation.

Retrieving Your Developer Central Password

If you already have a Developer Central account but have forgotten your password, you can click a link on Developer Central to have your password reset. It's a fairly straightforward process, with one twist. Oftentimes developers will never see the email containing the link to reset their password. If this happens to you, check your spam or junk email folder. Many spam filters are very sensitive to any PayPal email message, due to the huge amount of spoof messages floating around. PayPal Developer Central messages are often picked up by spam filters as a possible fake message and are subsequently sent to the junk mail folder.

PayPal Transaction Fees

It is always free to send money using PayPal, but receiving money is a different story. There is no cost associated with accepting money through a Personal account, but you are restricted by the monthly receiving limit as described earlier in this chapter. Premier and Business accounts are subject to the fees in Table 2-1 for all received payments. As you can see, the fees you are charged decrease as the amount of monthly revenue you receive increases.

Table 2-1. *PayPal Transaction Fees (U.S. Accounts)*

Monthly Revenue	Transaction Fee
$0–$3,000	2.9% + $0.30
$3,001–$10,000	2.5% + $0.30
$10,001–$100,000	2.2% + $0.30
> $100,000	1.9% + $0.30

If your PayPal account receives $3,000 or more in monthly revenue, you can qualify for the better rate. It won't happen automatically, though; PayPal won't lower your transaction rate until you fill out an online application and are approved for the lower rate. You must have a sustained history of high transaction volume to get the lower rate.

Account Status

Your PayPal account has a status associated with it, and depending on the status of your account, you are or aren't able to perform certain actions. The various PayPal account statuses are described in the sections that follow.

Verified

A PayPal account is Verified when the owner has validated the primary email address and confirmed a bank account associated with the account. An account can also become Verified if PayPal confirms the owner's identity in some other way. Essentially, being Verified means PayPal knows that you are who you say you are. When your account becomes Verified, PayPal offers you a Verified seal that you can place on your website. When users click the seal, they are taken to a page on the PayPal site that confirms that you own a Verified account. Having this seal on your website is a positive sign to potential buyers that you have passed PayPal's verification standards.

Confirmed

A PayPal address is Confirmed when the owner has validated the account's mailing address. If you sell goods online and accept payment through your PayPal account, it is recommended that you only ship to a buyer's Confirmed address. This is not a requirement to be covered under PayPal's Seller Protection Policy (SPP), however. Since some PayPal users are unable to confirm their address, the requirement to be covered under the SPP is that you ship to the address on the Transaction Details page, regardless of whether or not that address is confirmed. You can have multiple addresses attached to a PayPal account, each of which can become Confirmed.

Limited

PayPal regularly screens all accounts to look for unusual activity. Examples of unusual activity are sudden changes in transaction volume, potential violations of the User Agreement, or the use of incorrect bank routing information. If your account becomes Limited, notification is sent to your account's primary email address, and the next time you log in to your PayPal account, you will receive instructions on how to lift the Limited status from your account. This usually involves faxing over some official documentation that proves that everything that's been going on with your account is OK. When your account is Limited, you do not have access to certain functionality, such as the ability to send and receive funds.

Closed

Closing your PayPal account means you can't use it ever again. There is no way to reopen a PayPal account once it's been closed, and there is no real benefit to closing a PayPal account. So make sure you really want to close your account before doing so!

Countries

At the time of this writing, PayPal is available in 103 countries, with plans to continue expanding into more countries in the future. The functionality available to users is different depending on the country. Table 2-2 lists all of the countries where PayPal is currently available and the functions users in each country can perform with their PayPal account.

Table 2-2. *Countries Where PayPal Is Available*

Country	Withdraw to Local Bank Account	Withdraw to U.S. Bank Account	Withdraw by Check	Send Money
Andorra	—	—	—	X
Anguilla	—	—	—	X
Argentina	—	X	X	X
Aruba	—	—	—	X
Australia	X	X	X	X
Austria	X	X	X	X
Bahamas	—	—	—	X
Bahrain	—	—	—	X
Barbados	—	—	—	X
Belgium	X	X	X	X
Bermuda	—	—	—	X
Botswana	—	—	—	X
Brazil	—	X	X	X
British Virgin Islands	—	—	—	X
Brunei	—	—	—	X
Canada	X	X	X	X
Cape Verde	—	—	—	X
Cayman Islands	—	—	—	X
Chile	—	X	X	X
China	X	X	X	X
Costa Rica	—	X	—	X
Croatia	—	—	—	X
Cyprus	—	—	—	X
Czech Republic	X	X	X	X
Denmark	X	X	X	X

Country	Withdraw to Local Bank Account	Withdraw to U.S. Bank Account	Withdraw by Check	Send Money
Dominican Republic	—	X	—	X
Ecuador	—	X	X	X
Estonia	—	—	—	X
Falkland Islands	—	—	—	X
Fiji	—	—	—	X
Finland	X	X	X	X
France	X	X	X	X
French Guiana	X	X	X	X
French Polynesia	—	—	—	X
Germany	X	X	X	X
Gibraltar	—	—	—	X
Greece	X	X	X	X
Guadeloupe	X	X	X	X
Hong Kong	X	X	X	X
Hungary	X	X	X	X
Iceland	—	X	—	X
India	—	X	X	X
Indonesia	—	—	—	X
Ireland	X	X	X	X
Israel	—	X	—	X
Italy	X	X	X	X
Jamaica	—	X	X	X
Japan	X	X	X	X
Jordan	—	—	—	X
Latvia	—	—	—	X
Liechtenstein	—	—	—	X
Lithuania	—	—	—	X
Luxembourg	—	—	—	X
Malaysia	—	X	—	X
Maldives	—	—	—	X
Malta	—	—	—	X
Martinique	X	X	X	X
Mayotte	—	—	—	X
Mexico	X	X	X	X
Namibia	—	—	—	X
Netherlands	X	X	X	X

Continued

Table 2-2. *Continued*

Country	Withdraw to Local Bank Account	Withdraw to U.S. Bank Account	Withdraw by Check	Send Money
New Caldonia	—	—	—	X
New Zealand	X	X	X	X
Norway	X	X	X	X
Philippines	—	—	—	X
Pitcairn Islands	—	—	—	X
Poland	X	X	X	X
Portugal	X	X	X	X
Qatar	—	—	—	X
Reunion	X	X	X	X
Russia	—	—	—	X
Samoa	—	—	—	X
Singapore	X	X	X	X
Slovakia	—	—	—	X
Slovenia	—	—	—	X
Solomon Islands	—	—	—	X
South Africa	—	—	—	X
South Korea	X	X	X	X
Spain	X	X	X	X
St. Helena	—	—	—	X
St. Kitts and Nevis	—	—	—	X
St. Lucia	—	—	—	X
St. Pierre and Miquelon	—	—	—	X
Sweden	X	X	X	X
Switzerland	X	X	X	X
Taiwan	X	X	X	X
Thailand	X	X	X	X
Togo	—	—	—	X
Tonga	—	—	—	X
Trinidad and Tobago	—	—	—	X
Tunisia	—	—	—	X
Turkey	—	X	—	X
Ukraine	—	—	—	X
Uruguay	—	X	X	X
United Arab Emirates	—	—	—	X
United Kingdom	X	X	X	X
United States	X	X	X	X

Country	Withdraw to Local Bank Account	Withdraw to U.S. Bank Account	Withdraw by Check	Send Money
Venezuela	—	X	—	X
Vietnam	—	—	—	X
Wallis and Futuna Islands	—	—	—	X

Currencies

One of PayPal's advantages is its capability to transact business in multiple currencies, which greatly increases the convenience of doing business internationally. PayPal will automatically handle the conversion of funds from one currency to another (for a fee), so you don't have to worry about maintaining account balances in each currency. PayPal also offers you the ability to withdraw multiple currency funds to your local bank account with no exchange costs. PayPal currently supports the following currencies:

- American dollar (USD)
- Canadian dollar (CAD)
- Australian dollar (AUD)
- Euro (EUR)
- Pound sterling (GBP)
- Yen (JPY)
- Swiss franc (CHF)
- Czech koruna (CZK)
- Danish krone (DKK)
- Hong Kong dollar (HKD)
- Hungarian forint (HUF)
- Norwegian krone (NOK)
- New Zealand dollar (NZD)
- Polish zloty (PLN)
- Swedish krona (SEK)
- Singapore dollar (SGD)
- Thai baht (THB)

Account Settings

You can set a number of preferences in your PayPal account. You access these preferences by logging in to your account and clicking the Profile subtab on the Account Overview page (see Figure 2-4). Depending on your account type, some settings may not be available. A Personal account has the least number of settings available, and a Business account has the most. This section describes all settings that are available within the PayPal Profile.

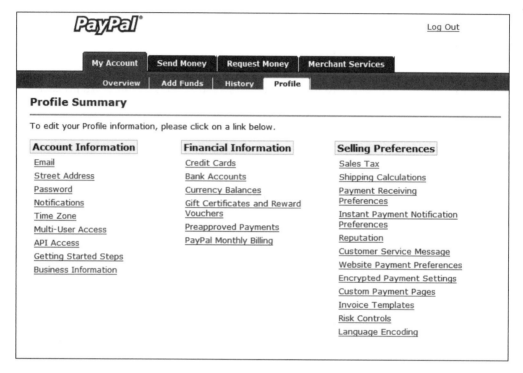

Figure 2-4. *The PayPal Profile settings page*

Account Information

Account Information settings manage your basic account information. The sections that follow describe what you can manage in each area.

Email

You can attach up to eight email addresses to your PayPal account. The Email section of your Profile is where you add additional email addresses, and it's also where you select the primary address. When PayPal sends an email notification to you, it sends the email to your primary address. If you use Multi-User Access for your account, this is the area where you specify which email address is the Administrative address for the account.

Street Address

In the Street Address section of your Profile, you enter in the various physical locations that you use. You can enter multiple addresses, but only specify one address as your official home address and one address as your official business address. Each address can become Confirmed by following the usual steps for confirming an address.

Password

The Password section of your Profile is where you can update the password used to log in to your PayPal account. Your password should generally not be based on a word that can be found in the dictionary, and it should contain one or more special characters, such as a number or other keyboard symbol. This helps increase the security of your password, to prevent anyone from accessing your account without your permission. In the Password section, you can also update the two security questions used to validate your identity to PayPal in case you forget your password or need to contact customer service for any other reason.

Notifications

In the Notifications section of your Profile, you can specify when and how you want PayPal to email you. When you first create your PayPal account, your account is configured with some default values for certain email notifications, such as to receive an email whenever you send or receive money. You can disable these notifications, but it is not recommended. You can also add notifications to receive email about PayPal third-party promotions, PayPal policy updates, auction seller tips, updates from the PayPal Developer Network (PDN), and more. You can also specify whether you want to receive email notifications in HTML or plain text format.

Tip The Notifications section of your Profile is where you register to receive DevTalk, PayPal's email newsletter for developers. DevTalk contains announcements and information that are relevant to developers of all skill levels, as well as promotional offers from PayPal partners. If you are a developer involved with building websites at any level, I encourage you to sign up to receive DevTalk.

Since PayPal is the most spoofed company in the world, you should always take steps to ensure an email you receive from PayPal is legitimate. See the "Recognizing a Spoof Email" sidebar to educate yourself on some red flags that you should be aware of when trying to determine if an email that claims to be from PayPal is legitimate.

RECOGNIZING A SPOOF EMAIL

PayPal is the most spoofed site in the world, for obvious reasons. Every day, thousands of fraudulent emails claiming to be from PayPal are sent to unsuspecting individuals, but these emails are actually sent by fraudsters who hope that the recipient will believe the email is legitimate and provide the sender with the username and password to the recipient's PayPal account. Once a fraudster has access to someone's PayPal account, he or she has direct access to the PayPal customer's bank accounts and other financial records.

Here are some red flags to watch out for when you receive an email that claims to be from PayPal:

- *Generic greeting*: Official PayPal emails will always address you by your first and last name. An email that begins with "Dear PayPal member," or something similar, is fraudulent.

- *False sense of urgency*: Spoof emails will attempt to trick you by saying that a certain action must take place ASAP, or by a certain date.

- *Fake links*: Spoof emails will almost always have a URL for you to click that will take you to a page that looks just like the PayPal homepage. If the link looks suspicious, don't click it. You should only ever enter your password on a web page that begins with the URL https://www.paypal.com.

- *Request for personal information*: An official email from PayPal will never ask you for any personal information, such as your PayPal account password, contact information, or financial information.

- *Insecure URL*: Any URL that asks you for personal information should begin with https://. If "http" is not followed by "s", the site is not secure, and you should not enter any personal information.

- *Pop-up boxes*: PayPal never uses pop-up boxes in email notifications.

- *Attachments*: PayPal never includes attachments in email notifications.

The following image shows an example PayPal spoof email that contains many of the red flags just listed. If you receive an email that you believe to be fraudulent, forward it to spoof@paypal.com.

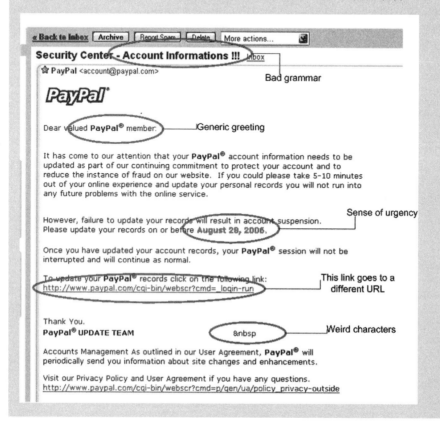

Time Zone

The Time Zone section of your Profile is where you specify the time zone you live in. This ensures that the times for your transactions are stored correctly in the PayPal system.

Multi-User Access

Multi-User Access is a feature that is only available to Business accounts. It is useful if you want to provide access to your PayPal account to multiple people, but allow them to perform only specified actions once they are inside your account. For example, you may want to provide access to someone in your shipping department to view the shipping addresses for completed orders, but you may not want to give that person access to add a bank account or send money from your account.

The following sections describe how to set up and use Multi-User access.

Creating an Administrator

To set up Multi-User Access, you must first specify a single administrator who will grant permissions to other users as well as receive notifications for all other users' activity on the account. It is required that this address be different than the email address that receives payments for the account, so if you have only one email address attached to your PayPal account, you will first need to add a second email address. Once you have added that additional email address, you can specify it as the administrative email address for Multi-User Access.

Adding Users

Once you have specified an administrator for Multi-User Access, you can begin adding additional users. You create a user by specifying the person's first and last name, and creating a *user ID* that the person will use to log in to your account, as well as a password. The user ID is not an email address, but simply a string between 10 and 16 characters in length that contains only English and German letters and numbers. No special characters are allowed, and the user ID is not case sensitive. The administrator should tell users what their user ID and password is, and inform them that they will not log in to the PayPal account with an email address, but instead with this user ID.

Specifying Privileges

The administrator has fine-grained control over which permissions to grant the user. The following list outlines the permissions that an administrator may grant a user:

- *Send Money*: Send money from this account to another.

- *Request Money*: Request money from another user to be sent via PayPal.

- *Add Funds*: Add funds to the PayPal account via an attached bank account.

- *Refunds*: Refund a previous payment transaction.

- *Withdraw Funds*: Withdraw funds to an attached bank account.

- *Cancel Payments*: Cancel a pending payment from the account.

- *View Balance*: View the balance of the account.

- *View Profile*: View details on the Profile tab.

- *Edit Profile*: Edit details on the Profile tab.

- *Settlement Files & Scheduled Downloads*: Access settlement files and scheduled download logs via direct HTTP post. For more information on using these features, see Chapter 8.

- *Authorization & Settlements*: View and capture transaction authorizations.

- *Use Virtual Terminal*: Process credit card transactions in real time via your PayPal account. (You must be approved for Virtual Terminal.)

- *Discuss Account with Customer Service*: Contact PayPal customer service to discuss account issues.

API Access

PayPal's API allows developers to leverage PayPal's payments platform in their own applications by remotely calling PayPal operations from within their own code. The API is covered in detail in Chapter 6. This section of your Profile allows you to request API credentials, which are used to identify your API calls to PayPal.

Business Information

The Business Information section of your Profile is where you update information about your business, such as the contact information, category of business, average monthly volume, and when the business was established. The one item you cannot change is your business name. For security reasons, PayPal does not allow you to update the business name once it has been initially set up. There's a web form you can submit to make a change if you make a typographical error, but you cannot automatically change the business name through the Profile section of your PayPal account, so make sure you get it right the first time!

Financial Information

This section describes your PayPal account's financial information settings.

Credit Cards

The Credit Card section of your Profile allows you to manage the credit cards associated with your PayPal account. You can add multiple credit cards to your account, but one credit card will always be flagged as the primary card to be used. Each credit card may go through a confirmation process, called the Expanded Use Enrollment Process, in order to validate that you are in fact the owner of the card. The Expanded Use Enrollment Process involves making a small charge to your credit card and including a four-digit Expanded Use number that will appear on your statement. If you have online access to your credit card account, you should be able to view this charge and retrieve the Expanded Use number within three or four business days. If you don't have online access, you have to wait for your next paper statement to come in the mail.

This section of your Profile also lets you specify if you want to require someone to log in before using one of your credit card numbers to pay. Some sellers let you check out and pay with PayPal without logging in to your PayPal account, but this is an extra layer of security PayPal offers to make sure that only you use your credit card number to check out.

Bank Accounts

The Bank Accounts section of your Profile allows you to manage the bank accounts associated with your PayPal account. You can add multiple bank accounts to your account, but one bank account will always be flagged as the primary bank account to be used. For each account, you specify the bank name, whether it is a checking or savings account, the bank routing number, and the account number.

Whenever you add a new bank account, PayPal takes specific steps to confirm that you are the owner of the bank account. PayPal accomplishes this by its unique "random deposit" process. PayPal will put two random deposits, each between $0.01 and $0.99, into your account within two to three days of you entering in the bank account information. Once you receive these deposits, you confirm the bank account by logging in to your PayPal account and entering the amounts of the deposits. Once your bank account is confirmed through this method, you can use it to add and withdraw funds to and from your PayPal account.

Currency Balances

PayPal offers support for 17 currencies, listed previously in the "Currencies" section. Your PayPal account can have a separate balance for each type of supported currency. While it is not required to have a balance in Euros to make a transaction with a user whose primary currency is Euros, you have the option to maintain a separate balance just for Euro-based transactions. The Currency Balances section of your Profile allows you to open and close balances in multiple currencies, as well as transfer funds between currencies. Be aware that PayPal does charge an exchange rate fee for transferring between currencies.

Gift Certificates and Reward Vouchers

If you have a Premier or Business account, PayPal allows you to create gift certificates to offer on your website. It's free to create PayPal gift certificates, and this is a great way to help increase sales on your website. It's extremely easy to create a gift certificate, and you can customize it in numerous ways to make it unique to your website.

Through the Gift Certificates and Reward Vouchers section of your Profile, you can create gift certificates as well as view a report to see which gift certificates have been redeemed and which have not. PayPal offers a form that allows you to configure the gift certificate you would like to create, including options such as the currency and amount of the gift certificate, as well as settings that control the appearance of the gift certificate, such as its color and button style. Then PayPal generates some HTML code for you to copy and paste into your website to easily make your gift certificates available for new customers.

Preapproved Payments

PayPal offers select businesses the option to create flexible billing arrangements with their customers. These arrangements involve the creation of a billing agreement between the business and a customer that, once accepted, allows the business to bill the customer's PayPal account on an as-needed basis. One example of this is Apple iTunes. If you are an iTunes customer, you can choose PayPal as your payment option and accept the iTunes Billing Agreement. Then Apple can take money from your PayPal account as you shop for music with iTunes, and you do not need to log in to your PayPal account to approve every purchase.

The Preapproved Payments section of your Profile lists the companies with which you have billing agreements established. In this section, you can view the billing agreements you have with each company, edit the funding sources you use with each agreement, and cancel an agreement at any time if you no longer wish to maintain the billing agreement with the company.

If you want to offer a Preapproved Payments arrangement on your own website, you must contact a PayPal account manager to see if you qualify for this feature.

PayPal Monthly Billing

The PayPal Monthly Billing section of your Profile lists the agreements you have with PayPal that allow PayPal to bill you on a monthly basis. Currently, the only agreement that qualifies for this is the monthly fee that PayPal charges for use of the Direct Payment credit card processing API, which is included as part of Website Payments Pro. That fee is currently $20 per month, and it can be canceled by accessing this section of your Profile. If you do not have any monthly billing arrangements with PayPal, this section will not appear in your Profile.

Selling Preferences

This Profile section describes the settings available to you regarding the preferences for using your PayPal account to sell goods or services.

Sales Tax

The Sales Tax section of your Profile allows you to set a sales tax rate for a particular geographic region that will be applied to all payments sent to you from your customers' PayPal accounts. You can specify a different tax rate for each of the 50 U.S. states, and also for each country. You can also choose to apply the sales tax to either the sum total of the items purchased or the sum total of the items plus the shipping and handling fees.

■Note If you sell a specific item that requires a special tax rate (or no tax at all), you can override your Profile-based tax settings by passing in a special tax variable in the form data you post to PayPal when initiating the checkout.

Shipping Calculations

In the Shipping Calculations section of your Profile, you can specify shipping charges that will automatically be applied to certain types of PayPal purchases. PayPal will add shipping charges to purchases made through the PayPal Shopping Cart, Buy Now buttons, and Donations. PayPal will *not* add shipping charges to payments made with PayPal Subscriptions and Recurring Payments, Winning Buyer Notification, or Instant Purchase on eBay listings.

You can specify different shipping preferences for each type of currency: you can choose to charge a flat amount based on the total amount of purchase, or you can choose to charge a percentage of the total amount of purchase. Once you've selected the method of shipping costs, you can specify the various levels of shipping costs and the price ranges for which each level applies. Figure 2-5 shows the screen where you specify the price ranges and the associated shipping cost for each range.

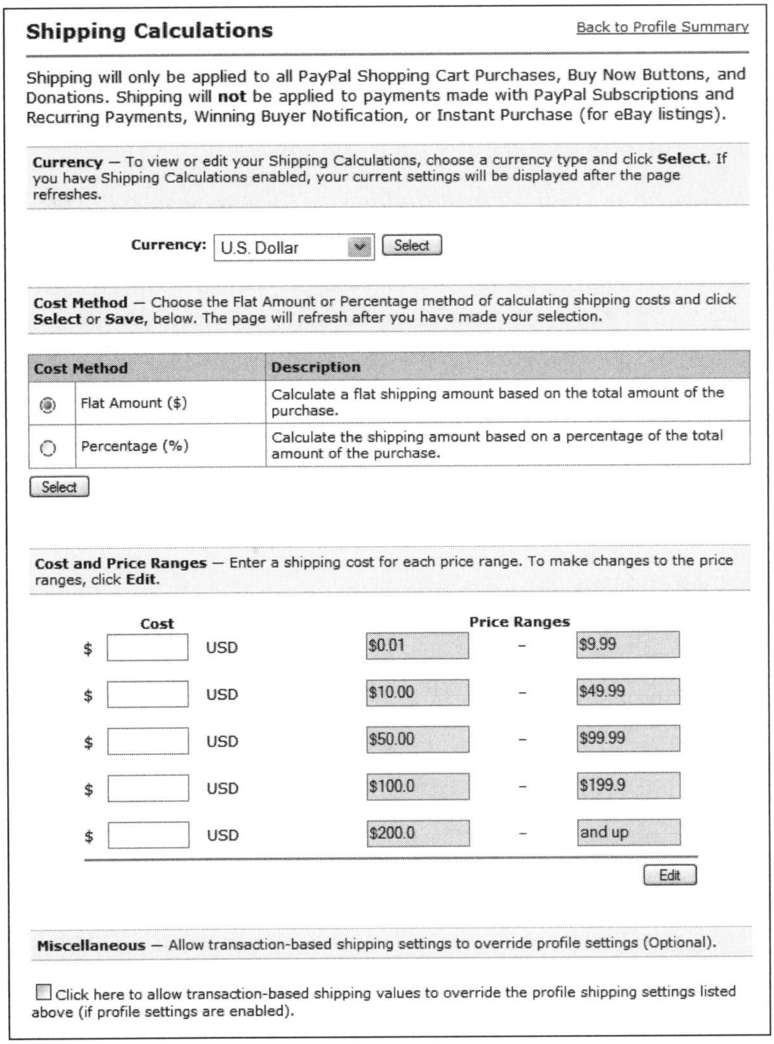

Figure 2-5. *Specifying shipping costs*

There is also a setting in the Shipping Calculations section of your Profile that, if enabled, allows you to override the values listed in this section on a per-transaction basis, if you have an item that requires special shipping charges. This is done by passing in the new shipping value in the form data that you post to PayPal when initiating the checkout.

Payment Receiving Preferences

The Payment Receiving Preferences section of your Profile allows you to configure some specific PayPal options that allow you to further customize your customers' buying experience. You can configure the following options in this section of your Profile:

- *Block payments from U.S. users who do not provide a Confirmed Address.*

- *Block payments sent to me in a currency I do not hold.* You can choose to block payments sent to you in a currency you do not hold, or you can choose to convert them to U.S. dollars.

- *Block accidental payments.*

- *Block payments from users who have non-U.S. PayPal accounts.*

- *Block payments from users who initiate payments from the Pay Anyone subtab of the Send Money tab.*

- *Block payments from users who pay with eCheck for website and Smart Logo payments, or German bank transfer for all website payments except eBay.* You can require customers to pay with eCheck for website and Smart Logo payments.

- *Add Instructions to Seller.* You can choose whether to offer your customers the ability to send you specific instructions when placing an order.

- *Credit Card Statement Name.* You can specify the name that will appear on your customers' credit card statements when they pay you with a credit card.

Instant Payment Notification Preferences

PayPal's Instant Payment Notification (IPN) allows you to automate certain aspects of your business by enabling a server-to-server communication to automatically take place whenever you receive a PayPal payment or whenever a status changes occurs on a transaction. This section of your Profile allows you to turn on IPN and specify the URL to which PayPal posts the notifications. For more information on IPN, see Chapter 5.

Reputation

Similar to eBay's notion of a user's feedback score, you can earn a reputation in the PayPal system through your *reputation score.* Your reputation score indicates the number of unique verified PayPal members who have paid you. Your score is updated 30 days after a transaction takes place, to ensure that your reputation reflects successful exchanges. Your score is displayed on your Account Overview page, next to your Account Status. The Reputation section of your Profile allows you to cap this number at 1,000, if you would like to do so for security reasons.

Website Payment Preferences

The Website Payment Preferences section of your Profile allows you to configure a number of PayPal features that you can use to further customize a customer's buying experience. The features that are configured through this area of your Profile are as follows:

- *Auto Return*: When enabled, Auto Return will send customers back to your website immediately following payment completion. When Auto Return is disabled, customers will need to click a button to return to your website.

- *Payment Data Transfer*: When Payment Data Transfer is enabled and implemented correctly, customers will be able to view details of their just-completed transaction after they are returned to your website following their checkout on the PayPal site. For more information on Payment Data Transfer, see Chapter 8.

- *Encrypted Website Payments*: For added security, you can choose to block payments that originate from nonencrypted HTML buttons. For more information on Encrypted Website Payments, see Chapter 7.

- *PayPal Account Optional*: When this option is enabled, your customers do not have to have a PayPal account in order to pay you through the PayPal website. They will be given the option to create a PayPal account, but if they choose not to, they can still submit payment by entering their credit card details.

- *Contact Telephone Number*: When this option is enabled, your customers will be prompted to include a telephone number where they can be reached to discuss details of the transaction. You can make this field required, optional, or not include it at all.

Encrypted Payment Settings

Through PayPal's Encrypted Website Payments (EWP) feature, you can encrypt the code in your HTML buttons so that a fraudulent third party is unable to modify information contained in the code, such as item prices and quantities. In the Encrypted Payment Settings section of your Profile, you can download the PayPal public certificate, which is needed to encrypt your code. You can also upload your public certificate to the PayPal site, which uses it to verify the digital signature that you used when creating the encrypted button code. For more details on EWP, see Chapter 4.

Custom Payment Pages

You can customize the checkout screens that your customers see in order to match the style of your website. In the Custom Payment Pages section of your Profile, you can create new page styles and specify settings such as the image users see at the top of the pages, the background color for the pages, and the border colors. You can create and maintain multiple page styles, but only one style at a time can be the primary style used. Every account comes with a default style: the traditional blue-and-white pages that PayPal customers are used to seeing.

Invoice Templates

PayPal offers an easy way to create and send itemized invoices to your customers via email. In the Invoice Templates section of your Profile, you can create templates that contain pre-populated data for invoices that you commonly send out to multiple customers. This time-saving measure prevents you from having to type in the same invoice information every time you want to send a new invoice.

Risk Controls

PayPal Risk Controls allow eligible sellers the ability to set their risk preferences to accept or decline payments based on certain criteria. Before using Risk Controls, you must accept a user agreement that explains the terms under which you use the controls. The types of controls available to you are explained in the sections that follow. In addition to enabling you to configure these settings, the Risk Controls section of your Profile also allows you to search for payments that were declined or accepted and flagged for risk by your Risk Control settings.

Country Monitor

The Country Monitor control allows you to specify which countries you will and will not accept payments from. You can also choose to accept payments from certain countries, but have PayPal send you a special notification whenever such a payment occurs.

Maximum Amount

The Maximum Amount control allows you to specify a maximum amount for any PayPal payment you receive. You can apply this maximum to all PayPal payments or only payments made from customers with an unconfirmed U.S. address. That option gives you added protection, since PayPal's address verification checks help to reduce fraud. For transactions above the maximum amount you specify, you can choose to deny the transaction, accept the transaction, or accept the transaction but receive special notification when it occurs.

Direct Payment/Virtual Terminal

The Direct Payment/Virtual Terminal control allows you to specify settings that control whether credit card payments made through PayPal's Direct Payment or Virtual Terminal products are accepted or denied.

Language Encoding

The Language Encoding section of your Profile allows you to select the language used on your website. This setting determines the encoding used on the payment buttons used to send data to PayPal. Currently, there are six options for this value:

- Western European languages (including English)
- Chinese (traditional)
- Chinese (simplified)
- Japanese
- Korean
- Russian

Summary

This chapter was all about the PayPal account. It provided an overview of the different types of PayPal accounts, and the various features and settings associated with each one. You learned which countries and currencies that currently work with PayPal and how to set up Sandbox testing accounts through Developer Central (`https://developer.paypal.com`). Remember when working with Sandbox accounts, if you are having trouble logging in to Developer Central, then clear the cookies on your browser. Also remember that you will never receive an actual email for a Sandbox account; these accounts will always only be accessed via Developer Central. It's amazing how many questions come in to PayPal technical support on these two topics alone.

PayPal offers a multitude of configuration options through the Profile section of an account, and you examined the various options and what they all mean. From basic contact information, to your bank account and credit card information, to preferences you can set for specifying selling preferences, you can fine-tune your account to meet the needs of your business, no matter how large or small.

Now that you know all about PayPal accounts, it's time to start looking at what you can actually do with them. In the coming chapters, you'll get your hands dirty with the technology behind PayPal and explore all the things you can do to help buyers and sellers make secure online transactions. You'll start with the simple, straightforward standard payment options that have been around for ages, and then progress through the more advanced APIs that PayPal offers developers.

CHAPTER 3

■■■

Basic Website Payments

Accepting payments on a website with PayPal is as simple or as complex as you want to make it. At the basic level, though, setting up an e-commerce site with PayPal is very straight-forward and requires only a working knowledge of the website's HTML code in order to be successful. Thousands of websites around the globe have used the technology outlined in this chapter to process millions of dollars in online transactions. These options will likely continue to remain PayPal's most popular choices, due to their simplicity.

This chapter covers the basic HTML payment options, collectively called Website Payments Standard:

- Buy Now button for single-item purchases

- Donations for charity payments

- Subscriptions for recurring payments

- PayPal Shopping Cart for multi-item purchases

- Cart Upload for submitting third-party shopping cart contents

When a quick and easy solution is needed, Website Payments Standard is the way to go. To make things even easier, PayPal also offers an area on its website that generates all the HTML code for you, as well as offers you the ability to encrypt the buttons if you want to provide an added layer of security to your website. The encryption is performed through a PayPal technology known as Encrypted Website Payments (EWP). EWP, which is discussed in full detail in Chapter 4, prevents a fraudster from modifying the details of your button code before the data is sent to PayPal.

In this chapter you'll learn how to automatically and manually generate the code you need to successfully process payments through PayPal.

Website Payments Standard

When PayPal rolled out its Website Payments Pro payment solution in 2005, the company took the existing basic payment options and collected them under the name Website Payments Standard. The way in which you integrate Standard and Pro is very different: Standard is generally much easier to use, but it doesn't offer as much flexibility as Pro. Pro requires API programming ability and increases integration complexity (see Chapter 6 for more details).

With Website Payments Standard, you give buyers the ability to pay you by leaving your site and completing the transaction on the PayPal website. Your customer is then (optionally) returned to your website after the transaction is complete. While some might say that you should never have your customer leave your website, PayPal users are accustomed to the basic PayPal checkout flow and assume they will return to your site after they complete their purchase. In general, the business advantages to offering the PayPal payment option outweigh any disadvantages inherent with redirecting users away from your site.

Figure 3-1 shows the basic checkout flow for Website Payments Standard transactions.

Figure 3-1. *The checkout flow for Website Payments Standard*

The Buy Now Button

PayPal's ubiquitous Buy Now button can be found on thousands of websites worldwide. It's accessible and easy to use, so as a result, PayPal has seen rapid adoption of this technology around the globe. The Buy Now button is the best solution to implement when you are selling individual items on a website, and you do not need the advanced functionality that a shopping cart offers.

A Sample Button

Let's dive right in and take a look at some HTML for a Buy Now button. Just reviewing Listing 3-1 should give you a sense of how simple it would be to modify this for your needs.

Listing 3-1. *Buy Now Button Example Code*

```
<form action="https://www.paypal.com/cgi-bin/webscr" method="post">
  <input type="hidden" name="cmd" value="_xclick"/>
  <input type="hidden" name="business" value="seller@apress.com"/>
  <input type="hidden" name="item_name" value="Red Jacket"/>
  <input type="hidden" name="item_number" value="7601"/>
  <input type="hidden" name="amount" value="125.00"/>
  <input type="hidden" name="no_shipping" value="2"/>
  <input type="hidden" name="no_note" value="1"/>
  <input type="hidden" name="currency_code" value="USD"/>
```

```
<input type="hidden" name="bn" value="PP-BuyNowBF"/>
<input type="image" src="https://www.paypal.com/en_US/i/btn/x-click-but23.gif"➥
    border="0" name="submit"➥
    alt="Make payments with PayPal - it's fast, free and secure!"/>
<img alt="" border="0" src="https://www.paypal.com/en_US/i/scr/pixel.gif"
    width="1" height="1"/>
</form>
```

■Note If you want to test the code in Listing 3-1 with a Sandbox account that you created in the last chapter, make sure you have confirmed your account by opening the account verification email located in the Email tab of Developer Central (`https://developer.paypal.com`).

As you can see, the entire button is wrapped in a `<form>` element, which posts the payment information to PayPal at the URL `https://www.paypal.com/cgi-bin/webscr` when this link is clicked. If you inspect the code, you will notice a number of hidden variables with corresponding values. Here are the most important variables:

- `business`: The email address of the PayPal account selling the item

- `item_name`: The name of the item for sale

- `item_number`: An identifier you can use to track an internal inventory number

- `amount`: The price of the item

- `currency_code`: The currency of the value specified in `amount`

- `image`: The URL of the button's image

By modifying the values of these variables, you can adapt the code in Listing 3-1 to create a payment button for your website. It's that simple!

Testing a Buy Now Button

To test your Buy Now button, just save it as an HTML file on your computer. When you open the file with a web browser, you should see your button. Clicking the button will take you to the PayPal Sandbox, where you can log in using the Personal account you created in the previous chapter. Complete the checkout flow, and you will see the funds appear in your Business account.

If you pay with an eCheck in the Sandbox, obviously the check will not clear on its own since it's fake money to begin with. So in order to clear eCheck transactions in the Sandbox, you must log in to the buyer's Sandbox account, find the transaction in your Account History, and then click to view the details of the transaction. At the bottom of the transaction details for the bank transfer are links to clear the eCheck and to have the eCheck be denied (see Figure 3-2).

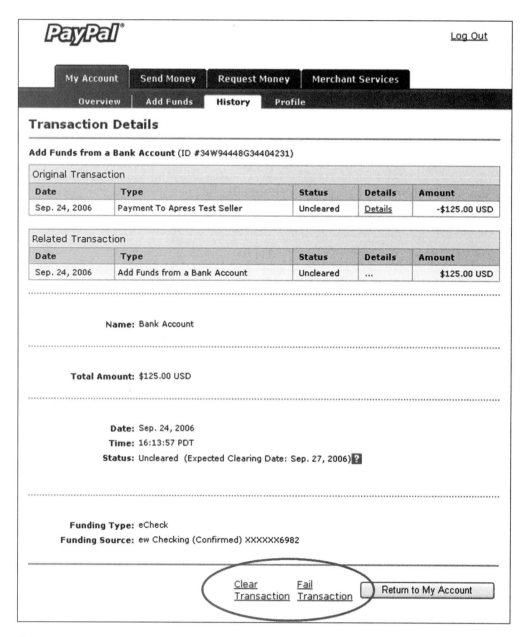

Figure 3-2. *Location of links to clear or deny pending eCheck transactions in the Sandbox*

Button Factory

PayPal provides a place on its website where you can enter some basic information about the product or service you're selling and have the HTML code generated for you. Then, all you have to do is copy and paste that code into your website. This site is commonly called the Button Factory, although the actual page doesn't display that name anywhere. To get to the Button

Factory, type the following URL into your browser: https://www.paypal.com/us/cgi-bin/
webscr?cmd=_web-tools (note that you must be logged in to your PayPal account to access
this page).

Figure 3-3 shows the first page of PayPal's Button Factory.

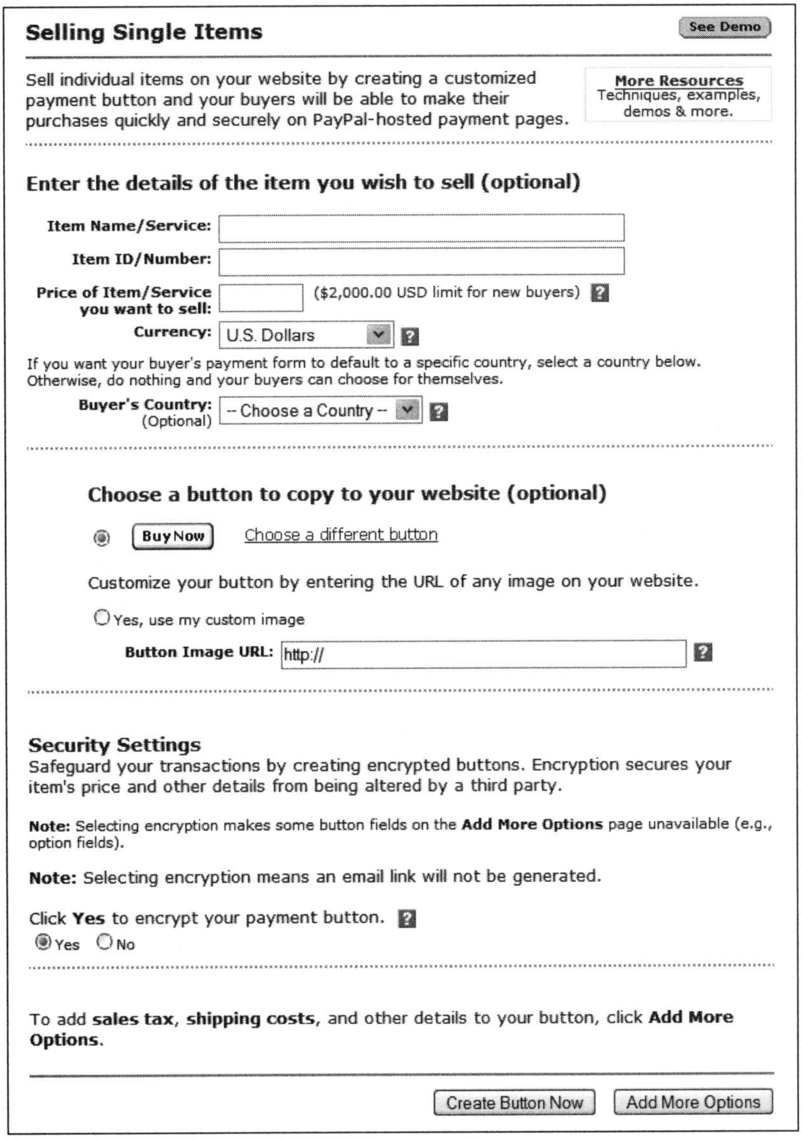

Figure 3-3. *Buy Now Button Factory*

This page asks for information about three aspects of the payment button:

- Details about the item being sold

- The button image that will be shown to users

- Whether or not you want to encrypt the button parameters

If these basic parameters are all you want to specify about your payment button, you can choose to have the code generated for you right then and there by clicking the Create Button Now button at the bottom of the page. There is, however, a second page of settings where you can input additional details about the item for sale (see Figure 3-4). You can get there by clicking the Add More Options button at the bottom of the page.

This page of options lets you specify the following information about the item for sale:

- URL where a buyer will be returned to after purchasing this item

- URL where a buyer will be returned to if the buyer cancels the transaction

- Whether you want to allow a buyer to purchase more than one of the item

- Whether you want a buyer to provide a shipping address

- Whether you want to allow a buyer to attach a note to their order

After completing the form on this page, you can click the Create Button Now button at the bottom of the page and have the HTML generated for you. Just copy and paste the code into the web page where you want to offer the item for sale, and then wait for some sales! You can also click the Preview button to get a sense of what a customer who has just completed a transaction using this new Buy Now button would see upon completion of a successful payment.

The Button Factory, while effective for quickly generating some code for simple items, does not offer much flexibility if you want to start adding a lot of additional parameters to your code, such as item color or size. There are many additional parameters you can set in your HTML that are not offered through the Button Factory. The next section describes the types of parameters you can include to further customize your button.

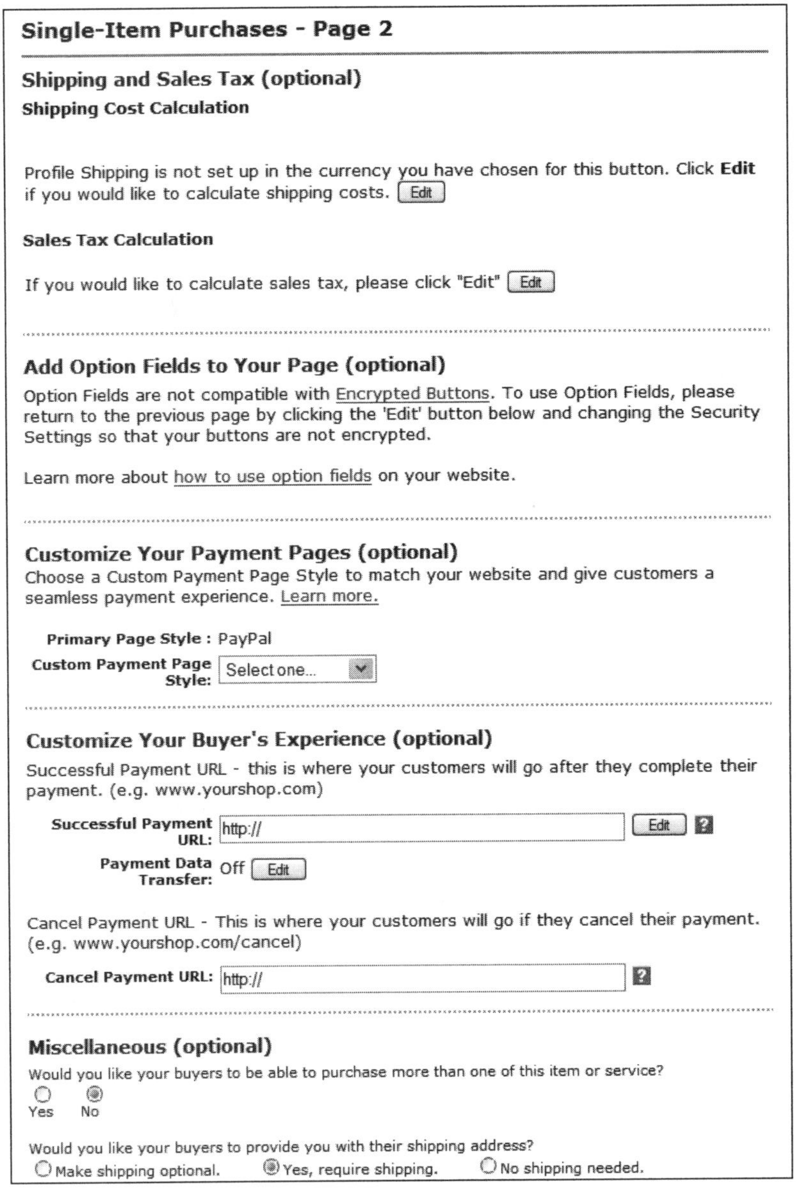

Single-Item Purchases - Page 2

Shipping and Sales Tax (optional)

Shipping Cost Calculation

Profile Shipping is not set up in the currency you have chosen for this button. Click **Edit** if you would like to calculate shipping costs. [Edit]

Sales Tax Calculation

If you would like to calculate sales tax, please click "Edit" [Edit]

....

Add Option Fields to Your Page (optional)

Option Fields are not compatible with Encrypted Buttons. To use Option Fields, please return to the previous page by clicking the 'Edit' button below and changing the Security Settings so that your buttons are not encrypted.

Learn more about how to use option fields on your website.

....

Customize Your Payment Pages (optional)

Choose a Custom Payment Page Style to match your website and give customers a seamless payment experience. Learn more.

Primary Page Style : PayPal

Custom Payment Page Style: [Select one... ▾]

....

Customize Your Buyer's Experience (optional)

Successful Payment URL - this is where your customers will go after they complete their payment. (e.g. www.yourshop.com)

Successful Payment URL: [http://] [Edit] [?]

Payment Data Transfer: Off [Edit]

Cancel Payment URL - This is where your customers will go if they cancel their payment. (e.g. www.yourshop.com/cancel)

Cancel Payment URL: [http://] [?]

....

Miscellaneous (optional)

Would you like your buyers to be able to purchase more than one of this item or service?
○ ◉
Yes No

Would you like your buyers to provide you with their shipping address?
○ Make shipping optional.   ◉ Yes, require shipping.   ○ No shipping needed.

Figure 3-4. *Specifying optional information for a Buy Now button*

Additional Button Parameters

Earlier in this section, you saw some sample code for a Buy Now button. It contained a few hidden variables that specified basic details about the item for sale. In addition to these variables, you can include many optional parameters in your button code to add additional functionality to the button. The "Standard Variable Reference" section in this book's appendix contains a complete list of all possible button parameters, but for now, just be aware that the basic categories that the parameters fall into are as follows:

- *Checkout page appearance customization*: With these options, you can add a header image to the PayPal-hosted page, change the background colors, and more.

- *Descriptive information about the item*: This category contains the name, quantity, price, and optional variables.

- *Financial details about the transaction*: These parameters relate to shipping and handling charges, tax, invoice number, and currency code.

- *Contact information about the buyer*: You can override the address stored in the buyer's PayPal account with information they have already entered on your website, before being redirected to checkout on PayPal's website.

- *Shopping cart–specific parameters*: There are varying ways that shopping carts can interact with PayPal; these are covered in the "Cart Upload" section later in this chapter.

Donations

PayPal's ability to allow people to easily set up their website to accept donation payments has had an impact on thousands of individuals and organizations worldwide. People with little to no technical know-how have been able to use the Button Factory to create a button or a link that allows anyone to donate to their cause. Creating a Donate button is very similar to creating a Buy Now button, except you have the option of leaving the payment amount blank if you want to let someone donate an arbitrary amount to you. The other main difference is the URL of the button image, which points to an image of a Donate button instead of a Buy Now button.

The URL to access the Donations Button Factory is `https://www.paypal.com/us/cgi-bin/webscr?cmd=_xclick-donations-factory`.

A Sample Donations Button

Listing 3-2 shows some sample code for a Donate button.

Listing 3-2. *Donate Button Example Code*

```
<form action="https://www.paypal.com/cgi-bin/webscr" method="post">
  <input type="hidden" name="cmd" value="_xclick"/>
  <input type="hidden" name="business" value="donations@example-business.com"/>
  <input type="hidden" name="item_name" value="School Fundraiser"/>
  <input type="hidden" name="item_number" value="2006"/>
  <input type="hidden" name="amount" value="50.00"/>
  <input type="hidden" name="no_shipping" value="2"/>
  <input type="hidden" name="no_note" value="1"/>
  <input type="hidden" name="currency_code" value="USD"/>
  <input type="hidden" name="tax" value="0"/>
  <input type="hidden" name="bn" value="PP-DonationsBF"/>
```

```
<input type="image"
        src="https://www.paypal.com/en_US/i/btn/x-click-but21.gif"
        border="0" name="submit"
        alt="Make payments with PayPal - it's fast, free and secure!"/>
    <img alt="" border="0" src="https://www.paypal.com/en_US/i/scr/pixel.gif"
        width="1" height="1"/>
</form>
```

As you can see, the code is very similar to that of a Buy Now button, except the `image` parameter now references the location of a Donate button instead of a Buy Now button. If you want to let the donator specify the amount to donate, just remove the line with the `amount` parameter. Listing 3-2 is set to specify a donation amount of $50.

Subscriptions and Recurring Payments

PayPal lets you set up recurring payments with the Subscriptions and Recurring Payments feature. You can't use this if you have a Personal account; you must first upgrade to a Premier or Business account. Use your Sandbox Business account if you want to test out Subscriptions and Recurring Payments and do not have a Premier or Business account on the main PayPal site.

A Sample Subscription Button

Listing 3-3 shows code for a sample Sandbox subscription button.

Listing 3-3. *Sandbox Subscription Button Example Code*

```
<form action="https://www.sandbox.paypal.com/cgi-bin/webscr" method="post">
    <input type="image" src="https://www.paypal.com/en_US/i/btn/x-click-but20.gif"
        border="0" name="submit"
        alt="Make payments with PayPal - it's fast, free and secure!"/>
    <img alt="" border="0"
        src="https://www.sandbox.paypal.com/en_US/i/scr/pixel.gif" ➥
        width="1" height="1"/>
    <input type="hidden" name="cmd" value="_xclick-subscriptions"/>
    <input type="hidden" name="business" value="test2@test22.com"/>
    <input type="hidden" name="item_name" value="Magazine Subscription"/>
    <input type="hidden" name="item_number" value="1212"/>
    <input type="hidden" name="no_shipping" value="1"/>
    <input type="hidden" name="no_note" value="1"/>
    <input type="hidden" name="currency_code" value="USD"/>
    <input type="hidden" name="bn" value="PP-SubscriptionsBF"/>
    <input type="hidden" name="a3" value="20.00"/>
    <input type="hidden" name="p3" value="10"/>
    <input type="hidden" name="t3" value="W"/>
    <input type="hidden" name="src" value="1"/>
    <input type="hidden" name="sra" value="1"/>
</form>
```

As you can see, Listing 3-3 is just basic HTML. PayPal provides a place on its website where you can enter some basic details about the subscription for sale and have the HTML code generated for you: `https://www.paypal.com/us/cgi-bin/webscr?cmd=_xclick-sub-factory`. A screenshot of part of that page is shown in Figure 3-5.

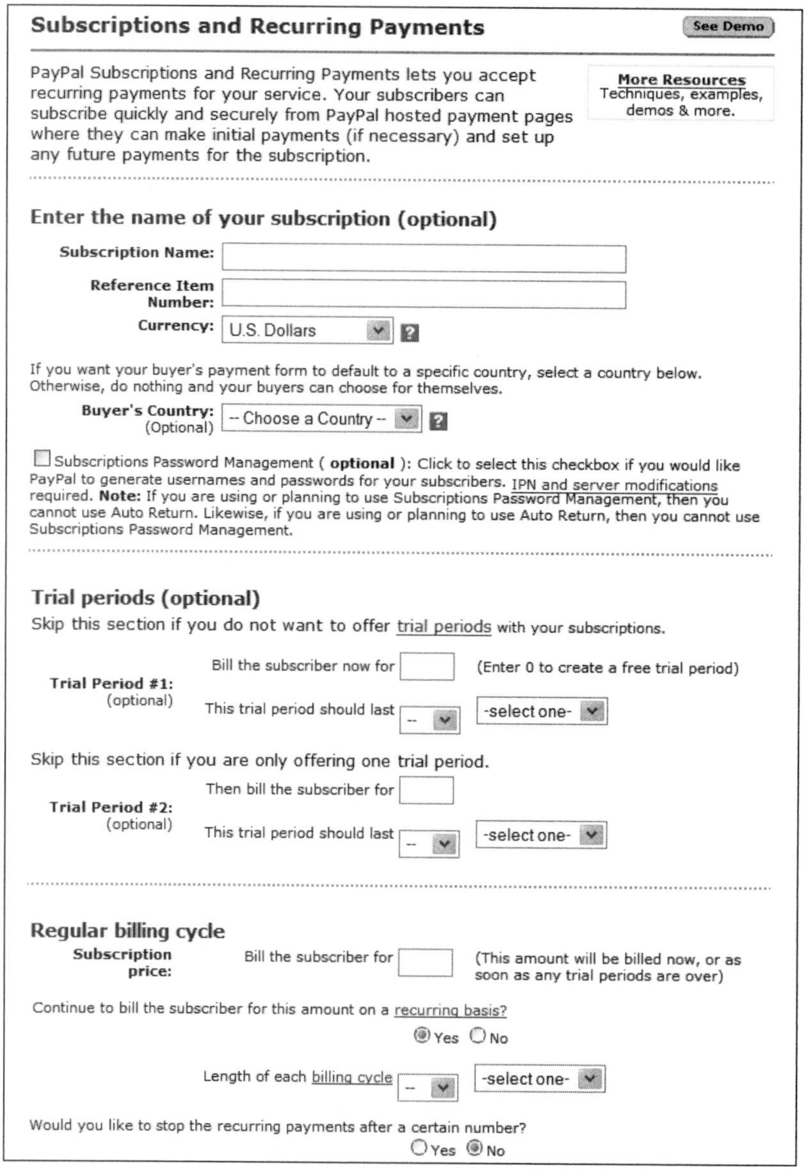

Figure 3-5. *Subscription and Recurring Payments information*

On this page, you can specify a number of details about your subscription:

- The name of the subscription

- An internal item number for the subscription

- The currency that subscription payments will be made in

- Whether you want PayPal to generate a username/password combination for your customer

- Whether you want to offer a lower price for an initial/trial period of the subscription

- How often you want to bill the subscriber

- Whether to reattempt the payment if it fails

- The subscription button image

- Whether you want PayPal to encrypt the button parameters

- URL where a buyer will be returned to after subscribing

- URL where a buyer will be returned to if the buyer cancels the transaction

- Whether you want a buyer to provide a shipping address

PayPal limits the amount you can process during a single subscription payment. The maximum transaction amount for each supported currency is shown in Table 3-1.

Table 3-1. *Maximum Transaction Amounts for PayPal Subscription Payments*

Currency	Maximum Transaction Amount
American dollar	10,000 USD
Australian dollar	12,500 AUD
Canadian dollar	12,500 CAD
Euro	8,000 EUR
Japanese yen	1,000,000 JPY
Pound sterling	5,500 GBP

Reattempting Failed Subscription Payments

When a subscription payment is made, you will receive an email notification at the primary email address on your PayPal account. If a subscription payment fails, you have the option to have PayPal reattempt the payment before the user's subscription is cancelled. If you choose to have PayPal reattempt the payment, it will be reattempted three days later. If that also fails, PayPal will reattempt again five days later. If it fails again, the subscription is automatically cancelled. Reattempts will not occur if another subscription payment is scheduled within 14 days of the failed payment, so payments do not overlap.

The subscription variable that specifies whether or not to reattempt failed subscription payments is sra. If set to 1, PayPal will reattempt the payment as described in the previous paragraph. If sra is omitted or set to any value other than 1, PayPal will cancel the subscription upon the first failed payment.

Canceling Subscriptions

If you wish to cancel one or more subscription agreements that your customers have with you, you can do this via the PayPal website. Click the History subtab on your Account Overview page, choose Subscriptions from the drop-down box, and then click Search. You'll see a list of recent subscription payments. Click the Details link next to the customer that you'd like to cancel. All of the subscription payment details will appear on the next page, and at the bottom of that page is a Cancel Subscription button.

If you wish to cancel several subscribers at once, click the "Cancel several subscribers" link at the bottom of the Subscription Payment Details page. After clicking this link, you are taken to a page where you can upload a text file that contains one email address per line. All of the subscriptions for the accounts listed in the text file will be cancelled. It may take up to an hour for PayPal to process all of the cancellations. When the process is complete, you can download a log file of the results by clicking the View Details link on the Transaction History page for the cancellation. The log file contains the results of the mass cancellation on a per-account basis.

Modifying Active Subscriptions

You can allow customers to modify their subscriptions by creating a Subscription button that has a hidden variable called modify. The only settings that you can modify on an active subscription are the subscription name, the item number, the subscription rate, and the billing cycle. There are two possible values for modify:

- modify = 1: Users can click the button to modify an existing subscription or create a new subscription.

- modify = 2: Users can click the button to modify only an existing subscription.

If you are sending the subscription modification information to your customers via email, create the new subscription information using the Button Factory, generate the email link, and then append either modify=1 or modify=2 to the end of the URL generated by PayPal.

Subscriptions Password Management

If you accept PayPal payments as a way for a subscriber to gain access to a secure, "members only" area of your website, PayPal offers a feature called Subscriptions Password Management that automatically generates a username and password for a new subscriber. If you use this feature, you must also use PayPal's Instant Payment Notification (IPN) to notify your website when a new user has registered. The IPN notification will contain the new subscriber's username and password, so that you can add the new subscriber to your web server's authentication mechanism. For more information on IPN, see Chapter 5.

If you use Apache as your web server, PayPal provides a Perl script you can copy into Apache's CGI directory to automate the process of updating your .htpasswd file with the new subscriber's information. There is a link on the first page of the Button Factory subscriptions page that allows you to access the script as well as a PDF document that gives step-by-step instructions on how to update your Apache installation and configure your PayPal account to correctly enable IPN.

To enable Subscriptions Password Management, click the appropriate check box on the Subscriptions Button Factory when creating your button. If you are creating your button manually and are not using the Button Factory, the variable that specifies the enablement of this feature is usr_manage. If you set usr_manage to 1, PayPal will generate usernames and passwords for your subscribers.

Subscription IPN Notifications

If you have IPN-enabled your account, your server will receive notifications upon the following events:

- Subscription creation
- Subscription cancellation
- Successful subscription payment
- Failed subscription payment
- End of subscription term

The End of Term IPN is sent when the subscription is completed. If a subscription is cancelled in the middle of a subscription term, the End of Term IPN will be sent at the end of the current term. If a subscription is recurring and is cancelled due to failed payment, the End of Term IPN will be sent right away. The list of variable names included in the IPN is included in the appendix. For more information on IPN, see Chapter 5.

Subscription Trial Periods

PayPal offers you the ability to create up to two trial periods for subscriptions. During a trial period, you can offer discounted rates for your product or service, or you can offer it for free. You specify this in your button code with the cryptic a, p, and t hidden variables. Table 3-2 lists the different variables you can use and their meanings.

Table 3-2. *Subscription Variables for Trial Periods*

Variable	Description
a1	Amount for the first trial period. For a free trial, use 0.
p1	Length for the first trial period. This modifies the unit of time specified by t1.
t1	Unit of time for the first trial period. Acceptable values are D (days), W (weeks), M (months), and Y (years).
a2	Same as a1, except for the second trial period.
p2	Same as p1, except for the second trial period.
t2	Same as t1, except for the second trial period.
a3	Regular rate of subscription.
p3	Regular length of subscription.
t3	Regular unit of time for subscription. See t1 for acceptable values.

Using the PayPal Shopping Cart

PayPal is pre-integrated into hundreds of shopping carts, but one of the most popular is the free shopping cart provided by PayPal. It is a hosted cart, which means that you do not have to download any software to use it. It operates in a similar fashion to the standard payment buttons discussed earlier in this chapter. Buyers interact with the PayPal website to manage the contents of their shopping cart.

The code to use the PayPal Shopping Cart is nothing more than basic HTML. The main difference between the PayPal Shopping Cart and the Buy Now buttons is that when your website uses the PayPal Shopping Cart, your customers click a button with the text Add to Cart instead of Buy Now. Customers can then choose to continue shopping on your website, or they can check out by paying with their PayPal account. If they choose to continue shopping on your website, they will return to the URL specified by the shopping_url variable in your HTML code.

Listing 3-4 shows sample code for an Add to Cart button. You will notice that it looks similar to code for a Buy Now button, with a few notable differences. First, the cmd variable now has a value of _cart. This tells PayPal that this is a shopping cart button, not a Buy Now button. The add variable, with a value of 1, tells PayPal that this is an Add to Cart button, not a View Cart button. To create a View Cart button, change the variable name add to display.

Listing 3-4. *Add to Cart Button Example Code*

```
<form target="paypal" action="https://www.paypal.com/cgi-bin/webscr"
      method="post">
  <input type="image"
         src="https://www.paypal.com/en_US/i/btn/x-click-but22.gif"
         border="0" name="submit"
         alt="Make payments with PayPal - it's fast, free and secure!"/>
  <img alt="" border="0" src="https://www.paypal.com/en_US/i/scr/pixel.gif"
       width="1" height="1"/>
  <input type="hidden" name="add" value="1"/>
  <input type="hidden" name="cmd" value="_cart"/>
  <input type="hidden" name="business" value="seller@apress.com"/>
  <input type="hidden" name="item_name" value="Cart Item 1"/>
  <input type="hidden" name="amount" value="5.00"/>
  <input type="hidden" name="no_shipping" value="2"/>
  <input type="hidden" name="no_note" value="1"/>
  <input type="hidden" name="currency_code" value="USD"/>
  <input type="hidden" name="bn" value="PP-ShopCartBF"/>
  <input type="hidden" name="shopping_url" value=www.myshop.com\products.html/>
</form>
```

For subsequent items that you want to list for sale on your website, just modify the values of item_name and amount. You can rapidly create a shopping cart–enabled website using this feature. The main disadvantage of using the PayPal Shopping Cart is having to redirect customers to PayPal's website every time they want to add something to their cart or view the cart contents. Also, if they cancel their shopping session with their cart full of items and come back the next day to continue, they'll have to start all over again—you can't maintain customers' cart contents and have a prefilled cart ready for them to check out when (and if) they return. Still, for many businesses, the PayPal Shopping Cart is a cost-effective and powerful solution to handle all of their e-commerce needs.

Cart Upload

If you have built your own shopping cart and only want PayPal to handle the checkout, the Cart Upload feature is a simple way to do this. When your customer arrives at the checkout page, you can let them know you offer PayPal as a payment option by displaying the PayPal Acceptance Mark, as shown in Figure 3-6. You can find more Acceptance Marks at `https://www.paypal.com/logocenter`.

Figure 3-6. *PayPal Acceptance Mark*

When a customer indicates that she wishes to pay with her PayPal account, you redirect her to the PayPal site and include all of the details of your shopping cart in a form post. There are two ways in which you can send this data to PayPal:

- Specify the sum total of all items in the shopping cart.

- Specify descriptions and prices of individual items in the shopping cart.

If you include the individual item details, the information about the items is included in the buyer's and seller's transaction history and notifications. The buyer will also see an itemized list on the PayPal checkout page after she is redirected to PayPal. We'll look at how to do both in this section.

Passing the Shopping Cart Total to PayPal

When you pass in the total amount of the shopping cart to PayPal, the customer will not have an individual breakdown of the items he purchased stored in his PayPal account. However, the code is a bit simpler to implement, as shown in Listing 3-5. Note the `cmd` value is still `_cart`, just like in the previous PayPal Shopping Cart examples. This example has an `upload` variable with a value of `1`. The `upload` variable tells PayPal that you are using the Cart Upload feature to pass in your shopping cart information.

Listing 3-5. *Example Code for Passing a Shopping Cart Total Amount to PayPal*

```
<form action="https://www.paypal.com/cgi-bin/webscr" method="post">
  <input type="hidden" name="cmd" value="_xclick"/>
  <input type="hidden" name="business" value="damon@example-business.com"/>
  <input type="hidden" name="item_name" value="Shopping Cart total"/>
  <input type="hidden" name="amount" value="250.00"/>
  <input type="submit" value="PayPal"/>
</form>
```

You may also use a `currency_code` variable that specifies the currency of the transaction. If you do not set a currency, the default is U.S. dollars.

Passing Individual Item Details to PayPal

When you post information on specific items in the customer's shopping cart, you get a bit more flexibility in what you're able to do with the cart. Listing 3-6 shows an example of a shopping cart with two items. Notice that `item_name` and `amount` have an integer appended to the variable names. This integer identifies the item number in the shopping cart. `item_name_1` and `amount_1` are associated with the first item in the cart, and so forth. You may optionally include a `quantity_x` variable if your customer has purchased multiple quantities of an item.

Listing 3-6. *Example Code for Passing Individual Shopping Cart Item Details to PayPal*

```
<form action="https://www.paypal.com/cgi-bin/webscr" method="post">
  <input type="hidden" name="cmd" value="_cart"/>
  <input type="hidden" name="upload" value="1"/>
  <input type="hidden" name="business" value="damon@example-business.com"/>
  <input type="hidden" name="item_name_1" value="Item Name 1"/>
  <input type="hidden" name="amount_1" value="1.00"/>
  <input type="hidden" name="quantity_1" value="1"/>
  <input type="hidden" name="item_name_2" value="Item Name 2"/>
  <input type="hidden" name="amount_2" value="2.00"/>
  <input type="hidden" name="quantity_2" value="3"/>
  <input type="submit" value="PayPal"/>
</form>
```

■**Note** The value of x when specifying individual items must begin with 1 and increase by 1 for each subsequent item. For example, if you specify an `item_name_4` and `amount_4` without specifying items 1, 2, and 3, PayPal will ignore this item and it will not be included in the total charge to your customer.

Specifying the Tax for the Shopping Cart

The examples in the preceding sections show the bare minimum variables you must submit in order to use the Cart Upload feature. One additional piece of information that is commonly used is the sales tax amount. There are two ways you can specify the sales tax when using Cart Upload. The simplest way is to specify a tax_cart variable with the total amount of sales tax for the purchase. The second way, available only if you pass individual item details to PayPal, is to specify a tax_x variable for each item. The value of x increments by 1 for each item in the cart (e.g., tax_1, tax_2, tax_3). This allows you to specify the sales tax for each item, and it makes sense if you sell some nontaxable items in addition to taxable items.

Summary

PayPal's basic HTML-based payment options provide the simplicity to allow for quick implementation as well as the flexibility to use as the basis for a complete payments solution. This chapter covered the main aspects of Website Payments Standard, including payment buttons for purchases, donations, and subscriptions, as well as PayPal's Shopping Cart feature. The chapter also discussed how to use PayPal's Cart Upload feature with a third-party shopping cart. There are dozens of optional variables that can be included in a Website Payments Standard payment button, all of which are listed in the "Standard Variable Reference" section of the appendix.

In addition, you learned how to use PayPal's Button Factory, an area on the PayPal website that generates HTML for payment buttons. The Button Factory also provides the ability to encrypt the button parameters so that they can't be modified by a malicious third party. It performs the encryption through a PayPal technology known as Encrypted Website Payments (EWP). EWP prevents a fraudster from modifying the details of your button code before the data is sent to PayPal. The next chapter digs deeper into EWP, so you can implement the technology directly without having to use the Button Factory.

CHAPTER 4

■ ■ ■

Encrypted Website Payments

As you learned in Chapter 3, creating a standard PayPal payment button is relatively fast and easy to do. Just copy and paste some basic HTML and change a couple of variables, and you're ready to go. You can put the code on your web server and start accepting online payments in a matter of minutes.

However, this technique also comes with a certain amount of risk. Put simply, your HTML is out there in plain text for the whole world to see—and believe me, people (and spiders) are looking. A fraudster could examine your button code and find out things such as

- The email address of your PayPal account

- The URL a buyer is returned to after making a purchase

- Any custom fields you have defined

The fraudster could then utilize or alter this data to attack your business. For example, say your website sells digital content via a Buy Now button that offers a $25 package of downloadable training materials. You also have a script at your `return_url` that makes the file available for download after completion of a successful PayPal transaction. If your button is unencrypted, a fraudster could copy the code and modify the price from $25 to $.01. The fraudster could then complete a 1-cent transaction to your PayPal account, and if your script is not savvy enough to double-check the purchase price of a transaction, the fraudster has just easily bought your $25 product for a penny.

That is just one example of how leaving unencrypted button code on your website makes your site vulnerable to attack. In this chapter, we will discuss how you can prevent this type of attack by using a feature that PayPal has created to counteract this type of activity: Encrypted Website Payments, or EWP. When customers click a payment button that has been encrypted with EWP, they have the exact same checkout experience as if they had clicked an unencrypted button. The difference is in the added security that you provide your business when using encrypted buttons.

This chapter covers the various technologies and processes that make up EWP and discusses the following topics:

- Understanding how EWP works

- Generating the necessary public certificates and private keys

- Uploading certificate information to PayPal

- Performing the button encryption

- Blocking unencrypted website payments

After reading this chapter, you will have a good understanding of how to create encrypted payment buttons for your application.

Overview of EWP

PayPal uses public key cryptography to encrypt your HTML button code. It's not necessary to have a full understanding of cryptography in order to use EWP, but since a basic knowledge of how public and private keys work together will help, this section begins with a brief overview of how public key cryptography works. If you are already familiar with this technology, skip ahead to the next section.

Public Key Cryptography

Public key cryptography is a common technology used to encrypt data that is sent from one place to another on the Internet and ensure that the identity of the sender is guaranteed. It works through the use of *public keys* and *private keys*, which are bits of data that are mathematically related to one another through an algorithm. Their relationship is such that the private key cannot be derived from knowing the public key. For public key cryptography to work, the private key must be kept confidential, while the public key can be made widely available.

The way in which public keys are distributed is inside of a *digital certificate*. A digital certificate is a file that contains a public key and information about the key, such as the name of the company that owns that public key, a certificate expiration date, and the name of a third-party company that has validated the authenticity of the certificate. This third party is referred to as a *certificate authority* (CA). Common CAs include VeriSign and Thawte. The CA signs the digital certificate, and certificate consumers can then validate the authenticity of the public key by using the public certificate of the CA to verify the digital signature.

Encrypting Data with Public Key Cryptography

Encrypting a message so that it cannot be read or modified while in transit is the most common use of public key cryptography. In this scenario, the sender of the data uses the receiver's public key to encrypt the message. The resulting jumbled message is then sent to the receiver. The receiver, having a copy of the public key's corresponding private key, can then use the private key to decode the message. Figure 4-1 illustrates this process.

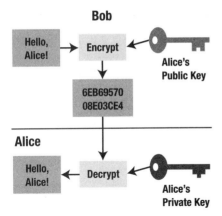

Figure 4-1. *Encrypting a message with public key cryptography. (After: David Göthberg.)*

Verifying a Sender's Identity with Public Key Cryptography

In addition to encrypting messages, public key cryptography can be used to verify the identity of the sender of a message. This technique uses a *digital signature* and works in a somewhat opposite way to message encrypting, in that the encryption is done with the private key, and not the public key (see Figure 4-2). Likewise, the decrypting is done with the public key, and not the private key. Obviously, the receiver of the message must have the public key of the person sending the message. When the receiver uses the public key to decrypt the message, the integrity of the sender's identity is proven. If the message was not sent by someone who had the correct private key, then the resulting decrypted message would be jumbled garbage and would not make any sense.

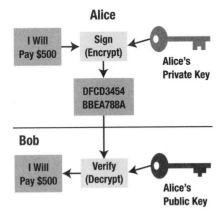

Figure 4-2. *Using a digital signature to validate the sender of a message. (After: David Göthberg.)*

Securing a Private Key

Both techniques rely on the secrecy of the private key being maintained. It can be quite costly for your business if the integrity of your private key is compromised. Not only do you have to generate a new private key, but you also have to replace all of the corresponding public keys. Additionally, the cost of losing your data could be huge. If you choose to use public key cryptography, there are some basic best practices you may wish to follow to increase the level of privacy and safety around your private keys:

- Use firewalls and intrusion detection software.

- Limit the number of people allowed to access private keys.

- Store private keys on a machine physically separate from your web server.

- Audit access logs to see which users access the private key.

- Configure all security aspects of your web server.

Obviously this is just a partial list, and the lengths you go to in order to secure your private keys will depend on your level of risk based on the value of the information you are protecting. But in short, if you are doing business online, then there is a good chance that someday someone is going to try and break in and cause havoc. The more prepared you are for these types of attacks, the higher your probability of being able to prevent the attackers from doing any damage.

Encrypted Code vs. Unencrypted Code

This section describes the difference between encrypted button code and unencrypted button code. Before the EWP encryption process, you may have code that looks something like that shown in Listing 4-1.

Listing 4-1. *Unencrypted Button Code*

```
<form action="https://www.paypal.com/cgi-bin/webscr" method="post">
  <input type="hidden" name="cmd" value="_xclick" />
  <input type="hidden" name="business" value="paypal@mywebsite.com" />
  <input type="hidden" name="return"
         value="http://www.mywebsite.com/thankyou.html" />
  <input type="hidden" name="item_name" value="Training Documents" />
  <input type="hidden" name="amount" value="25.00" />
  <input type="submit" value="Buy Now!" />
</form>
```

As you can see, all the settings are presented in plain text, which means they can be easily spoofed or modified by a fraudster. After the encryption process, your code will be impervious to attack and will look something like that shown in Listing 4-2.

Listing 4-2. *Encrypted Button Code*

```
<form action="https://www.paypal.com/cgi-bin/webscr" method="post">
  <input type="hidden" name="cmd" value="_s-xclick">
  <input type="hidden" name="encrypted" value="
-----BEGIN PKCS7-----
MIIG5QYJKoZIhvcNAQcDoIIG1jCCBtICAQAxggE6MIIBNgIBADCBnjCBmDELMAkG
A1UEBhMCVVMxEzARBgNVBAgTCkNhbGlmb3JuaWExETAPBgNVBAcTCFNhbiBKb3Nl
...
wkTGxwAxwWownnk9yzWnyPpK7InDhQIGFrobpf/kpfw9tkORgYR+Ufa9gcOa3Xg/
KpWp9N88uBHP/W225LYHH3AMgHiOHqQJum+8JdfWvvt5NSdJJMfTz9Y=
-----END PKCS7-----
" />
  <input type="submit" value="Buy Now!" />
</form>
```

In Listing 4-2, all of the button variables have been encrypted so that they cannot be viewed or modified by a third party. This feature greatly increases the security of your payment buttons and your business.

How PayPal Reads Encrypted Code

The actual encryption of your code is done with use of the PayPal public certificate, which is available for download from the PayPal website. When a user clicks the encrypted button, PayPal uses the corresponding private key to decrypt the code. Instructions for accessing the PayPal public certificate are provided later in the chapter.

Anyone can access the PayPal public certificate, so PayPal takes an additional step to make sure that you are the person who performed the encryption: it has you digitally sign your code before encrypting it. You perform this step using a private key that you generate on your own, and then you provide PayPal with the corresponding public certificate to verify your digital signature. This process is described in more detail later in the chapter.

Blocking Unencrypted Website Payments

If you use EWP to encrypt the payment buttons on your website, you should consider blocking any payments that someone tries to send you from an unencrypted button. This is an additional antispoof mechanism that PayPal provides to help protect you from fraudsters. If you are positive that your site contains only encrypted payment buttons, it makes sense to add this extra layer of security.

Follow these steps to block unencrypted website payments:

1. Log in to your Business or Premier account at www.paypal.com.

2. Click the Profile subtab.

3. Click the Website Payment Preferences link in the right-hand menu.

4. Click the On radio button next to Block Non-encrypted Website Payments.

5. Click Save.

Once you have configured this option in your account, anyone attempting to pay you with a nonencrypted button will receive an error message.

Creating Encrypted Buttons

There are two ways you can go when creating encrypted buttons. The easiest and fastest way to create an encrypted button is by using the PayPal Button Factory. This method has some limitations that are explained in the next section. Alternatively, you can choose to use third-party encryption utilities such as OpenSSL, in addition to libraries provided by PayPal, to generate the public certificates and private keys necessary to perform the encryption. Both methods are described in more detail shortly.

EWP with the Button Factory

The simplest and most straightforward way to create an encrypted payment button is to use PayPal's Button Factory. The Button Factory is an area on the PayPal website where you can automatically generate HTML code by entering a few simple details about the item you are selling. For selling single items, the URL for the Button Factory is `www.paypal.com/us/cgi-bin/webscr?cmd=_web-tools`. Figure 4-3 shows a partial screenshot of the Button Factory, focusing on the area that deals with encryption.

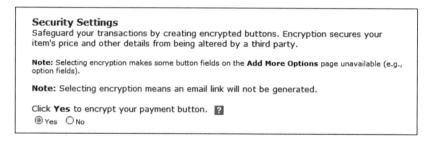

Figure 4-3. *Security Settings area of the PayPal Button Factory*

Under the Security Settings header, you can click the Yes radio button (which is selected by default) to create encrypted button code.

While this is the easiest method of creating a secure payment button, the drawback is that you can't use custom input fields, such as item size, color, and so forth. If you need these parameters defined in your button code, you will not be able to use the Button Factory to create encrypted code. The remainder of this chapter deals with creating payment buttons outside of the Button Factory context.

Creating Certificates and Keys

The Button Factory is great if you need a simple and quick way to create a secure payment button. A more flexible but slightly more difficult method for creating encrypted button code involves the use of public key cryptography, as described earlier in this chapter. The process can be somewhat confusing, but if you follow the steps in this section, you should be able to generate your own encrypted button code in no time flat.

Creating a Private Key and Public Certificate

When using EWP, you sign your button code using your private key, and PayPal verifies your digital signature when someone clicks your button. PayPal requires you to upload your public certificate so that your digital signature can be verified. PayPal accepts only X.509 public certificates, not public keys. The difference between a key and a certificate is that a certificate includes the public key along with information about the key, such as the owner of the key and when the key expires.

PayPal accepts public certificates in Privacy Enhanced Mail (PEM) format from any established certificate authority, such as VeriSign. However, you can freely create public/private key pairs using an encryption tool such as OpenSSL. For the sake of digitally signing your button code, you can use a self-signed public certificate and do not need to purchase one from a CA. Most Linux and Unix operating systems already have the OpenSSL utility built in. If you are a Windows user, you can download the Windows version of OpenSSL by visiting `www.slproweb.com/products/Win32OpenSSL.html`.

Once you have OpenSSL or a similar encryption tool available to you in your environment, you can create the public/private key pair that will be used to digitally sign your button code. The examples that follow are for use with OpenSSL.

Creating a Private Key and Public Certificate

Use the following OpenSSL command to create your private key. The command creates a 1,024-bit RSA private key stored in the file `private-key.pem`.

```
openssl genrsa –out private-key.pem 1024
```

Use the following OpenSSL command to create your public certificate. Run the command from the same directory that you ran the previous command to generate your private key. You will be prompted to enter some basic information for inclusion in the certificate, such as your name. The command generates a public certificate stored in the file `public-cert.pem`.

```
openssl req –new –key private-key.pem –x509 –days 365 –out public-cert.pem
```

Now that you have created your private key and public certificate, you must upload the public certificate to PayPal so that PayPal can use it to verify your digital signature. That process is described shortly in the section titled "Uploading a Public Certificate to PayPal."

Creating a PKCS12 File

PKCS12 is a cryptography standard developed by RSA Laboratories (`www.rsasecurity.com/rsalabs`) that defines a file format used to store both a private key and the corresponding public certificate, encrypting them both with a password-based key. You need to perform this step to create a PKCS12 file that combines and encrypts the private key and public certificate you just created. You will need this file when you perform your button encryption.

Use the following OpenSSL command to create your PKCS12 file. Run the command from the same directory that you ran the previous commands to generate your private key and public certificate. You will be prompted for an encryption password; make sure to remember to write it down somewhere! The command generates a PKCS12 file stored at my_pkcs12.p12.

```
openssl pkcs12 -export -in public-cert.pem -inkey private-key.pem -out my_pkcs12.p12
```

Uploading a Public Certificate to PayPal

PayPal ensures that you are the person who used the PayPal public certificate to encrypt your payment button by validating the digital signature you applied to your code when you signed it using your private key. In order to do this, PayPal needs a copy of your public certificate. This section describes how to upload your public certificate to the PayPal website.

Follow these steps to upload your public certificate to PayPal:

1. Log in to your Business or Premier account at www.paypal.com.

2. Click the Profile subtab.

3. In the Selling Preferences column, click Encrypted Payment Settings.

4. Click Add under Your Public Certificates.

5. Click Browse, and select your public certificate file (public-cert.pem if you followed the previous instructions).

6. When your public certificate is successfully uploaded, it appears on the next screen under Your Public Certificates, as shown in Figure 4-4.

In Figure 4-4, notice the column titled Cert ID. This contains the certificate ID that PayPal has assigned to your public certificate. Copy and paste this value somewhere into your development environment. You will need it when it comes time to generate your encrypted button code.

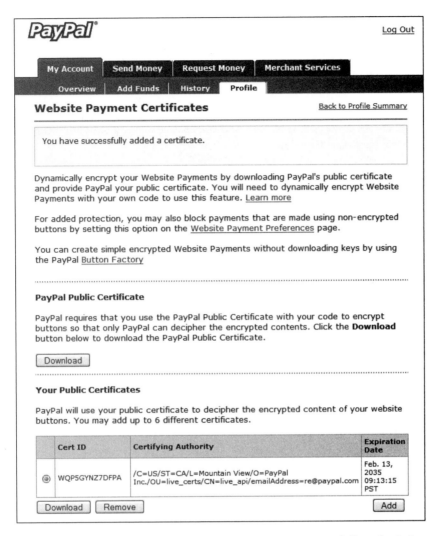

Figure 4-4. *Screenshot after a public certificate has been successfully uploaded*

Downloading the PayPal Public Certificate

PayPal's public certificate is used to turn your plain text button code into the encrypted jumble of text that can be read by nobody except PayPal. The process of performing the actual encryption is described later in this chapter.

Follow these steps to download the PayPal public certificate:

1. Log in to your Business or Premier account at www.paypal.com.

2. Click the Profile subtab.

3. In the Selling Preferences column, click Encrypted Payment Settings.

4. Click Download in the PayPal Public Certificate area.

The file will be called `paypal_cert_pem.txt`. Store this file in a secure location.

■**Note** Make sure you do not confuse the PayPal public certificate with your own public certificate. Give the two files distinctly different file names.

Encrypting Buttons

In the previous section, you created the public and private key pair used to digitally sign your code, uploaded your public certificate to PayPal, and downloaded the PayPal public certificate. Now it's time to actually do some encryption!

The Encrypted "Blob"

When you create an encrypted button, your HTML code will look similar to that shown in Listing 4-2. The encrypted string that is specified as the value for the `encrypted` hidden variable contains the rest of the button variables. Before this string is encrypted, you create an unencrypted version of it that contains all of the button parameters listed as name/value pairs, with each pair separated by `\n`. For example, an unencrypted variable string might start off like this: `cmd=_xclick\nbusiness=seller@apress.com\ncurrency_code=USD\nitem_name=Brown Shoes\namount=69.95\n...`

Java Developers

Java developers have two software packages available to them for encrypting their payment buttons: the ButtonEncryption application and the PayPal Java SDK, available at `www.paypal.com/sdk`. The ButtonEncryption application was the first code released to help developers encrypt code. Then PayPal decided to bundle that functionality into its Java SDK, which was released originally in 2004. If you are more familiar with object-oriented programming, I recommend using the Java SDK for your encryption needs. If you prefer the command-line approach, the ButtonEncryption application will suit your needs. Both methods are described in the sections that follow.

Using the ButtonEncryption Application

You can download the ButtonEncryption application from the PayPal Integration Center at `www.paypal.com/integration`. Click the Website Payments Standard link, and then follow the link to Encrypted Website Payments. Scroll to the bottom of the page, and you'll find the files located under the Sample Code header.

To use the ButtonEncryption application, you must have the following software packages installed on your computer:

- J2SE version 1.4.2 or higher, available at `http://java.sun.com`.

- The Bouncy Castle JCE provider and SMIME/CMS libraries, available at `www.bouncycastle.org/latest_releases.html`. You'll need `bcprov-jdk<java_version>-<current version>.jar` and `bcmail-jdk<java_version>-<current version>.jar`. Add these JAR files to your Java environment. You can find full installation instructions for Bouncy Castle at `www.bouncycastle.org/specifications.html#install`.

- The Java Cryptography Extension (JCE) Unlimited Strength Jurisdiction Policy Files, available at `http://java.sun.com/javase/downloads/index.jsp` in the Other Downloads section. Copy the JAR files to your `$JAVA_HOME/jre/lib/security` directory.

- An OpenSSL distribution. You can obtain this from `www.openssl.org`.

Building the ButtonEncryption Application

On Windows, use `build-window.bat` to build the ButtonEncryption application. On Unix platforms, use `build-app.sh` to build the application.

Note There is a bug in the existing build script, in that the Java installation is expected to be in certain locations (`C:\j2sdk1.4.2_04` for Windows and `/x/contrib./j2sdk1.4.0` for Unix). You'll need to replace these values with your environment's values for the code to compile properly.

Running the ButtonEncryption Application

From a command line, use the following command and parameters to execute the ButtonEncryption application:

```
java ButtonEncryption <CertFile> <PKCS12File> <PPCertFile> <Password> ➥
    <CmdTxt> <OutputFile>
```

Each of the preceding parameters should be replaced with the following:

- `<CertFile>`: Location of your public certificate

- `<PKCS12File>`: Location of your PKCS12 file

- `<PPCertFile>`: Location of the PayPal public certificate

- `<Password>`: Password used to encrypt your PKCS12 files

- `<CmdTxt>`: Comma-separated, double quote–enclosed list of button parameters

- `<OutputFile>`: Name of the encrypted output file

An example of the command with filled-in values looks like this:

```
java ButtonEncryption public-cert.pem my_pkcs12.p12 paypal_pubcert.pem password
"cmd=_xclick,business=example@test.com,amount=55.00,currency_code=USD,item_name=ewp
example,cert_id=ZWTMUVWGGH8T8" encrypted_button.html
```

Optionally, you can add a sandbox parameter to the end of the list if you want to test EWP in the Sandbox. To create a Sandbox button, just add sandbox to the end of the command line.

The other parameter to note is cert_id. This value is the certificate ID that your public certificate was assigned from PayPal when you uploaded your public certificate into your Profile.

Using the PayPal Java SDK

If you don't like the command-line stand-alone format that the ButtonEncryption application provides, the PayPal Java SDK provides a more object-oriented approach that makes things a bit easier if you're embedding this functionality into a larger application. The basic way that EWP works within the Java SDK is by providing all of your certificates, keys, passwords, and other credentials to an EWPProfile object, and then invoking the encryptButton() method of an EWPServices object.

Listing 4-3 shows how to do just that. It reads the button properties in from a properties file by iterating over the contents of the file. For this code to work, you must have a few of the JAR files included with the SDK in your classpath. To compile the code, you must have paypal_base.jar in your classpath. To execute it, you need commons-logging-1.0.4.jar and the libraries downloaded from Bouncy Castle in your classpath. Additionally, all the necessary SDK classes must be listed in import statements in your code.

Listing 4-3. *Using the Java SDK to Encrypt a Button*

```
//
package com.apress.paypal;

import java.util.Properties;
import java.util.Enumeration;

import com.paypal.sdk.profiles.EWPProfile;
import com.paypal.sdk.profiles.ProfileFactory;

import com.paypal.sdk.services.EWPServices;

import  com.paypal.sdk.exceptions.PayPalException;

public class CreateButton {

  // the button properties
  public static final String PROPERTIES_FILE = "button.params.properties";

  // path to your PKCS12 file
  public static final String PKCS12 = "./my_pkcs12.p12";

  // path to PayPal's public certificate
  public static final String PAYPAL_CERT = "./paypal_cert_pem.txt";
```

```java
// use https://www.sandbox.paypal.com if testing
public static final String URL = "https://www.paypal.com";

public static void main (String args[]) {

  // Check to see if the user provided a password
  if (args.length != 1) {
    System.out.println("You must provide a password.");
    System.exit(0);
  }

  // password used to encrypt your PKCS12 files
  // obtained from the command line
  String USER_PASSWORD = args[0];

  // Read properties file with a custom loader
  PropertiesLoader loader = new PropertiesLoader(); // custom loader
  Properties properties = loader.loadProperties(PROPERTIES_FILE);

  // First we will create the EWPProfile object
  try {
    EWPProfile ewpProfile = ProfileFactory.createEWPProfile();

    ewpProfile.setCertificateFile(PKCS12);
    ewpProfile.setPayPalCertificateFile(PAYPAL_CERT);
    ewpProfile.setPrivateKeyPassword(USER_PASSWORD);
    ewpProfile.setUrl(URL);

    StringBuilder buttonParameters = new StringBuilder();

    // Now we will define the button parameters for our payment button
    for (Enumeration e = properties.keys(); e.hasMoreElements();) {
      String key = (String)e.nextElement();
      buttonParameters.append(key + "=" + properties.getProperty(key) + "\n");
    }

    // Next we will create the EWPServices object
    // and tell it which EWPProfile object to use
    EWPServices ewpServices = new EWPServices();
    ewpServices.setEWPProfile(ewpProfile);

    // Finally we are ready to call the method to perform the button encryption
    String encryptedButton =
      ewpServices.encryptButton(buttonParameters.toString().getBytes());
```

```
            System.out.println(encryptedButton);
        } catch (PayPalException ppe) {
            System.out.println("An exception occurred when creating the button.");
            ppe.printStackTrace();
        }
    }
}
```

After this code has executed, you will see the full contents of the encrypted button, and you can then save them in an HTML file for use on a web server. Here is a sample properties file of button properties:

```
cmd=_xclick
business= example@test.com
amount=55.00
currency_code=USD
item_name= ewp example
cert_id= ZWTMUVWGGH8T8
no_shipping=2
no_note=1
item_number=7601
bn=PP-BuyNowBF
```

Windows Developers

The following sections provide code samples for Windows developers interested in using PayPal's EWP feature. Samples are provided in Visual Basic 6 for the COM and classic ASP platforms, and also in C# for the .NET 2.0 platform.

■**Note** Thanks to Harry Xue for providing the classes in this section.

Visual Basic 6

The class in Listing 4-4 can be used to perform EWP under both COM and ASP. It requires Microsoft CAPICOM, which you can download from www.microsoft.com. CAPICOM can be used to do things like digitally sign data, sign code, verify digital signatures, envelop data for privacy, hash data, encrypt/decrypt data, and more. The button parameters must be formatted as name/value pairs separated by a line feed (vbLf or chr(10)).

Listing 4-4. *Visual Basic 6 Sample for EWP*

```
Private mRecipientPublicCertPath As String
Private mSignerCert As CAPICOM.Certificate
Private mRecipientCert As CAPICOM.Certificate

Public Sub Class_Terminate()
```

```vb
    Set mSignerCert = Nothing
    Set mRecipientCert = Nothing

End Sub

Property Get RecipientPublicCertPath() As String

    RecipientPublicCertPath = mRecipientPublicCertPath

End Property

Property Let RecipientPublicCertPath(value As String)

    mRecipientPublicCertPath = value
    Set mRecipientCert = New CAPICOM.Certificate
    mRecipientCert.Load value

End Property

Public Sub LoadSignerCredential(signerPfxCertPath As String, ➥
    signerPfxCertPassword As String)

    Set mSignerCert = New CAPICOM.Certificate
    mSignerCert.Load signerPfxCertPath, signerPfxCertPassword

End Sub

' This function takes an unencrypted variable string as a parameter and returns ➥
    a string that has been signed and encrypted
Public Function SignAndEncrypt(ustr As String) As String

    Dim bstr As String
    Dim signed As String
    Dim enveloped As String
    Dim result As String

    bstr = UnicodeStringToBinaryString(ustr)
    signed = Sign(bstr)
    enveloped = Envelope(signed)
    result = FormatForTransport(enveloped)

    SignAndEncrypt = result

End Function

' This function performs the digital signature on the encrypted string
Private Function Sign(bstr As String) As String
```

```
        Dim result As String
        Dim signer As CAPICOM.ISigner
        Dim signed As CAPICOM.SignedData

        Set signer = New CAPICOM.signer
        signer.Certificate = mSignerCert

        Set signed = New CAPICOM.SignedData
        signed.Content = bstr
        result = signed.Sign(signer, False, CAPICOM_ENCODE_BINARY)

        Sign = result

        Set signed = Nothing
        Set signer = Nothing

End Function

' This function encrypts the button variables
Private Function Envelope(bstr As String) As String

        Dim result As String
        Dim enveloped As CAPICOM.EnvelopedData

        Set enveloped = New CAPICOM.EnvelopedData
        enveloped.Content = bstr
        enveloped.Recipients.Add mRecipientCert
        result = enveloped.Encrypt(CAPICOM_ENCODE_BINARY)

        Envelope = result

        Set enveloped = Nothing

End Function

' This function creates the encrypted variable string that will be assigned ➡
    to the encrypted hidden form variable in your button code
Private Function FormatForTransport(bstr As String) As String

        Dim result As String
        Dim util As CAPICOM.Utilities
        Dim b64 As String
```

```
    Set util = New CAPICOM.Utilities
    'First we Base64-encode the variables
    b64 = util.Base64Encode(bstr)
    'Next we remove all of the line breaks
    result = Replace(b64, vbCrLf, "")
    'Finally we add the PKCS7 header and footer
    result = "-----BEGIN PKCS7-----" & result & "-----END PKCS7-----"

    FormatForTransport = result

    Set util = Nothing

End Function

' Utility function to convert unicode to binary
Private Function UnicodeStringToBinaryString(ustr As String) As String

    Dim bstr As String
    Dim bytes() As Byte
    Dim utils As CAPICOM.Utilities

    bytes = StrConv(ustr, vbFromUnicode)
    Set utils = New CAPICOM.Utilities
    bstr = utils.ByteArrayToBinaryString(bytes)

    UnicodeStringToBinaryString = bstr

    Set utils = Nothing
End Function
```

Listing 4-5 is an example of how to use the class presented in Listing 4-4.

Listing 4-5. *Using the Visual Basic 6 Class for EWP*

```
Private Function Encrypt() As String
    Dim paypalCertPath As String
    Dim myCertPath As String
    Dim myCertPassword As String
    Dim paymentData As String

    Dim ewp As clsEWP
    Dim encrypted As String
```

```
paypalCertPath = "C:\paypal_cert_pem.txt"
myCertPath = "C:\ewp_cert.p12"
myCertPassword = GetCertPassword() ' retrieve your password securely here
paymentData = "cmd=_xclick" & vbLf & _
              "business=your@email.com" & vbLf & _
              "currency_code=GBP" & vbLf & _
              "item_name=Tennis Balls ßü (£12 umlot OK)" & vbLf & _
              "amount=15.00" & vbLf & _
              "return=https://www.yourdomain.com/return" & vbLf & _
              "cancel_return=https://www.yourdomain.com/cancel" & vbLf & _
              "cert_id=C2XRTSNRF7E2S"

Set ewp = New clsEWP
ewp.RecipientPublicCertPath = paypalCertPath
ewp.LoadSignerCredential myCertPath, myCertPassword
encrypted = ewp.SignAndEncrypt(paymentData)

Encrypt = encrypted

End Function
```

C#

The ButtonEncryption class shown in Listing 4-6 can be used to perform EWP. You can download this class, as well as all the sample code from this book, from the Source Code/Download
section of the Apress website (www.apress.com).

Listing 4-6. *C# Sample for EWP Under .NET 2.0*

```
using System;
using System.Collections.Generic;
using System.Text;
using System.Security.Cryptography;
using Pkcs = System.Security.Cryptography.Pkcs;
using X509 = System.Security.Cryptography.X509Certificates;

namespace com.apress.paypal
{
    public class ButtonEncryption
    {
        private Encoding _encoding = Encoding.Default;
        private string _recipientPublicCertPath;

        private X509.X509Certificate2 _signerCert;
        private X509.X509Certificate2 _recipientCert;
```

```
public ButtonEncryption()
{
}


#region Properties

/// <summary>
/// Character encoding, e.g. UTF-8, Windows-1252
/// </summary>
public string Charset
{
    get { return _encoding.WebName; }
    set
    {
        if (value != null && value != "")
        {
            _encoding = Encoding.GetEncoding(value);
        }
    }
}


/// <summary>

/// Path to the recipient's public certificate in PEM format
/// </summary>
public string RecipientPublicCertPath
{
    get { return _recipientPublicCertPath; }
    set
    {
        _recipientPublicCertPath = value;
        _recipientCert =
          new X509.X509Certificate2(_recipientPublicCertPath);
    }
}

#endregion

/// <summary>
///  Loads the PKCS12 file which contains the public certificate
/// and private key of the signer
/// </summary>
/// <param name="signerPfxCertPath">
/// File path to the signer's public certificate plus private key
/// in PKCS#12 format</param>
/// <param name="signerPfxCertPassword">
/// Password for signer's private key</param>
```

```csharp
public void LoadSignerCredential(string signerPfxCertPath,
                                 string signerPfxCertPassword)
{
    _signerCert =
      new X509.X509Certificate2(signerPfxCertPath, signerPfxCertPassword);
}


/// <summary>
/// Sign a message and encrypt it for the recipient.
/// </summary>
/// <param name="clearText">Name value pairs
/// must be separated by \n (vbLf or Chr(10)),
/// for example "cmd=_xclick\nbusiness=..."</param>
/// <returns></returns>
public string SignAndEncrypt(string clearText)
{
    string result = null;

    byte[] messageBytes = _encoding.GetBytes(clearText);
    byte[] signedBytes = Sign(messageBytes);
    byte[] encryptedBytes = Envelope(signedBytes);

    result = Base64Encode(encryptedBytes);

    return result;
}


private byte[] Sign(byte[] messageBytes)
{
    Pkcs.ContentInfo content = new Pkcs.ContentInfo(messageBytes);
    Pkcs.SignedCms signed = new Pkcs.SignedCms(content);
    Pkcs.CmsSigner signer = new Pkcs.CmsSigner(_signerCert);
    signed.ComputeSignature(signer);
    byte[] signedBytes = signed.Encode();

    return signedBytes;
}


private byte[] Envelope(byte[] contentBytes)
{
    Pkcs.ContentInfo content = new Pkcs.ContentInfo(contentBytes);
    Pkcs.EnvelopedCms envMsg = new Pkcs.EnvelopedCms(content);
    Pkcs.CmsRecipient recipient =
      new Pkcs.CmsRecipient(
        Pkcs.SubjectIdentifierType.IssuerAndSerialNumber, _recipientCert);
    envMsg.Encrypt(recipient);
    byte[] encryptedBytes = envMsg.Encode();
```

```
            return encryptedBytes;
        }

        private string Base64Encode(byte[] encoded)
        {
            const string PKCS7_HEADER = "-----BEGIN PKCS7-----";
            const string PKCS7_FOOTER = "-----END PKCS7-----";

            string base64 = Convert.ToBase64String(encoded);
            StringBuilder formatted = new StringBuilder();
            formatted.Append(PKCS7_HEADER);
            formatted.Append(base64);
            formatted.Append(PKCS7_FOOTER);

            return formatted.ToString();
        }
    }
}
```

Listing 4-7 shows an example of how to use the ButtonEncryption class.

Listing 4-7. *C# Example of Using the ButtonEncryption Class*

```
string paypalCertPath = Server.MapPath("App_Data/paypal_cert_pem.txt");
string signerPfxPath = Server.MapPath("App_Data/my_cert.p12");
string signerPfxPassword = GetSignerPfxPassword(); // retrieve your password
string clearText = "cmd=_xclick\n" +
                   "business=your@domain.com\n" +
                   "currency_code=GBP\n" +
                   "item_name=Tennis Balls ßü (£12 umlot OK)\n" +
                   "amount=15.00\n" +
                   "return=https://www.yourdomain.com/return\n" +
                   "cancel_return=https://www.yourdomain.com/cancel\n" +
                   "cert_id=C2XRTSNRF7E2S";

ButtonEncryption ewp = new ButtonEncryption();
ewp.LoadSignerCredential(signerPfxPath, signerPfxPassword);
ewp.RecipientPublicCertPath = paypalCertPath;

string result = ewp.SignAndEncrypt(clearText);
```

You can then take the value of result and insert it into your button form as shown in Listing 4-8.

Listing 4-8. *Buy Now Button with Encrypted Text*

```
<form action="https://www.sandbox.paypal.com/cgi-bin/webscr" method="POST">
  <input type="hidden" name="cmd" value="_s-xclick">
  <input type="hidden" name="encrypted" value="<% result %>">
  <input type="submit" name="submit" value="Pay Now">
</form>
```

PHP Developers

PayPal does not provide libraries or sample code for PHP, but members of PayPal's developer community have contributed some code for PHP that performs PayPal EWP encryption. Chris Hogben generated the original versions of this code, and it has since been updated by Dave Burchell. You can download this source code from www.paypaltech.com/Dave/api_sourcebook/html/ewp/ewpphp.html or from the Source Code/Download section of the Apress website (www.apress.com), where many of the source code examples in this book can be accessed.

This code uses two files: Config.php to enclose all of the configuration settings (see Listing 4-9) and EncryptedButtons.php to perform the actual encryption (see Listing 4-10). Comments for the code are provided inline.

Listing 4-9. *Config.php*

```
<?php
class PayPal_EncryptedButtons_Config {

// {{{ properties

/***************************************
 *
 * Please edit the options below to reflect
 * your system configuration. If they are
 * incorrect, this program may not work as
 * expected.
 *
 ***************************************/


        /* Certificate ID */
        var $cert_id = "PZ9MJJTPW9NP8";

        /* PayPal E-mail Address */
        var $business = "seller@testaccount.com";

        /* Receiver E-Mail - E-Mail Address Payment will be sent to */
        /* Leave blank if the same as above */
        var $receiver = "";
```

```php
    /* Base Directory - Base directory where all files will be stored */
    /* This should be outside the website root, and only readable by you */
    /* The trailing slash is REQUIRED */
    var $basedir = "/var/www/php_paypal/";

    /* Certificate Store - Directory in which all certificates are stored */
    /* Can be the name of a subdirectory under basedir, or another path */
    /* The trailing slash is REQUIRED */
    var $certstore = "certificates/";

    /* Temporary Directory - Where temporary files are stored regarding  ➥
the transaction.  This should be under the base directory OR outside  ➥
the webroot, and only readable by you/the web server. Files from this  ➥
directory are automatically removed after use. The trailing slash is REQUIRED */
    var $tempdir = "/var/www/php_paypal/temp/";

    /* OpenSSL Path - Path to the OpenSSL Binary */
    /* If openssl isn't in your PATH, then change this to where  ➥
it's located, otherwise leave it as it is */
    /* No trailing slash */
    var $openssl = "openssl";

    /* Certificate Names - Names of all the certificates required */

    /* Your Private Key Filename */
    var $my_private = "/var/www/php_paypal/certificates/cert_key.pem";

    /* Your Public Certificate Filename */
    var $my_public = "/var/www/php_paypal/certificates/cert_key.pem";

    /* PayPal's Public Certificate Filename */
  var $paypal_public = "/var/www/php_paypal/certificates/paypal_public_cert.pem";


// }}}

}

?>
```

Listing 4-10. *EncryptedButtons.php*

```php
<?php

// {{{ constants
// {{{ error codes

 define("PP_ERROR_OK", 0);
 define("PP_ERROR_FILE", 1);
 define("PP_ERROR_OPENSSL", 2);
 define("PP_ERROR_DATA", 3);
 define("PP_ERROR_PARAMS", 4);
 define("PP_ERROR_NOTFOUND", 5);
 define("PP_ERROR_UNKNOWN", 6);

// }}}
// }}}

require_once "Config.php";

 class PayPal_EncryptedButtons {

        // {{{ properties

        /** Button Data Array */
        var $buttonData = array();

        /** Config Pointer */
        var $config;

        /** Internal Data Handler */
        var $_data;

        /** Random Transaction ID */
        var $_rnd;

        var $debug = true;

        // }}}

        // {{{ constructor
        /**
        * Constructs a new PayPal_EncryptedButtons object
        *
        * @access public
        */
```

```php
    function PayPal_EncryptedButtons($config = array()) {
            $this->config = new PayPal_EncryptedButtons_Config;
            return;
    }


    // }}}
    // {{{ changeConfig()
    /**
     * Change a Configuration Directive after the class has been loaded
     *
     * @param string $name
     * @param string $value
     * @return bool
     * @access public
     *
     */
    function changeConfig($name, $value = "") {
            if ($this->config->$name) {
                    $this->config->$name = $value;
                    return true;
            }
            else {
                    return false;
            }
    }
    // }}}


    // {{{ addButtonParam()
    /**
     * Add parameters to the button code
     *
     * @param mixed $names
     * @param mixed $values
     * @return int
     * @access public
     */
    function addButtonParam($names = "", $values = "") {
            if ((is_array($names) && !is_array($values)) || ➥
(!is_array($names) && is_array($values))) {
                    return PP_ERROR_PARAMS;
            }
            elseif (is_array($names) && is_array($values)) {
                    if (count($names) !== count($values)) {
                            return PP_ERROR_PARAMS;
                    }
```

```
                                    $i = 0;
                                    while ($i < count($names)) {
                                            $this->buttonData[$names[$i]] = $values[$i];
                                            $i++;
                                    }
                                    return PP_ERROR_OK;
                    }
                    else {
                            if ($names == "" || $values == "") {
                                    return PP_ERROR_PARAMS;
                            }
                            else {
                                    $this->buttonData[$names] = $values;
                                    return PP_ERROR_OK;
                            }
                    }
            }
            // }}}

            // {{{ delButtonParam()
            /**
             * Deletes a Button Parameter
             *
             * @param string $name
             * @return int
             * @access public
             */
            function delButtonParam($name = "") {
                    if ($name == "") {
                            return PP_ERROR_PARAMS;
                    }
                    if ($this->buttonData[$name] !== null) {
                            $this->buttonData[$name] = null;
                            return PP_ERROR_OK;
                    }
                    return PP_ERROR_NOTFOUND + 10;
            }
            // }}}

            // {{{ encryptButtonData()
            /**
             * Encrypts the data in buttonData
             *
             * @return int
             * @access public
             */
```

```php
    function encryptButtonData() {
            $this->encryptedButton = null;
            if (!is_dir($this->config->basedir)) {
                    if (!mkdir($this->config->basedir)) {
                            return PP_ERROR_NOTFOUND + 20;
                    }
            }
            @chdir($this->config->basedir);
            $this->_data = "cmd=_xclick\n";
            $this->_data .= "business=".$this->config->business."\n";
            $this->_data .= "receiver_email=".$this->config->➥
receiver_email."\n";
            foreach ($this->buttonData as $name => $val) {
                    if ($val == null) { continue; }
                    $this->_data .= $name."=".$val."\n";
            }
            $this->_data .= "cert_id=".$this->config->cert_id;
            $this->_rnd = rand(100000, 999999);
            if (!is_dir($this->config->tempdir)) {
                    if (!@mkdir($this->config->tempdir)) {
                            return PP_ERROR_NOTFOUND + 30;
                    }
            }
            $f = @fopen($this->config->tempdir.$this->_rnd.".1", "w");
            //if (!$f) { return PP_ERROR_FILE; }
            if (!$f) { return 41; }
            fwrite($f, trim($this->_data), strlen(trim($this->_data)));
            fclose($f);
            if (!file_exists($this->config->my_private)) {
                    return 145;
            }
            if (!file_exists($this->config->my_public)) {
                    return 245;
            }
            if (!file_exists($this->config->paypal_public)) {
                    return 345;
            }
            if (!file_exists($this->config->my_private) || ➥
!file_exists($this->config->my_public) || ➥
!file_exists($this->config->paypal_public)) {
                    return PP_ERROR_NOTFOUND + 40;
            }
            $exec = $this->config->openssl." smime -sign -in ".$this->config->➥
tempdir.$this->_rnd.".1 -signer ".$this->config->my_public." -inkey ".$this->➥
config->my_private." -outform der -nodetach -binary > ".$this->config->➥
tempdir.$this->_rnd.".2";
```

```
                    $status1 = `$exec`;
                    $exec = $this->config->openssl." smime -encrypt -des3 -binary ➥
        -outform pem ".$this->config->paypal_public." < ".$this->config->➥
        tempdir.$this->_rnd.".2 > ".$this->config->tempdir.$this->_rnd.".3";
                    $status2 = `$exec`;
                    $this->encryptedButton = trim(file_get_contents($this->config->➥
        tempdir.$this->_rnd.".3"));
                    @unlink($this->config->tempdir.$this->_rnd.".1");
                    @unlink($this->config->tempdir.$this->_rnd.".2");
                    @unlink($this->config->tempdir.$this->_rnd.".3");
                    if (strpos($status1, "No such file or directory") !== false || ➥
        strpos($status2, "No such file or directory") !== false) {
                            return PP_ERROR_OPENSSL;
                    }
                    if (!$this->encryptedButton) {
                            return PP_ERROR_DATA;
                    }
                    return PP_ERROR_OK;
            }
            // }}}

            // {{{ getButton()
            /**
            * Returns the Encrypted Button Contents
            *
            * @return string
            * @access public
            */
            function getButton() {
                    if (!$this->encryptedButton) {
                            return "";
                    }
                    return $this->encryptedButton;
            }
            // }}}

    }
    // }}}

?>
```

Perl Developers

PayPal does not offer any sample code for Perl, but a member of the PayPal developer community has stepped up to fill in the gap. Gray Watson from 256 (http://256.com) has provided a Perl version of an EWP encryption script that calls OpenSSL directly (see Listing 4-11). This script depends on the use of a flat file named params.txt to contain your configuration parameters, although it could easily be modified to include the values directly in the script. You can download the script from http://256.com/gray/docs/paypal_encrypt or from the Source Code/Download section of the Apress website (www.apress.com), along with many other samples from this book.

Listing 4-11. *Perl EWP Script*

```perl
#!/usr/bin/perl
#
# Script which uses openssl to encrypt Paypal payment buttons
#
# More details: http://256.com/gray/docs/paypal_encrypt/
#

use FileHandle;
use IPC::Open2;
use strict;

# private key file to use
my $MY_KEY_FILE = "sample_key.pem";

# public certificate file to use - should correspond to the $cert_id
my $MY_CERT_FILE = "sample_cert.pem";

# Paypal's public certificate
my $PAYPAL_CERT_FILE = "paypal_public_cert.pem";

# File that holds extra parameters for the paypal transaction.
my $MY_PARAM_FILE = "params.txt";

# path to the openssl binary
#my $OPENSSL = "/usr/bin/openssl";
#my $OPENSSL = "C:\\OpenSSL\\Bin\\openssl.exe";
my $OPENSSL = "/usr/local/bin/openssl";

# make sure we can execute the openssl utility
die "Could not execute $OPENSSL: $!\n" unless -x $OPENSSL;

##############

# Send arguments into the openssl commands needed to do the sign,
# encrypt, s/mime magic commands.
my $pid = open2(*READER, *WRITER,
    "$OPENSSL smime -sign -signer $MY_CERT_FILE " .
    "-inkey $MY_KEY_FILE -outform der -nodetach -binary " .
    "| $OPENSSL smime -encrypt -des3 -binary -outform pem " .
    "$PAYPAL_CERT_FILE")
  || die "Could not run open2 on $OPENSSL: $!\n";
```

```perl
# Write our parameters that we need to be encrypted to the openssl process.
open(PARAMS, "< $MY_PARAM_FILE")
  || die "Could not open '$MY_PARAM_FILE': $!\n";
while (<PARAMS>) {
  chomp;
  next if (m/^\#/ || m/^$/);
  print WRITER "$_\n";
}
close(PARAMS);

# close the writer file-handle
close(WRITER);

# read in the lines from openssl
my @lines = <READER>;

# close the reader file-handle which probably closes the openssl processes
close(READER);

# combine them into one variable
my $encrypted = join('', @lines);

####################

# print our encrypted HTML button code
print qq[
<html>
<head><title> Sample.html </title></head>
<body>
<h1>Donate</h1>
<form action="https://www. paypal.com/cgi-bin/webscr" method="post">
<input type="hidden" name="cmd" value="_s-xclick">
<input type="hidden" name="encrypted" value="
$encrypted" />
<input type="submit" value="Buy Now" />
</form>
</body>
</html>
];
```

Summary

Placing plain-text HTML buttons on your website can leave your site open to attack from fraudsters. Using PayPal's Encrypted Website Payments (EWP) feature, you can encrypt the variables in your button code so that they are protected from attack by a malicious third party. In this chapter, we discussed the steps involved to acquire the necessary public certificate and private key files to use EWP. Sample code for multiple languages was also provided and discussed.

One other major takeaway from this chapter is that PayPal offers the ability to encrypt your button code directly on the PayPal website by using PayPal's Button Factory. If you do not have any custom variables in your button, such as item color or size, you can just check a box in the Button Factory and PayPal will perform the EWP process for you. The rest of the chapter offered techniques to use when this simple, straightforward process does not suit your needs.

In the next chapter, we will discuss postpayment processing, which deals with the PayPal options available to you after your customer has completed a PayPal purchase.

CHAPTER 5

■ ■ ■

Postpayment Processing

Up until this point, I've mainly discussed how to set up your website to accept standard PayPal payments. I've kept it pretty simple and shown some examples of adding Buy Now buttons or even a simple shopping cart to your website. A little complexity was added during the discussion of the encryption aspect of button parameters, but even this function can be automated by the PayPal Button Factory, as shown in Chapter 4.

For some individuals and small businesses, these basic options may be enough to satisfy all of their e-commerce needs, but for many other businesses that handle a high transaction volume or need to tie into a back-end database, it's not enough to just accept payments. To develop a true end-to-end application, what you do after the sale is made is just as important as the sale itself. This function, which we'll refer to as *postpayment processing*, is what this chapter addresses.

Over the years, PayPal has pioneered a number of secure technologies to assist developers in improving their postpayment processing capabilities, in regard to both order fulfillment automation and improved user experience. This chapter covers the range of options available, provides examples of when it makes sense to use a given option, and presents general best practices to consider when designing an e-commerce solution. The specific technologies covered in this chapter are as follows:

- Auto Return

- Payment Data Transfer (PDT)

- Instant Payment Notification (IPN)

These technologies work closely together and are often combined for the best results. By the end of this chapter, you'll understand how these features work and when it makes sense to use them. You'll also realize their importance in creating a robust e-commerce solution that goes beyond the basics. PayPal offers code samples on its website that you can download and modify for your needs, so if you do choose to begin working with these features, you'll already have some scripts to work from. I'll tell you how to access those as well.

One of the first questions people ask when determining their postpayment processing strategy is, "How can I get notified about new payments as they occur?" And indeed, that's an excellent place to start. PayPal offers a number of different answers to that question that go beyond the basic email sent to the primary email address on the account whenever a new payment is made. We'll begin with a look at the Auto Return feature.

Auto Return

One of the ways PayPal allows you to control the checkout experience for your customers is with the Auto Return feature. By default, customers see a page similar to Figure 5-1 after they pay you with their PayPal account.

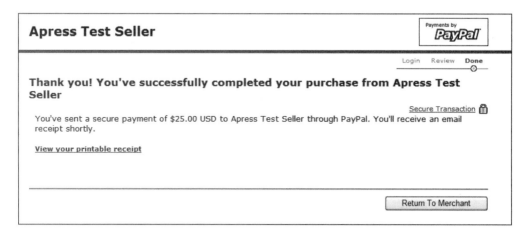

Figure 5-1. *A standard payment confirmation page without Auto Return*

As you can see, customers have to click the Return to Merchant button to return to your website, which is ultimately what you want. Once they return, you can display a thank you message, and let them know that their order is on its way. You can also direct them to continue browsing on your website and offer them additional content, products, and services.

But what if a customer doesn't click the Return to Merchant button? That person will browse off to some other site, and although the transaction has been completed, you've lost the user. There's no chance for an upsell or any additional activity on your website.

The Auto Return feature addresses this problem by automatically redirecting your customer's browser to your return URL. After a couple of seconds go by on the payment confirmation page, PayPal initiates a HTTP redirect to a URL that you specify. The buyer is then taken back to your website for continued browsing.

Auto Return Account Settings

If you want PayPal to automatically redirect your customers back to your website at the end of a successful transaction, follow these steps to turn on Auto Return for your account:

1. Log in to your Premier or Business account at `www.paypal.com`.

2. Click the Profile subtab.

3. Click Website Payment Preferences in the Selling Preferences column.

4. Click the On radio button next to the Auto Return label.

5. Enter the URL where you want your users to return in the text box labeled Return URL. The web page at this URL should display text to users that lets them know that the transaction was successfully completed, and that they will receive transaction details via email.

6. Click the Save button at the bottom of the page.

In addition to setting the Return URL as described in step 5, you can include a `return` variable with your button code or API call that will override this value on a per-transaction basis.

■**Note** If you have Account Optional turned on for your account, which means that buyers who don't have PayPal accounts can still check out through PayPal by paying with a credit card, those buyers will not be automatically returned to your website after checkout. They will, however, be given the choice to return to your site by clicking a button, in addition to being presented with the option to create a PayPal account.

The rm Variable

The next section on Payment Data Transfer (PDT) describes a way that you can use HTTP to programmatically retrieve transaction details from PayPal upon a customer's return to your website following a successful PayPal purchase. But if you only need barebones information about the transaction, there is a little-known variable you can use in your button code that allows you to retrieve some core transaction details without having to get involved in the multistep PDT process. That variable is `rm`, which stands for "return method."

The default return method used when PayPal sends a customer back to your website is HTTP GET. And indeed, if you do not include the `rm` variable in your button code, a GET is what you'll get. But over time, developers began asking to have this redirect be made via HTTP POST. PayPal listened to this feedback and provided a way to make it possible. And since the redirect can now be made via HTTP POST, a number of variables can easily be included with the URL. The variables that PayPal includes in the URL include the transaction ID, amount, status, and currency of the purchase.

To enable this feature and have PayPal make a POST to your return URL instead of a GET, set the `rm` variable to 2. To have PayPal make a GET, set `rm` to 1 or do not include it at all. One other caveat is that if you pass in a `notify_url` or have IPN enabled on your account, the IPN data is posted to the return URL even if `rm` is set to 1. Table 5-1 summarizes the possible values of `rm` and the corresponding return method used by PayPal.

Table 5-1. `rm` *Variable Values and Corresponding PayPal Return Methods*

`rm` **Value**	**Return Method**
Default/0	HTTP GET
1	HTTP GET
2	HTTP POST

Table 5-2 summarizes the variables included by PayPal in the POST. A basic script at your return URL can easily parse these variables and take appropriate action, such as updating a database or making a subsequent call to the GetTransactionDetails API for complete transaction details. See Chapter 6 for more information on the GetTransactionDetails API.

Table 5-2. *Variables Included in the POST Back from PayPal*

Variable	Meaning
tx	Transaction ID
st	Payment status
amt	Payment amount
cc	Currency code
sig	Deprecated (has no meaning but is still included for backward compatibility)

■**Note** Use of the rm variable only works if you have Auto Return disabled in your account.

Payment Data Transfer

PayPal's Payment Data Transfer (PDT) feature arose from a need to fix a fundamental shortcoming of PayPal's hosted checkout process: when a customer is sent back to your site after paying, how do you know who it is? This inability to distinguish which customer has returned to your site prevents you from, among other things, displaying a customized thank you message to the buyer. PayPal recognized that online businesses want to not only identify the customer returning to their site, but also know what the customer purchased and the location where the items should be shipped. PayPal's Express Checkout has since handled this problem via the PayPal API, but with standard checkout, a solution was needed.

To solve this problem, PayPal developed PDT. To use PDT, you must have Auto Return enabled (see the previous section titled "Auto Return"). When you enable PDT for your account, PayPal will append a transaction ID to the Auto Return URL you specified in your Profile. A *transaction ID* is a unique alphanumeric string that identifies an individual PayPal transaction. You use that transaction ID to query PayPal about the details of the transaction, which you then display to your customer. Buyers enjoy a better checkout experience by ending up on your website with a customized message that personally thanks them for their purchase, tells them what they just bought, and lets them know both where it will be shipped and when it is likely to arrive.

■**Note** PDT works only with Website Payments Standard. It does not work with Express Checkout.

How PDT Works

PDT is a front-end technology, meaning that there is a web flow involved. After a transaction has been successfully completed, PayPal automatically redirects the customer's browser back to your website at your Auto Return URL via HTTP GET. The transaction ID will be appended to this URL with the variable `tx`. Here's an example of how this URL will look:

Auto Return URL: `http://www.my-test-store.com/thank-you.php`

URL with appended transaction ID: `http://www.my-test-store.com/thank-you.php?tx= 6DF258882T143510R`

At this point, you know that a new transaction has taken place, but you don't know anything about it except for the transaction ID. You then use the transaction ID to query PayPal for the complete list of transaction details. You do this by submitting a HTTP POST request to PayPal, in which you include the transaction ID along with your *identity token*, a secure string that uniquely identifies you to PayPal (instructions on how to obtain your identity token are described in the upcoming "PDT Account Settings" section). The format of the HTTP POST should be as follows (example values are provided for the transaction ID [tx] and the identity token [at]):

```
<form method="POST">
    <action="https://www.paypal.com/cgi-bin/webscr"/>
    <input type="hidden" name="cmd" value="_notify-synch"/>
    <input type="hidden" name="tx" value="6DF258882T143510R"/>
    <input type="hidden" name="at" value="YourIdentityToken"/>
    <input type="submit" value="PDT"/>
</form>
```

The `cmd` variable, with a value of `_notify-synch`, tells PayPal that this is a PDT request. The `tx` variable contains the transaction ID value that PayPal just sent to you, and the `at` variable contains your identity token. PayPal will then respond to your POST, and the first line will be either SUCCESS or FAIL. If it is FAIL, PayPal was not able to validate the transaction. Either your transaction ID, identity token, or account profile settings are not correct. But if you have everything set up correctly, you will receive SUCCESS as the first line, followed by a series of name/value pairs that contain information about the transaction, as shown in Listing 5-1.

Listing 5-1. *Example of a Successful PDT HTTP Response*

```
SUCCESS
first_name=Bob
last_name=Wilson
payment_status=Completed
payer_email=bigbobwilson%40hotmail.com
payment_gross=75.00
mc_currency=USD
custom=A+custom+message+can+go+here
more...
```

Your code can then parse the response, line by line, and retrieve the transaction details. More fields are returned than those shown in Listing 5-1. The meaning of most of the fields is fairly self-explanatory, but for a complete list of the variables that can be returned in a PDT response, check this book's appendix.

Figure 5-2 provides a graphical representation of the various interactions that take place in PDT.

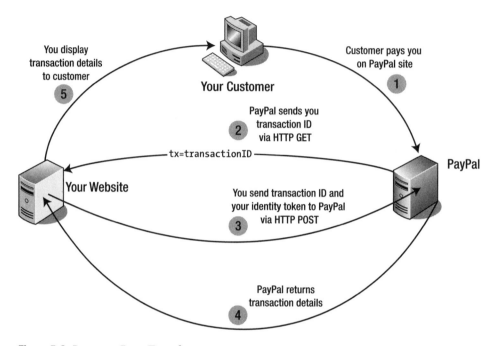

Figure 5-2. *Payment Data Transfer process*

Now that you have a general overview of the PDT process, next you'll see how to activate PDT for your account, and you'll also take a look at some code that performs all the necessary steps involved.

PDT Account Settings

To enable PDT for your account and acquire your identity token, take the following steps:

1. Log in to your Premier or Business account at www.paypal.com.

2. Click the Profile subtab.

3. Click Website Payment Preferences in the Selling Preferences column.

4. Click the On radio button next to the Auto Return label.

5. Enter the URL of the script that will process the PDT HTTP request sent from PayPal (step 2 in Figure 5-2).

6. Under Payment Data Transfer, click the On radio button.

7. Click Save.

If you do everything correctly, you will be taken back to your account Profile page and shown a success message (see Figure 5-3). This message contains your identity token, which you will then include in your PDT script. You include your identity token when you query PayPal to retrieve details for a new transaction. Since you are the only one who knows your identity token, PayPal uses it to authenticate you when you make your HTTP request for transaction details.

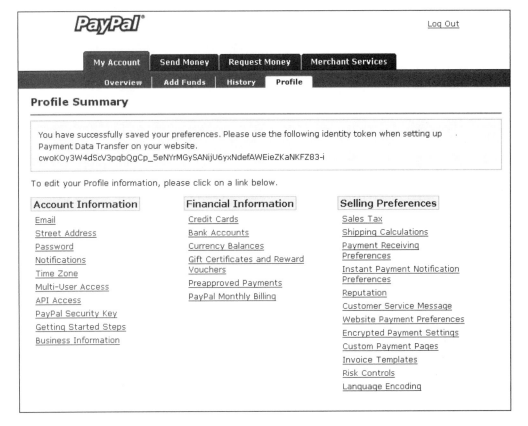

Figure 5-3. *Successful creation of an identity token*

Sample PDT Script

If you're looking for a quick way to generate a PDT script, PayPal's technical support staff maintains a script generation tool at www.paypaltech.com/PDTGen. The code in Listing 5-2 is based on a PHP sample that comes from the generator. It has been slightly modified and inline explanations have been added. There are also places where additional code should be added that is based on the specific website it is used for.

Listing 5-2. *Sample PDT Script*

```php
<?php

// PayPal Payment Data Transfer (PDT) Script

// Begin to form the HTTP request that will be sent to PayPal
$req = 'cmd=_notify-synch';

// Read the Transaction ID from the 'tx' variable sent by PayPal
$transaction_id = $_GET['tx'];

// Define your identify token
$identity_token = "o97T9kcQ5skO847fk7CLyjTmIDqh4nG9vAonIS1IbQxnhG5gPUgBFMv8Pw8";

// Append the Transaction ID and Identify Token to the request string
$req .= "&tx=$transaction_id&at=$identity_token";


// Post back to PayPal system to validate the transaction ➥
// and retrieve transaction details
// First, form the HTTP Header
$header .= "POST /cgi-bin/webscr HTTP/1.0\r\n";
$header .= "Content-Type: application/x-www-form-urlencoded\r\n";
$header .= "Content-Length: " . strlen($req) . "\r\n\r\n";

// This code posts to the PayPal Sandbox testing environment, and not the live site
// If your server is SSL enabled, use 443 instead of 80 to make a secure post
$fp = fsockopen ('www.sandbox.paypal.com', 80, $errno, $errstr, 30);

if (!$fp) {
  // HTTP ERROR
}
else {
  // Make the POST
  fputs ($fp, $header . $req);

  // Read the body data
  $res = '';
  $headerdone = false;
  while (!feof($fp)) {
    $line = fgets ($fp, 1024);
    if (strcmp($line, "\r\n") == 0) {
      // Read the header
      $headerdone = true;
    }
```

```php
      else if ($headerdone) {
        // Header has been read, now read the contents
        $res .= $line;
      }
    }


    // Parse the response from PayPal. Create a string array of values.
    $lines = explode("\n", $res);
    $keyarray = array();
    // Check the first line to see if it reads SUCCESS or FAIL
    if (strcmp ($lines[0], "SUCCESS") == 0) {
      for ($i=1; $i<count($lines);$i++) {
        list($key,$val) = explode("=", $lines[$i]);
        $keyarray[urldecode($key)] = urldecode($val);
      }
      // At this point, you have an array of values
      // that tell you a lot about the transaction
      // You may want to add logic to perform the following checks:
      // * the payment_status is Completed before processing an order
      // * the transaction ID has not been previously processed
      // * the receiver_email is your primary PayPal email
      // * the payment_amount and payment_currency are correct

      $firstname = $keyarray['first_name'];
      $lastname = $keyarray['last_name'];
      $itemname = $keyarray['item_name'];
      $amount = $keyarray['mc_gross'];

      // Display a customized thank you message to your customer
      echo ("<b> Dear $firstname $lastname ,</b>\n");
      echo ("Thank you for your purchase of $itemname \n");
      echo ("Your order has been processed for the amount of $amount \n");
      echo ("");
    }
    else if (strcmp ($lines[0], "FAIL") == 0) {
      // PayPal could not validate the transaction. Log and investigate!
    }
}

fclose ($fp);
?>


<p>
Your transaction has been completed, and a receipt for your purchase has been
emailed to you. You may log into your account at www.paypal.com to view details of
this transaction.</p><br/>
```

You can obviously modify this code to meet your needs, but as you can see, it is a fairly straightforward process. By combining the transaction ID with your identity token, you can securely retrieve details for any transaction that has occurred in your account.

PDT Shortcomings

PDT is useful for giving your customer an improved checkout experience, but it has a few shortcomings that prevent it from being reliably used as a sole solution for postpayment processing. Two specific times when PDT does not prove to be an optimal solution is when you are paid with an eCheck and when your user browses away from the PayPal payment confirmation screen before being redirected back to your site.

eCheck Pending Payments

Unless you have specifically set in your profile to not accept eCheck payments, customers can pay you via a bank draft from their checking or savings account. However, because this process relies on the traditional ACH payment network, it can take up to four days to complete. If you rely on PDT notification to fulfill new orders for your customers, you'll have to manually check to see when the payment clears. Unless you are using IPN or the PayPal API, you can't automatically know if and when the eCheck clears. When you do receive payment via eCheck, the payment_status variable in the PDT response will have a value of Pending. If you are offering a downloadable product to your customer after he or she returns to your site, you should double-check to make sure the payment_status is Completed before providing access to the download.

User Abandonment After Checkout

Although the Auto Return feature is reliable, there are a couple of seconds after buyers see the payment confirmation page and before they are returned to your site. During this time, they may close their browser or click to visit another website. As far as they are concerned, the order is complete. But if you're relying on that return and the subsequent PDT request to update your order database, you won't find out about the transaction unless you manually reconcile with your account history.

The next section covers how PDT and Auto Return can be used as part of a larger solution when combined with IPN.

Instant Payment Notification

The advent of PDT was an improvement for the PayPal buyer experience, but some inherent shortcomings left something to be desired in designing an automated order-processing application. Businesses needed a way to reliably receive an automatic notification every time a transaction took place. PDT came close, but didn't completely fit the bill. To solve this conundrum, in 2004 PayPal introduced Instant Payment Notification (IPN).

IPN is a server-to-server communication mechanism that securely sends a message from PayPal to a URL you specify. A message is sent whenever a new transaction takes place, the status of a prior transaction changes, or a new dispute is filed against your account in the Resolution Center (for more on the Resolution Center, see Chapter 9). By hosting a script at the URL that processes the IPN (called the *notification URL*), businesses can automate certain aspects of their order fulfillment process to perform such tasks as automatically updating a database with a new customer order, sending a confirmation email, and triggering an investigation into a claim made by a dissatisfied customer.

■**Caution** Since IPN messages can sometimes be delayed—hence not exactly "instant"—IPN should not be exclusively relied on when immediate order fulfillment is necessary, such as in the case of a digital download service.

How IPN Works

IPN is different from PDT in that it is not a front-end technology; there are no web flows involved. IPN is a multistep process that involves a series of communication points between your server and PayPal servers. It was designed to be absolutely secure, yet easy enough to use so that even a novice web programmer can deploy a simple script to process notifications.

When an IPN-triggering event happens, such as the arrival of a new payment, PayPal posts an IPN to your server at your notification URL. This is done via HTTP POST. Included in this notification are all of your customer's payment details as well as an encrypted string. The transaction details are sent as a series of name/value pairs. The set of variable names used is the same set used for a PDT request. This book's appendix contains a complete list of IPN/PDT variable names.

Upon receiving the notification, you post the body of the message back to PayPal at a secure URL. This is done so that PayPal can verify that the IPN message is authentic and not sent by a fraudster to simulate a purchase. The URL that you post to is `https://www.paypal.com/cgi-bin/webscr`.

■**Tip** If you are testing in the Sandbox, change the URL to `https://www.sandbox.paypal.com/cgi-bin/webscr`.

When you send this post to PayPal, you include all form variables exactly as you received them (and in the same order), and you also append a variable named `cmd` with the value `_notify-validate` to tell PayPal that this request is for IPN validation. PayPal verifies the transaction by checking the encrypted string and sends confirmation back to your server with a single word, VERIFIED or INVALID, in the body of the response. Your IPN script should make sure to respond to the HTTP response with a 200 OK message to prevent additional attempts by PayPal to send the IPN. If a 200 OK response is not received from your server, PayPal will continue to resend the original IPN four seconds later, then eight seconds after that, then 16 seconds, then 32 seconds, and so on, for up to four days. Most web servers will handle the 200 OK response automatically.

If you receive an INVALID response, then either you've done something wrong or the original IPN should be treated as suspicious and investigated. See the "IPN Troubleshooting Tips" section later in this chapter for common causes of this error. If you receive a VERIFIED response, it means that PayPal could validate that the original IPN message you received was authentic. You're almost out of the woods at this point, but not quite. There are a few additional sanity checks that you should perform before completing and fulfilling the order:

- Confirm that the payment_status is Completed, since IPNs are also sent for other payment status updates, such as Pending or Failed.

- Check that the txn_id is unique, to prevent a fraudster from reusing an old, completed transaction. It's especially important to perform this check if you use PDT with IPN and update your database with data from each.

- Validate that the receiver_email is an email address registered in your PayPal account, to prevent the payment from being sent to a fraudster's account.

- Check other transaction details, such as the item number and price, to confirm that the price has not been changed by a malicious third party.

Figure 5-4 describes the order in which the various steps in IPN take place. This example is for a new transaction.

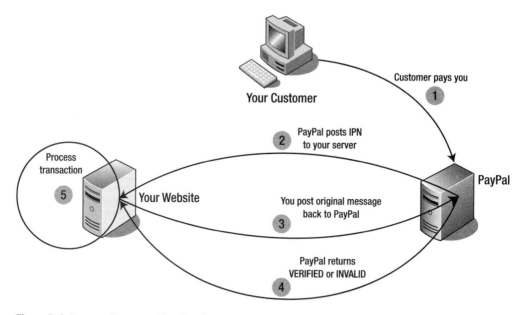

Figure 5-4. *Instant Payment Notification process*

IPN Account Settings

To configure your PayPal account with the appropriate settings to use IPN, follow these steps:

1. Log in to your Premier or Business account at www.paypal.com.

2. Click the Profile subtab.

3. Click Instant Payment Notification Preferences in the Selling Preferences column. You can see that IPN is turned off by default.

4. Click the Edit button to update your settings.

5. Check the activation check box and enter the URL of the script that will process the IPN notifications. This is your notification URL.

6. Click Save, and you should get a message that you have successfully activated IPN.

The notification URL, the location of your script that will process IPN notifications, should be a different URL than that of the web page where your customers return after completing a purchase on the PayPal site. In fact, the notification URL shouldn't even be a web page at all; it should just process the notifications and execute the corresponding business logic.

If you want the web page that your customer sees after completing the transaction to show details of the purchase, you should use PDT in combination with IPN. If you have a need for more than one notification URL to be used, such as the case where you want to handle different types of transactions with different IPN scripts, you can dynamically set the notification URL on a per-transaction basis. See the "Dynamically Setting the Notification URL" section later in this chapter for more information on how to do this.

IPN Sample Code

You can search "PayPal IPN scripts" on the Web and find a number of sites that offer free code samples that will parse your IPN posts, and handle the postback to PayPal and the ensuing verification response. But above all others, I recommend the scripts provided by the PayPal Merchant Technical Support staff. These scripts, which you can access at www.paypaltech.com/SG2, are most likely to be up to date and ready to go out of the box with little modification. You have the option to generate IPN scripts for Perl, PHP, ASP/VBScript, ASP.NET (both VB and C#), ColdFusion, and Java/JSP.

Listing 5-3 contains a slightly modified PHP sample IPN script that processes an IPN notification and sends the buyer a custom email with details about his or her purchase. This is a very simple and straightforward script, but it should give you a general sense of the process.

Listing 5-3. *Sample IPN Script in PHP*

```php
<?php

// Read the post from PayPal system and add 'cmd'
$req = 'cmd=_notify-validate';

foreach ($_POST as $key => $value) {
  $value = urlencode(stripslashes($value));
  $req .= "&$key=$value";
}
```

```php
// post back to PayPal system to validate
$header .= "POST /cgi-bin/webscr HTTP/1.0\r\n";
$header .= "Content-Type: application/x-www-form-urlencoded\r\n";
$header .= "Content-Length: " . strlen($req) . "\r\n\r\n";
$fp = fsockopen ('www.paypal.com', 80, $errno, $errstr, 30);

// assign posted variables to local variables
$item_name = $_POST['item_name'];
$item_number = $_POST['item_number'];
$payment_status = $_POST['payment_status'];
$payment_amount = $_POST['mc_gross'];
$payment_currency = $_POST['mc_currency'];
$txn_id = $_POST['txn_id'];
$receiver_email = $_POST['receiver_email'];
$payer_email = $_POST['payer_email'];
$payment_date = $_POST['payment_date'];
$first_name = $_POST['first_name'];
$last_name = $_POST['last_name'];
$payment_type = $_POST['payment_type'];
$payment_status = $_POST['payment_status'];
$payment_gross = $_POST['payment_gross'];
$payment_fee = $_POST['payment_fee'];
$settle_amount = $_POST['settle_amount'];
$memo = $_POST['memo'];
$payer_email = $_POST['payer_email'];
$receiver_email = $_POST['receiver_email'];
$txn_id = $_POST['txn_id'];
$txn_type = $_POST['txn_type'];
$payer_status = $_POST['payer_status'];
$address_street = $_POST['address_street'];
$address_city = $_POST['address_city'];
$address_state = $_POST['address_state'];
$address_zip = $_POST['address_zip'];
$address_country = $_POST['address_country'];
$address_status = $_POST['address_status'];
$item_name = $_POST['item_name'];
$item_number = $_POST['item_number'];
$tax = $_POST['tax'];
$option_name1 = $_POST['option_name1'];
$option_selection1 = $_POST['option_selection1'];
$option_name2 = $_POST['option_name2'];
$option_selection2 = $_POST['option_selection2'];
$for_auction = $_POST['for_auction'];
$invoice = $_POST['invoice'];
$subscr_id = $_POST['subscr_id'];
```

```
if (!$fp) {
  // HTTP ERROR
} else {

  fputs ($fp, $header . $req);

  while (!feof($fp)) {

    $res = fgets ($fp, 1024);

    if (strcmp ($res, "VERIFIED") == 0) {

      // check the payment_status is Completed
      // check that txn_id has not been previously processed
      // check that receiver_email is your Primary PayPal email
      // check that payment_amount and payment_currency are correct
      // process payment

      // Send a custom email to the value of payer_email

      // Set variables needed for email.
      $from = "Damon's Desks";
      $subject = "Thanks for your purchase";
      $msg =  "Thank you for your purchase. ➥
Your order will be delivered in the next 14 days. We appreciate your business.";

      mail($payer_email, $subject, $msg, "From: $from");

    }

    else if (strcmp ($res, "INVALID") == 0) {
      // log for manual investigation
    }
  }
  fclose ($fp);
}
?>
```

Dynamically Setting the Notification URL

You may have a need to use multiple IPN scripts, depending on the complexity of the application you are building. If this is the case, PayPal offers a second way to set the notification URL in addition to setting it in your account profile. You can specify the notification URL on a per-transaction basis by using the notify_url variable.

■**Note** The value of `notify_url` must be URL encoded.

The `notify_url` parameter will override the URL you have set in your PayPal account profile. It can be passed in via a Website Payments Standard payment button as an additional hidden form variable, or it can be passed in using the PayPal API during an Express Checkout transaction. In the latter case, the variable is called `NotifyURL`. For more information on Express Checkout and the PayPal API, see Chapter 6.

Dispute Resolution with IPN

If a buyer files a chargeback with his or her credit card company or a complaint on the PayPal Resolution Center about a purchase made with you, you will receive an IPN notification to alert you in addition to an email. You will receive information about whether it is a new case or updated information on an existing case, a unique `case_id` to identify the dispute, the reason for the dispute, when it was registered, and the transaction ID of the purchase in question. For more information on dealing with chargebacks and disputes, see Chapter 9.

Using IPN and PDT Together

For a more robust strategy, you can get the best of both worlds by using IPN and PDT together. It's a more complex way to go, but this approach has a number of advantages. You can rely on IPN notifications to make sure you always get customer information for every transaction, and you can also take advantage of PDT and give customers an improved checkout experience by displaying transaction details to them upon their return to your website.

Additionally, since IPNs can be delayed from time to time, data returned to you from PDT can be used to update your customer database. If you use both PDT and IPN to handle post-payment processing, the main thing you will have to take into account is double-checking to make sure you do not process the same transaction twice—once each for both the PDT data and the IPN data.

IPN Troubleshooting Tips

IPN is a very popular technology used by thousands of developers and websites, but it is a nontrivial process to get it up and going. There are a number of places you can trip up along the way, and troubleshooting IPN scripts can be no easy task. This section contains some common errors to check for when your IPN script isn't working as expected.

Not Receiving IPN POSTs

So you've got your IPN script all written and deployed, and you've configured your PayPal profile to activate IPN. You create a test transaction to see how your shiny new script works, and . . . nothing happens. Don't fret—this is a common problem that can be caused by many things. Here's a list of some things to double-check before throwing up your hands in frustration:

- Confirm the PayPal account. IPN won't work if you haven't confirmed the PayPal account to which the money is being sent.

- Check firewall settings. An IPN is an HTTP POST that is sent from PayPal's servers. If your application is behind a firewall, make sure it is not blocking the POST.

- Check server logs. If you have access to your web server's log files, check the access logs to see if IPN traffic is even showing up to your server, and check the error logs to see if it contains any error messages that may help you debug your script.

- Check the path. You'd be amazed at how often a simple missing slash or mistyped directory name causes headaches for developers.

Debugging an INVALID IPN Response

After you receive a new IPN, you post it back to PayPal, which then returns either VERIFIED or INVALID. If you receive INVALID for a message and can't quite figure out why, make sure you aren't being tripped up by any of the following common obstacles:

- *Not posting back* all *variables*: Even if your script is concerned with processing only one or two variables, you must pass back every single variable, in the order they were received, for PayPal to return VERIFIED.

- *Posting to the wrong URL*: As obvious as this seems, developers will often forget to update the URL they are posting to, and post a live IPN to a Sandbox URL or vice versa.

- *Using the wrong character encoding*: Not only do you have to post back all variables, but also you have to post them back in the same character encoding that they were sent to you in. If your script alters the character encoding in any way, this may cause an INVALID response. A common symptom of this is receiving sporadic INVALID responses when most return VERIFIED.

When all else fails, there are a few places to go to get further assistance with IPN. A great place to start is the knowledge base at the PayPal Integration Center at `www.paypal.com/integration`. Another good place to ask a question is the PayPal Developer Community (`http://paypal.lithium.com`), which has a dedicated discussion forum for IPN.

Summary

What happens after a sale is complete is just as important as the sale itself. Auto Return, Payment Data Transfer (PDT), and Instant Payment Notification (IPN) are three technologies you can use to improve your customers' experience and programmatically handle certain tasks in response to a new transaction. This chapter discussed the benefits and limitations of each technology, and proposed an approach that combines all three to offer a fairly robust solution. The `rm` variable was also presented as a handy way to get core transaction details without going through the complexity of PDT or IPN.

Although a lot of information was presented in this chapter, it was not quite complete. There are additional postpayment processing options that I did not cover, and they involve the use of the PayPal API. The PayPal API is the focus of the next chapter, and it takes a different approach to communicating with PayPal. The API provides a number of administrative functions, such as search and refunds, that can help you create a true end-to-end order-processing system. Additionally, the PayPal API offers advanced payment options that you can provide to customers to offer an even more powerful and complete e-commerce solution. Getting interested? Good. Delving into the API is when things really start to get interesting.

CHAPTER 6

■■■

The PayPal API

In 2004, PayPal opened up a range of functionality to developers with the release of the first version of the PayPal API. For those unfamiliar with the term, "API" stands for *application programming interface*. Wikipedia defines an API as "the interface that a computer system, library or application provides in order to allow requests for services to be made of it by other computer programs, and/or to allow data to be exchanged between them."[1] And this is essentially what PayPal added to its repertoire with the public API: a way to programmatically make requests of the PayPal system and receive data in return. Put another way, the API allows you to interact with the PayPal system without needing to use a web browser to log in to your PayPal account.

This chapter is all about the PayPal API: how to use it, what it's good for, pitfalls to be aware of, and how to integrate APIs into your application to start taking advantage of one of PayPal's most powerful features. PayPal offered only a few APIs at first, but it has since gradually added to the list, which now consists of over a dozen APIs that can be used to send money, receive money, refund money, search transaction histories, and more. Upon completion of this chapter, you'll have a good idea of whether the API is something you want to tinker with or leave for another project. Topics this chapter covers include the following:

- Understanding the functionality available through the PayPal API

- Configuring your PayPal account for API access

- Looking at the two interfaces you can use to make API calls

- Developing with the PayPal SDK

- Searching transactions and issuing refunds through the API

- Sending money with the MassPay API

- Implementing PayPal's Express Checkout solution

- Processing credit cards directly with Website Payments Pro

At first glance, the API can be somewhat intimidating. There are some confusing variable names and options that you may not be sure if you need to use, and there's no straightforward "Hello World" code that can have you successfully making an API call in the first five minutes of work. However, once you get your hands a little bit dirty and start to become comfortable

---

1. See http://en.wikipedia.org/wiki/Application_programming_interface.

with how the API works, you'll find that it is actually very well designed. You'll discover flexible options that you hadn't even considered when you first decided to crack open the API. It may even cause you to rethink parts of your application to become even more rich and robust. I hope this chapter can start those lines of thinking for you and spark enough interest to have you put this book down for a few minutes so you can get neck deep with the code behind the PayPal API.

Note This chapter does not cover the APIs used with the Payflow Gateway. The Payflow APIs are covered in Chapter 7.

Overview of the PayPal API

OK, the PayPal API sounds great, but what can you do with it? This section gives a quick overview of the operations available to you and the life cycle of an API call. The remainder of the chapter goes into more detail on each operation, such as the request and response variables, but Table 6-1 is intended to give you a quick overview of the functionality available.

API Operations

Table 6-1 lists all of the publicly available API calls that you can make to PayPal and provides a brief description of each. You can implement one or more of these API calls to add functionality to your application. As you continue reading through this chapter, you will learn how these operations work in more detail, and you will see examples of them in action.

Table 6-1. *PayPal API Operations*

API Operation	Description
TransactionSearch	Search your account history for transactions that meet your search criteria.
GetTransactionDetails	Get detailed information about a single transaction.
RefundTransaction	Issue a refund for a prior transaction.
MassPay	Pay one or more recipients with a single call.
DoDirectPayment	Process a Visa/MasterCard/Discover/American Express credit card payment.
DoAuthorization	Authorize (but don't charge) a credit card payment.
DoReauthorization	Reauthorize a previously authorized credit card payment.
DoCapture	Capture a previously authorized credit card payment.
DoVoid	Cancel a previously authorized payment.
SetExpressCheckout	Initiate an Express Checkout* transaction.
GetExpressCheckoutDetails	Get information about an Express Checkout transaction.
DoExpressCheckoutPayment	Complete an Express Checkout transaction.

* Express Checkout is covered extensively later in this chapter.

Life Cycle of an API Call

Every API call goes through the same steps, or life cycle. The API operates over a simple request/response protocol that most developers should have encountered at some point in their career. At the most basic level, the way a PayPal API call works is as follows:

1. You prepare an API request.

2. You make the API call by sending the request to PayPal.

3. PayPal receives the request and processes the API call.

4. PayPal returns a response to you.

5. You read the response and process the data.

Figure 6-1 shows a visual representation of the life cycle of a PayPal API call.

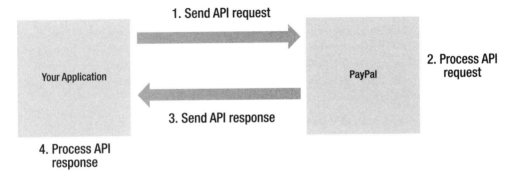

Figure 6-1. *Life cycle of a PayPal API call*

The remainder of this chapter deals with the implementation details involved in sending requests and processing responses. Before you can get to actually making API calls, though, you must first configure your PayPal account be able to access the PayPal API. By default, a PayPal account does not have the ability to use the API. The next section covers this process.

Accessing the PayPal API

For starters, to access the PayPal API, you must have a PayPal Premier or Business account. Personal accounts aren't allowed to use the API. If you have a Personal account and don't want to upgrade it since that would require you to start paying transaction fees for all the payments you receive, I recommend using a Sandbox testing account for your development. Chapter 2 goes into detail on creating and using Sandbox accounts.

Once you've logged in to your Premier or Business account (or have created a Sandbox testing account), you'll need to establish a set of API credentials, determine whether you want to use an API Certificate or API Signature, and decide if you will make first-party or third-party API calls. These topics are discussed in the sections that follow.

API Credentials

To use the PayPal API, you must establish a set of API credentials to identify yourself. Your credentials are included with every API call you make, so that PayPal knows who is making the call. API credentials consist of

- API Username

- API Password

- API Certificate *or* API Signature

Your API Username and API Password are completely different than the email address and password you use to log in to your PayPal account. This may sounds obvious, but some people actually get confused about this point. Your *API Username* is a string that PayPal generates for you, and it is based on your email address. For example, if your email address is developer@mysite.com, your API Username will be developer_api1.mysite.com. Your *API Password* is another string that PayPal generates for you. It is generally 16 characters in length and made up of random letters and numbers.

In addition to the API Username and API Password, a third security credential is required. You have the option of using either an *API Certificate* (a file) or an *API Signature* (a string) for this third option. The next section details the difference between the two and why I recommend using an API Signature for most cases. Before we get to that section though, here's how to get your API credentials:

1. Log in to your Premier or Business account at www.paypal.com.

2. Click the Profile subtab.

3. Click the API Access link under the Account Information header.

4. Click the link that says Request API Credentials.

5. Select either API Signature or API Certificate (read the next section before choosing).

After you choose to use either an API Signature or an API Certificate to authenticate your API calls, you will be shown a page that contains your API credentials. You should copy these credentials down somewhere secure, as you will need them when it comes time to write your code.

API Certificates vs. API Signatures

In the initial release of the API, PayPal took extra steps to make sure the security of the API was as strict as possible. API Certificates were the only option available. Unfortunately, this made the API too difficult to use for many developers.

The API uses the SSL protocol to secure communication. When using SSL, there is always a server-side certificate involved to securely identify the host. Additionally, there can optionally be a client-side certificate involved in the initial SSL handshake that identifies the client interacting with the host. Although rarely used, a client-side certificate adds an extra layer of security to SSL communication, and PayPal chose to require all API calls to use a client-side API Certificate for authentication.

While API Certificates are still supported (and always will be), developers complained about the complexity of using them. No other well-known enterprise—not even eBay or Amazon—required such stringent requirements to secure API calls. Sure, PayPal was directly accessing users' financial information, but eventually certificates became a big enough hurdle that they were preventing many less-experienced developers from gaining much traction with the API. These developers were throwing up their hands in frustration; they were not sure how to get their certificate, what to do with it once they did get it, or why they needed it in the first place. Some people even confused it with the SSL certificate used to secure their website traffic, and others couldn't figure out whether they needed separate certificates for their Sandbox account and their live account (you do).

Additionally, deploying an API Certificate in a shared hosting environment, such as GoDaddy or a similar ISP, is troublesome or impossible in some cases. ISPs don't want to deal with installing third-party certificates on their servers, even if they are from a trusted company such as PayPal. With API Certificates, PayPal had indeed gone the extra mile to secure their API, but in doing so, the company raised the barrier of entry by making the learning curve too steep for some developers to overcome, and making deployment literally impossible for some environments.

PayPal listened to the developer community's feedback on certificate complexity and responded in 2006 with the release of an alternate authentication mechanism meant to alleviate most of the issues surrounding the use of API Certificates. This response was the introduction of API Signatures, and a collective sigh of relief was heard from developers everywhere. An API Signature is a PayPal-generated string that can be used, in combination with an API Username and API Password, to authenticate a PayPal API call. Instead of dealing with encrypting and installing a file-based certificate, with API Signatures you now just need to include an additional string in your API requests.

Tip Unless you have a specific need to use an API Certificate, you should generally choose to use an API Signature instead. The use of an API Signature will save you development time and make your application easier to deploy. The tradeoff is that you must be especially careful to protect your API credentials.

So if you're using API Signatures and wondering why you're having to deal with this really long string that is essentially nothing more than a second password, now you know why. They were introduced to make life easier for you, the developer. And that's ultimately what an API Signature is—an additional password. So keep it safe!

Using API Certificates

If you choose to use an API Certificate instead of an API Signature to authenticate your API calls, there are a few steps you must follow to get your certificate ready to work. When you initially download your certificate, it is in PEM format (described shortly). The default file name is cert_key_pem.txt, which you should rename to something that makes sense to you, such as paypal_api_certificate.pem. If it's a Sandbox certificate, make sure to note that in the file name as well, by naming it something like paypal_sandbox_certificate.pem. You don't want to start confusing your live certificate with your Sandbox certificate.

If you use the PayPal SDK for Java, Classic ASP, or .NET, you need to encrypt the certificate before the SDK will be able to use it (PayPal's SDK, used to facilitate making API calls, is covered later in this chapter). The PayPal SDK for PHP does not require an encrypted certificate, and you can use the PEM format certificate directly as it is downloaded from PayPal.

Then, if you use the PayPal SDK for .NET, you need to take an additional step to install the certificate into the Windows store. This is a requirement imposed by the Windows operating system and the way it works with client-side SSL certificates. The remainder of this section describes how to encrypt and install your API Certificate.

Encrypting the API Certificate

■**Note** These steps are required only if you use the PayPal SDK for Java, .NET, or Classic ASP. The PayPal SDK for PHP does not require these steps.

The certificate you download from PayPal is in PEM format. It contains both your public certificate and the associated private key. Although the PEM certificate is not human-readable, the file is not encrypted. PayPal SDKs for Java, .NET, and Classic ASP require the additional step of encrypting the certificate into PKCS12 format, which is a secure format that cannot be decrypted without the password used to encrypt the file.

The following steps describe how to encrypt your API Certificate into PKCS12 format. These steps require the OpenSSL encryption utility, which is provided by default on Unix/Linux operating systems. Windows users will need to download this utility, which can be acquired from www.slproweb.com/products/Win32OpenSSL.html.

Once you have OpenSSL installed and in your system path, follow these steps to encrypt your API Certificate:

1. Open a command prompt.

2. Change the directory to the location of the API Certificate that you want to encrypt.

3. Execute the following command. This example assumes you have not changed the default file name from cert_key_pem.txt. The line wraps, but this should all be entered in one line:

   ```
   openssl pkcs12 -export -in cert_key_pem.txt -inkey cert_key_pem.txt ➥
   -out paypal_cert.p12
   ```

4. Enter an encryption password when prompted. Write this value down. This is your *private key password.*

5. The preceding command will create a file named paypal_cert.p12. This is your encrypted API Certificate.

You have now successfully encrypted your API Certificate. If you are using the PayPal SDK for .NET or Classic ASP, proceed to the following section and install the certificate into the Windows store.

Installing the API Certificate

■**Note** These steps are required only if you use the PayPal SDK for .NET or Classic ASP.

If you develop with the PayPal SDK for .NET or Classic ASP, you need to take additional steps before your API Certificate can be used. You must import the certificate into the Windows store and grant access to your private key to the user executing your web application. This is a Windows requirement, not a PayPal requirement.

Microsoft provides a utility that accomplishes all of these tasks in a single command. This utility is called the Windows HTTP Services Certificate Configuration Tool, or WinHttpCertCfg.exe. It is freely available as part of the Windows Server 2003 Resource Kit, which can be downloaded from Microsoft's website at a URL that is far too lengthy to reproduce in this book. Just search for "WinHttpCertCfg.exe" using your favorite search engine, and you'll get to the right page.

Once you have downloaded this utility, open a command prompt and enter the following command, making the appropriate replacements described after the code:

```
WinHttpCertCfg -i paypal_cert.p12 -p privateKeyPassword -c LOCAL_MACHINE\my ➥
-a username
```

For this example command, make the following replacements:

- Replace paypal_cert.p12 with the name of the PKCS12-encrypted API Certificate you generated in the previous section.

- Replace privateKeyPassword with the private key password you used to encrypt the certificate in the previous section.

- Replace username with the name of the user executing your application.

  - If you are testing with your Sandbox account, you can use Everyone for this value. Do not use Everyone with your live certificate, because granting private key access to all users on the server is insecure.

  - For an ASP.NET application, this value is ASPNET.

  - Under Windows IIS 5 (default configuration), this value is IWAM_<MACHINE NAME>, where <MACHINE NAME> is the appropriate computer name.

  - Under Windows IIS 6 (default configuration), this value is "NETWORK SERVICE" (make sure to include the quotation marks).

Once you've completed these steps, your API Certificate is ready to be used to make API calls. As you can see, it's a bit complicated. If your code is running on a shared server with an ISP, you'll be hard-pressed to accomplish these steps. This is one of the main reasons why API Signatures are a much easier alternative to API Certificates. Use API Signatures unless you really want to go through all the steps involved with certificates.

Third-Party API Calls

PayPal offers the ability for one PayPal account to make API calls on behalf of another PayPal account through the use of *third-party API calls*. In contrast, the traditional way of using the PayPal API, in which you make API calls directly with your own account and your own set of API credentials, is referred to as making *first-party API calls*. For most e-commerce sites that you build, the first-party model will be appropriate. But if you are building a product or service that uses the API, and you don't want your users to have to go through the process of creating their own set of API credentials, then the third-party model is designed to let you accomplish this.

In a third-party model, your code makes API calls to PayPal on behalf of other businesses. You only use a single set of API credentials for all API calls, no matter how many companies register to use your product or service. This introduces an obvious question: since API credentials identify a business to PayPal, how does PayPal know which company you are making calls for? This is accomplished through the use of an optional field included in every API request, called a *subject*. The subject is the primary email address of the PayPal account of the business on behalf of which the API call is made.

Hosted Shopping Carts Example

One example that illustrates the use of third-party API calls is a hosted shopping cart service such as Shopify (`http://shopify.com`). A hosted shopping cart is software that the user (a merchant) does not download, but instead interacts with via a remote, secure server. With a typical hosted shopping cart, a merchant might do things such as define inventory, set prices for various items, and customize the appearance of the shopping cart.

The hosted cart handles all of the PayPal API calls for its customer, the merchant. The merchant does not have to write any code to submit API calls to PayPal. The cart will actually make the API calls to PayPal and will specify the email address of the merchant in the subject field of each API call, so that PayPal knows which PayPal account to credit the funds.

Granting Third-Party Permission

Obviously, if an application is going to make API calls to PayPal on behalf of another user's PayPal account, that user must grant permission to the application to do so. Otherwise, the application could just go around making API calls on random PayPal accounts, and that wouldn't be too secure! The process by which the permission is granted involves setting appropriate values in your PayPal account Profile. When you click the API Access link in your PayPal Profile for the first time, you will see a screen similar to the one shown in Figure 6-2.

There are two main options on this page. The left option, Grant API Permission, is used to configure an account for third-party API calls. The right option, Request API Credentials, is used to get your API Username, API Password, and API Certificate or API Signature—in other words, the credentials needed for first-party API calls.

Selecting Grant API Permission takes you to the screen shown in Figure 6-3.

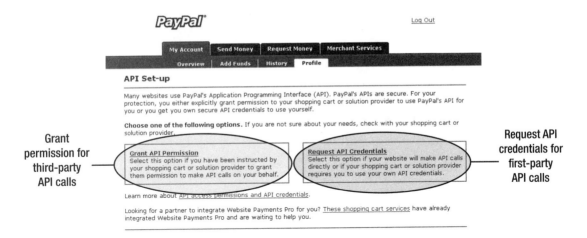

Figure 6-2. *PayPal API access setup page*

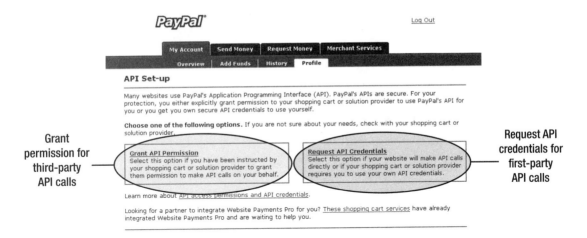

Figure 6-3. *Granting third-party API permission*

To grant another account access to make API calls on your behalf, on this page you must enter the API Username of the account you are granting the permission to in the Enter an API Partner Username text field. In the area beneath this text field are four check boxes where you can specify which API calls you are granting the other account to make. The four options and the API calls they represent are as follows:

- Direct_Payment
  - DoDirectPayment
- Express_Checkout
  - SetExpressCheckout
  - GetExpressCheckoutDetails
  - DoExpressCheckoutPayments
- Admin_API
  - RefundTransaction
  - TransactionSearch
  - GetTransactionDetails
- Auth_Settle
  - DoAuthorization
  - DoReauthorization
  - DoCapture
  - DoVoid

These four options were added as a convenience method to group similar API calls together and limit the number of choices a merchant has to make when granting third-party permissions. If you want to get down to the individual API call level, there's an additional link on this page, Custom API Authorization, that will take you to a page similar to the one shown in Figure 6-4.

This screen is similar to Figure 6-3, in that you have a text field where you specify the API Username of the account that you are granting third-party permission to. But instead of the list of API call categories shown on the prior screen, you have a comprehensive list of the individual PayPal API calls. This allows you to grant fine-grained permissions to another account.

Some API calls shown in Figure 6-4 are not covered in Figure 6-3, and there's also an entry for Encrypted Website Payments. The options presented here that are not covered in Figure 6-3 are as follows:

- *MassPay*: This option enables you to grant another account access to send money out of your account.

- *Encrypted Website Payments*: This option allows another account to create encrypted payment buttons. (This is not API related, but it's included here since you're still granting permission to a third party to take action on your behalf.)

- *BillUser, BillAgreementUpdate*: These are part of PayPal's Preapproved Payments feature, which is not publicly available and must be activated on a per-account basis.

- *CreateMobilePayment, GetMobileStatus*: These are PayPal Mobile APIs and are not publicly available.

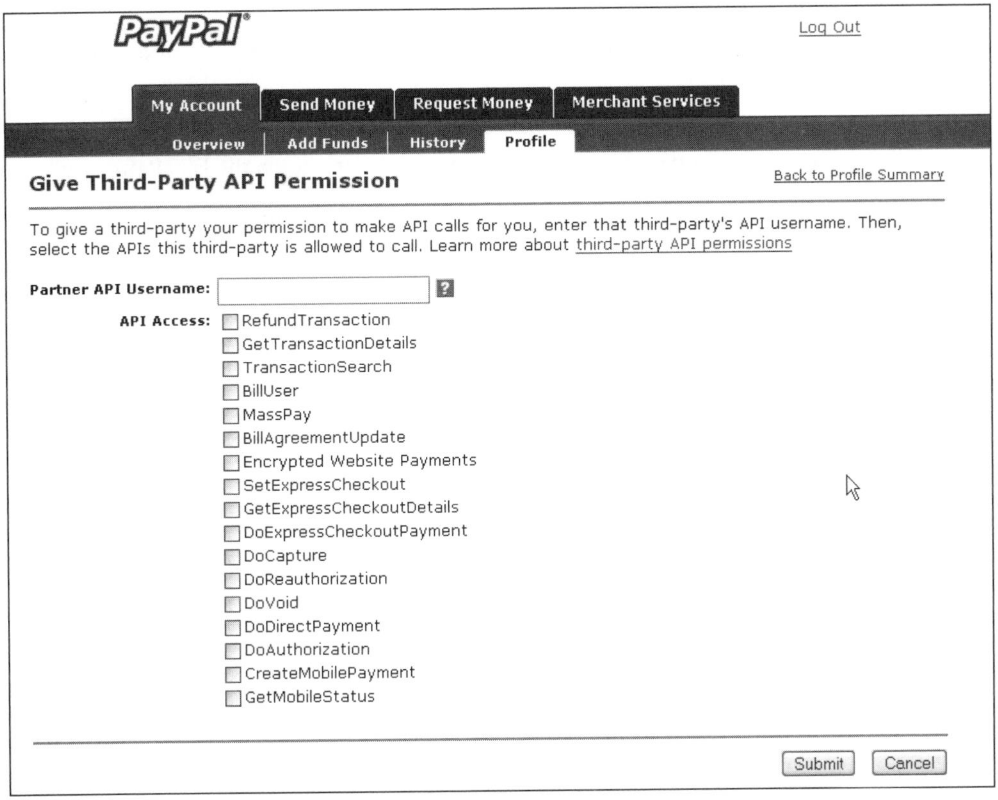

Figure 6-4. *Fine-grained third-party API permissions*

In general, you only need to set up your account to grant third-party API permissions if you are using an application that informs you that you will need to do this. If you are developing an application that relies on the use of third-party API calls, you need to provide explicit instructions to your users about how to grant your application the required permissions it needs in order to function correctly. The process should be clearly explained in your documentation in a step-by-step fashion, otherwise both you and PayPal will be dealing with confused customers who are wondering why they can't get your product or service to work.

This section is the only part of this chapter that discusses third-party API calls. The rest of this chapter deals strictly with first-party API calls. Keep in mind, however, that any of the examples or topics discussed in the remainder of this chapter can be made into a third-party call by simply populating the subject field of the API request.

Making API Calls

Once you have your account properly configured for API access, and you have established your API credentials, it's time to go about the business of making API calls. There are two main ways to send your requests to the PayPal API servers:

- *SOAP interface*: An object-oriented interface using data objects defined by the eBay Business Language (eBL) schema, where API requests and responses are sent as objects via the SOAP protocol

- *Name-Value Pair (NVP) interface*: Uses a similar but different data dictionary to eBL where API requests and responses are sent as simple strings via the HTTP protocol

You should use whichever method is easier for your programming style. The two interfaces are described in more detail in the sections that follow, but the essential choice you have to make is whether you want to form objects for your requests or compose long strings that contain all request parameters as name=value pairs, with all pairs separated by ampersands. Examples provided in this chapter are shown using both interfaces.

Using the SOAP Interface

The SOAP interface is the traditional way of making PayPal API calls. It uses the eBL schema to define request and response objects. eBL stands for eBay Business Language and refers to the set of API business objects defined in the PayPal XML Schema Definition (XSD) schema. The original plan with eBL was to build a common shared data language between eBay and PayPal. That ultimately didn't pan out, and the two schemas diverged. eBay has since evolved to a different schema and doesn't even support eBL anymore. It's strictly a PayPal schema, but the name eBL has stuck around. If you read the schema closely, you can even find some auction-related data types that are vestiges from the old days.

eBL includes the library of core data classes, request types, and response types used when making API calls. With over 100 different elements, often with similar but different naming, eBL is a beast. But thankfully it's a beast that can be tamed, and once you learn your way around it, you'll find that it's actually very well designed and quite flexible.

The locations of the PayPal Web Service Definition Language (WSDL), which defines the SOAP operations, and the accompanying XSD schema files, which define the eBL types, are as follows:

- WSDL: `https://www.paypal.com/wsdl/PayPalSvc.wsdl`

- eBL types: `https://www.paypal.com/wsdl/eBLBaseComponents.xsd`

- Additional types: `https://www.paypal.com/wsdl/CoreComponentTypes.xsd`

Using the Name/Value Pair Interface

Despite its flexibility, the complexity of using the SOAP interface created a barrier that prevented less-experienced developers from using the API. Developers with little to no object-oriented programming knowledge complained about having to work with the complex schema to make even the simplest of API calls. This barrier became apparent when PayPal released Website Payments Pro and the Direct Payment API, which handles the task of processing a credit card. Traditional payment gateways such as Authorize.net and VeriSign made this process extremely simple. You just sent in the credit card number, expiration date, and billing information as one long string, and you got an easy-to-understand value in return. Why did PayPal have to make it so complex? While some developers don't mind (and may actually prefer) the object-oriented SOAP interface, many expressed displeasure.

In response to this feedback, PayPal introduced the Name-Value Pair (NVP) interface in 2007 to offer an alternative to the SOAP interface. The NVP interface makes the API behave more like a traditional payment gateway interface; all API request parameters and response values are sent as a single string that can be easily constructed or parsed. It's sometimes referred to as a "flat" API since the object-oriented nature of the eBL is not present with the NVP interface.

Besides the request format, the protocol over which the API calls are made is the other major difference between the SOAP interface and the NVP interface. The SOAP interface uses the SOAP protocol, whereas making an API call with the NVP interface is done by simply making an HTTP POST request. All modern programming languages have a mechanism by which to make an HTTP POST. In the body of the post is a FORM element that contains your API credentials as well as the request parameters for the specific API call. The response to the API call arrives as the HTTP response to your POST request, and the response payload is the string containing the response values as a series of ampersand-delimited name/value pairs.

PayPal API Endpoints

The URLs listed in Table 6-2 are the endpoints that listen for API requests. Different endpoints are used depending on the environment (live or Sandbox), whether you're using API Certificates or API Signatures, and whether you're using the SOAP interface or the NVP interface.

Table 6-2. *PayPal API Endpoints*

Environment	Credential Type	Calling Type	Endpoint URL
Live	API Certificate	Name-Value Pair	`https://api.paypal.com/nvp`
Live	API Signature	Name-Value Pair	`https://api-3t.paypal.com/nvp`
Live	API Certificate	SOAP	`https://api.paypal.com/2.0`
Live	API Signature	SOAP	`https://api-3t.paypal.com/2.0`
Sandbox	API Certificate	Name-Value Pair	`https://api.sandbox.paypal.com/nvp`
Sandbox	API Signature	Name-Value Pair	`https://api.sandbox.paypal.com/nvp`
Sandbox	API Certificate	SOAP	`https://api.sandbox.paypal.com/2.0`
Sandbox	API Signature	SOAP	`https://api.sandbox.paypal.com/2.0`

■**Caution** While PayPal's live servers use a different endpoint for API Signatures and API Certificates, the Sandbox servers do not.

The PayPal SDK

As you have seen, making an API call is not as easy as simply setting up a standard Buy Now button. It can get complicated pretty quickly, and we haven't even taken a look at any code yet. To help developers manage these complexities, PayPal provides Software Development Kits, or SDKs, for a number of popular programming languages.

There are different SDKs for the SOAP interface and the NVP interface. If you are using the SOAP interface, I definitely recommend downloading an SDK to help hide the complexities of using the SOAP protocol. However, if you are using the NVP interface, I would think twice before choosing to use an SDK. Remember, the NVP interface just uses HTTP POSTs to submit API calls, and all modern programming languages provide a way to send HTTP requests simply. Using an SDK means that you have to download and install software onto your application server, and if you can figure out how to make HTTP requests on your own, you can bypass that installation hurdle as well as the learning curve for using the SDK by simply submitting HTTP requests directly to the PayPal endpoint.

Downloading the SDK

The SDKs that PayPal offers can be downloaded from the PayPal Integration Center at www.paypal.com/integration. Click the API Reference link in the navigation, and select either the SOAP interface or the NVP interface to be taken to a page that will show the platforms for which PayPal provides an SDK and links to download the latest SDK versions. The SDKs for the SOAP interface will have a version number that begins with 4, and the SDKs for the NVP interface will have a version number that begins with 5. The two versions of the SDK are extremely similar, with the only difference being in the way that API requests and responses are formed—SOAP uses objects, while NVP uses strings.

Important SDK Classes

The SDK contains many classes that work together to make API communication work for you, but you will never need to deal with most of them. A few classes, though, you will use heavily, and these classes are described in this section.

APIProfile

The APIProfile interface contains your API credentials. It provides methods for setting all aspects of your credentials, including

- API Username

- API Password

- API Signature

- Location of API Certificate file

- Private key password used to encrypt certificate

- Subject (if using third-party API calls)

Obviously if you are using an API Signature for your authentication, you would not use the methods provided for an API Certificate, and vice versa. The recommended way to get a new instance of an APIProfile class is not by instantiating one directly, but rather by using the ProfileFactory class described next.

ProfileFactory

The ProfileFactory class is used to generate new instances of APIProfile. It follows the traditional Factory design pattern that is documented in the classic book *Design Patterns: Elements of Reusable Object-Oriented Software* by Erich Gamma, Richard Helm, Ralph Johnson, and John Vlissides (Addison-Wesley, 1995). Two factory methods are provided that will create new APIProfile instances for you:

- createSSLAPIProfile(): For instantiating an APIProfile object that uses API Certificate as its authentication mechanism

- createSignatureAPIProfile(): For instantiating an APIProfile object that uses API Signature as its authentication mechanism

Both are static methods and can be used without instantiating a ProfileFactory object. Once you have created your APIProfile object and populated it with your API credentials, you can use the CallerServices class to make an API call.

CallerServices

The CallerServices class is the façade class used to interface with the SDK's API calling mechanism. It provides a simple call() method that makes API calls. Before you can use the call() method, you must first invoke the setApiProfile() method and pass in the instance of APIProfile that you have populated with your API credentials. This way, the CallerServices instance will know which credentials to send along with the API call. The call() method does not take any credentials information as parameters, so that's why you must use the setApiProfile() method first.

■**Caution** CallerServices is not a thread-safe class. You should either create a new instance of it every time you make an API call or synchronize the access to it.

A Simple Example of Making a PayPal API Call

OK, time to get into some code. Let's take a look at a code snippet that calls PayPal's GetTransactionDetails API. We'll take a look at the same API call made first with the SOAP interface using the PayPal SDK, and then with the NVP interface. The example using the NVP interface doesn't use the SDK; it just makes the HTTP POST directly.

■**Note** The examples in this chapter are very basic in nature. They are meant to convey the core steps that must take place in order to make API calls. They do not take into account thread-safety, API latency, database activity, or any other advanced functionality that you may need to consider if you are developing an enterprise-ready solution.

Example Using the SOAP Interface

The class in Listing 6-1 executes a GetTransactionDetails call for a Sandbox account using an API Signature as the means of authentication. The subsequent section gives the equivalent listing using the NVP interface. The samples are provided in Java primarily for ease of readability.

Listing 6-1. GetTransactionDetails *API Call Using the SOAP Interface*

```java
package com.apress.paypal;

import java.util.Calendar;

import java.text.DateFormat;

import com.paypal.sdk.profiles.APIProfile;
import com.paypal.sdk.profiles.ProfileFactory;

import com.paypal.sdk.services.CallerServices;

import com.paypal.sdk.exceptions.PayPalException;

import com.paypal.soap.api.AckCodeType;
import com.paypal.soap.api.GetTransactionDetailsReq;
import com.paypal.soap.api.GetTransactionDetailsRequestType;
import com.paypal.soap.api.GetTransactionDetailsResponseType;
import com.paypal.soap.api.BasicAmountType;
import com.paypal.soap.api.PaymentInfoType;
import com.paypal.soap.api.PaymentTransactionType;

public class ApiSamples {

    private static APIProfile profile;
    private static CallerServices caller = new CallerServices();

    /**
     * This method creates the API Profile object and populates it
     * with the API credentials for the account.
     *
     * @throws PayPalException If an error occurs while creating the profile.
     */
    private static final void setupProfile(String _username, String _password,
                                           String _signature,
                                           String _environment)
                                           throws PayPalException {
        profile = ProfileFactory.createSignatureAPIProfile();
        profile.setAPIUsername(_username);
```

```java
  profile.setAPIPassword(_password);
  profile.setSignature(_signature);
  profile.setEnvironment(_environment);
  caller.setAPIProfile(profile);
}


/**
 * This method makes a GetTransactionDetails API call
 * and displays the results to the command line.
 *
 * @throws PayPalException If an error occurs while making the API call.
 */
private static final void getTxnDetails(String _transactionId)
  throws PayPalException {
  GetTransactionDetailsReq request = new GetTransactionDetailsReq();
  GetTransactionDetailsRequestType requestType =
    new GetTransactionDetailsRequestType();
  requestType.setTransactionID(_transactionId);
  request.setGetTransactionDetailsRequest(requestType);
  GetTransactionDetailsResponseType response =
    (GetTransactionDetailsResponseType)caller.call("GetTransactionDetails",
                                                   requestType);
  if (response.getAck().equals(AckCodeType.Success) ||
      response.getAck().equals(AckCodeType.SuccessWithWarning)) {
    PaymentTransactionType paymentDetails =
      response.getPaymentTransactionDetails();
    PaymentInfoType paymentInfo = paymentDetails.getPaymentInfo();
    BasicAmountType transactionAmount = paymentInfo.getGrossAmount();
    Calendar transactionDate = paymentInfo.getPaymentDate();
    System.out.println("Transaction " + _transactionId + " was made on " +
      DateFormat.getDateTimeInstance(DateFormat.SHORT, DateFormat.SHORT)
      .format(transactionDate.getTime()) + " in the amount of " +
      transactionAmount.get_value() + " " +
      transactionAmount.getCurrencyID().toString());
  }
  if (response.getErrors() != null && response.getErrors().length > 0) {
    System.out.println("Errors/Warnings occurred while making the API call:");
    for (int i=0; i < response.getErrors().length; i++) {
      StringBuffer message =
        new StringBuffer(response.getErrors(i).getSeverityCode().toString());
      message.append(": ");
      message.append(response.getErrors(i).getShortMessage());
      message.append(" - ");
      message.append(response.getErrors(i).getLongMessage());
      message.append(" (");
      message.append(response.getErrors(i).getErrorCode().toString());
```

```
        message.append(")");
        System.out.println(message.toString());
      }
    }
  }

  /**
   * Main execution.
   */
  public static void main(String[] args) {
    try {
      setupProfile("test2_api1.test22.com",
                   "GLDXF6CFHEP93MT9",
                   "Av4O2NnzBevgVAx5aWX2KQREl7O2AYejRbdWdlEiq-vdOq9AIvPW-j3m",
                   "sandbox");
      getTxnDetails("8JL75876447207443");
    } catch (Exception e) {
      System.out.println(e.getMessage());
      e.printStackTrace();
    }
  }
}
```

Example Using the NVP Interface

The class in Listing 6-2 makes a GetTransactionDetails API call using the NVP interface. It does not use an SDK; the SDK is not really as useful with the NVP interface as it is with the SOAP interface. Methods such as call() and showErrors() are reused in code samples later in the chapter.

Listing 6-2. GetTransactionDetails *API Call Using the NVP Interface*

```
package com.apress.paypal;

import java.io.BufferedReader;
import java.io.DataOutputStream;
import java.io.InputStreamReader;

import java.net.URL;

import java.util.HashMap;
import java.util.Iterator;
import java.util.Set;
import java.util.StringTokenizer;

import java.net.URLDecoder;
import java.net.URLEncoder;
```

```java
import javax.net.ssl.HttpsURLConnection;

import org.apache.commons.logging.Log;
import org.apache.commons.logging.LogFactory;

import com.paypal.sdk.exceptions.FatalException;

public class NVPSamples {

  public static String call(String payload) throws Exception {
    StringBuffer request = new StringBuffer();
    request.append("USER=MyUser&PASSWORD=MyPassword&");
    request.append("SIGNATURE=9875lsjdf98734ljsdfks89lo9kfkld&").append(payload);

    // Change this URL to the correct PayPal URL
    URL url = new URL("https://api.sandbox.paypal.com/nvp/");
    HttpsURLConnection connection = (HttpsURLConnection)url.openConnection();
    connection.setDoOutput(true);
    connection.setUseCaches(false);
    connection.setRequestProperty("Content-Type", "text/namevalue");

    DataOutputStream out = new DataOutputStream(connection.getOutputStream());
    out.write(request.toString().getBytes());
    out.close();

    // Read the gateway response
    BufferedReader in =
      new BufferedReader(new InputStreamReader(connection.getInputStream()));
    StringBuffer sb = new StringBuffer();
    String line;

    while ((line = in.readLine()) != null) {
      sb.append(line);
    }

    in.close();
    return sb.toString();
  } // call

  public static void getTxnDetails() throws Exception {
    NVPEncoder encoder = new NVPEncoder();
    encoder.add("METHOD", "GetTransactionDetails");
    encoder.add("TRANSACTIONID", "8JL75876447207443");
    String strNVPString = encoder.encode();
    String ppresponse = call(strNVPString);
    NVPDecoder results = new NVPDecoder();
    results.decode(ppresponse);
```

```
    String transactionID = results.get("TRANSACTIONID");
    String amt = results.get("AMT");
    String paymentDate = results.get("PAYMENTDATE");
    if ("Success".equals(results.get("ACK"))) {
      System.out.println("Transaction " + transactionID + " was made on " +
        paymentDate + " in the amount of " + amt);
    } else {
      showErrors(results);
    }
  }

  // displays error messages
  private static void showErrors(NVPDecoder results) {
    int i = 0;
    while (results.get("L_LONGMESSAGE" + i) != null
          && results.get("L_LONGMESSAGE" + i).length() > 0) {
      System,out,println("Severity: " + results.get("L_SEVERITYCODE" + i));
      System.out.println("Error Number: " + results.get("L_ERRORCODE" + i));
      System.out.println("Short Message: " + results.get("L_SHORTMESSAGE" + i));
      System.out.println("Long Message: " + results.get("L_LONGMESSAGE" + i));
      i++;
    }
  }

  public static void main(String[] args) {
    try {
      getTxnDetails();
    } catch (Exception e) {
      System.out.println(e.getMessage());
      e.printStackTrace();
    }
  }
} // NVPSamples
```

Two classes used in Listing 6-2, NVPEncoder and NVPDecoder, handle the complexities associated with URL encoding. They are described in the next sections and provided for your use. They are also provided as part of the PayPal NVP SDK, but if you choose not to use an SDK, you can still use these classes directly to help with your URL encoding.

NVPEncoder

The NVPEncoder class encodes name/value pairs into an x-www-form-urlencoded string that is suitable for posting to PayPal. For every API request, create a new instance of NVPEncoder, and then invoke the add() method for each request parameter. add() has two parameters: the variable name and the corresponding value. Then, once you have added all of the request parameters, use the encode() method to get the encoded string that you will post to PayPal. You will see NVPEncoder used widely in the samples contained in this chapter.

NVPEncoder is included in the PayPal NVP SDKs for the Java and .NET platforms, but if you don't want to use an SDK, the class is shown in Listing 6-3 for your convenience.

Listing 6-3. NVPEncoder *Class to Handle URL Encoding*

```java
package com.apress.paypal;

import java.util.Set;
import java.util.HashMap;
import java.util.Iterator;

import java.net.URLEncoder;

import com.paypal.sdk.exceptions.FatalException;

class NVPEncoder {

  private HashMap nvps = new HashMap();

  /**
   * This method adds the given name and value as a pair as a new entity
   * @param pstrName  The String containing the name.
   * @param pstrValue The String containing the value for the given name.
   */
  public void add(String pstrName, String pstrValue)
  {
    nvps.put(pstrName, pstrValue);
  }

  /**
   * This method removes the given name along with the value for that name
   * @param pstrName  The String containing the name.
   */
  public void remove(String pstrName)
  {
    if(nvps.containsKey(pstrName)) {
      nvps.remove(pstrName);
    }
  }

  /**
   * This method clears all the name value pair data
   *
   */
  public void clear() {
    nvps.clear();
  }
```

```java
/**
 * This method forms an URL encoded string in the NVP format. To form the encoded
 * string it takes all the name and values added in this object.
 * @return String  The URL encoded string in the NVP format.
 */
public String encode() throws FatalException {
  String nvp = "";
  try {
    Set setKeysSet = nvps.keySet();
    Iterator iteKeys = setKeysSet.iterator();
    for(int i = 0 ; i < nvps.size(); i++) {
      if(iteKeys.hasNext()) {
        String lCurrentNameValue = "";
        String key = (String)iteKeys.next();

        if(nvps.get(key) == null || nvps.get(key).toString().equals("")) {
          continue;
        }

        lCurrentNameValue += URLEncoder.encode(key,"UTF-8") + "=" +
          URLEncoder.encode(nvps.get(key)+"","UTF-8") ;

        nvp += lCurrentNameValue;
        if(iteKeys.hasNext()) {
          nvp += "&";
        }
      }
    }
  } catch (Exception e) {
    e.printStackTrace();
    throw new FatalException(e.getMessage());
  }
  return nvp;
}
}
```

NVPDecoder

Just as NVPEncoder is used to form API requests, NVPDecoder is used to parse API responses. For each API response that you receive, create a new instance of NVPDecoder and call the decode() method, passing in the encoded string that you receive back from PayPal that contains the results of the API call. This will populate an internal hash of the variables contained in the API response. Then, you can call the get() method and pass in the name of the response variable you are interested in. The get() method returns the corresponding value, URL decoded. NVPDecoder is shown in Listing 6-4.

Listing 6-4. NVPDecoder *Class to Handle URL Decoding*

```java
package com.apress.paypal;

import java.util.HashMap;
import java.util.StringTokenizer;

import java.net.URLDecoder;

class NVPDecoder {
  private HashMap nvps = null;

  /**
   * This method returns the value for the given Name key.
   * @param pName    The name for which the value is required
   * @return String  The value for the given name, URL decoded
   */
  public String get(String pName) {
    return (String)nvps.get(pName);
  }

  /**
   * This method parses the string in the NVP format passed as the parameter
   * and stores them in a collection.
   * @param pPayload    The string in the NVP format.
   */
  public void decode(String pPayload) throws Exception {
    StringTokenizer stTok = new StringTokenizer(pPayload,"&");
    nvps = new HashMap();
    while(stTok.hasMoreTokens()) {
      StringTokenizer stInternalTokenizer =
        new StringTokenizer(stTok.nextToken(),"=");
      nvps.put(URLDecoder.decode(stInternalTokenizer.nextToken(), "UTF-8"),
                      stInternalTokenizer.hasMoreTokens() ?
                      URLDecoder.decode(stInternalTokenizer.nextToken(),
                                  "UTF-8") : "");
    }
  }
}
```

Handling PayPal API Responses

All API responses have some basic properties, regardless of the individual API call made and which interface you use. This section describes those properties.

Ack Code

All API responses return with an *Ack*, or acknowledgement, which contains the basic status of the call. The Ack will have one of four values:

- Success

- SuccessWithWarning

- Failure

- FailureWithWarning

Generally, the first thing your code should do is check the Ack value. If it's Success or SuccessWithWarning, the call was completed as expected. If it is Failure or FailureWithWarning, something went wrong. An array of error messages will accompany the response, and each error has an numerical error code, a short message, and a long message. These messages are meant to help you debug the problem, although they can sometimes be frustratingly ambiguous. The complete list of API error codes and their messages is presented in this book's appendix.

Correlation ID

Every response contains a *Correlation ID*. This is just a simple string that uniquely identifies the API call within the PayPal system. You should store the Correlation ID if your API call returns an error (especially if it's unexpected). PayPal technical support will use the Correlation ID to help debug the issue. The Correlation ID has no significance other than to identify a single API call.

Transaction Management with the PayPal API

One useful feature of the PayPal API is the ability to manage your PayPal account without having to log in to `www.paypal.com` and use the website. This can save you time and also allow you to add value to your application by building in PayPal administrative functionality. This section describes the various management functions that the PayPal API offers, including techniques for the following:

- Issuing full or partial refunds

- Searching your account history

- Retrieving detailed information about a specific transaction

- Authorizing a credit card but delaying the actual capture of funds

- Capturing funds for a previously authorized transaction

This section presents sample code for both methods of calling the PayPal API: the SOAP interface and the NVP interface.

Issuing Refunds with the RefundTransaction API

Refunds are a common occurrence in business. A product may be returned, a customer might have been overcharged, or perhaps the item purchased is not in stock. There are a multitude of possible causes for a refund, and PayPal provides the RefundTransaction API to handle them.

PayPal offers the ability to issue both full refunds and partial refunds. A *full refund* returns 100% of the transaction amount to the buyer, whereas a *partial refund* returns only a portion of the transaction. You can issue multiple partial refunds for a transaction, so long as the total amount of the partial refunds does not add up to more than the original transaction amount.

■**Note** You can issue a refund up to 60 days after a transaction has completed.

RefundTransaction API Using the SOAP Interface

The sample method in Listing 6-5 shows how to perform a RefundTransaction API call and access the results. It performs a full refund. If you want to perform a partial refund, you must also specify the amount of the refund.

This method is dependant upon Listing 6-1. Creation of the APIProfile and CallerServices objects is not shown here, or in the subsequent samples, to avoid displaying duplicate code.

Listing 6-5. *Making a* RefundTransaction *API Call Using the SOAP Interface*

```
import com.paypal.soap.api.RefundTransactionRequestType;
import com.paypal.soap.api.RefundTransactionResponseType;
import com.paypal.soap.api.RefundPurposeTypeCodeType;

...

/**
 * This method performs a full refund for a transaction
 *
 * @throws PayPalException If an error occurs while making the API call
 */
private static void refundTransaction(String _transactionId)
  throws PayPalException {
  RefundTransactionRequestType request = new RefundTransactionRequestType();
  request.setTransactionID(_transactionId);
  request.setRefundType(RefundPurposeTypeCodeType.Full);
  // caller is from the GetTransactionDetails example
  RefundTransactionResponseType response =
    (RefundTransactionResponseType)caller.call("RefundTransaction", request);
  if (response.getAck().equals(AckCodeType.Success)
      || response.getAck().getValue().equals(AckCodeType.SuccessWithWarning)) {
    System.out.println("Refund completed successfully");
  }
```

```
  if (response.getErrors() != null && response.getErrors().length > 0) {
    System.out.println("Errors/Warnings occurred while making the API call:");
    for (int i=0; i < response.getErrors().length; i++) {
      StringBuffer message =
        new StringBuffer(response.getErrors(i).getSeverityCode().toString());
      message.append(": ");
      message.append(response.getErrors(i).getShortMessage());
      message.append(" - ");
      message.append(response.getErrors(i).getLongMessage());
      message.append(" (");
      message.append(response.getErrors(i).getErrorCode().toString());
      message.append(")");
      System.out.println(message.toString());
    }
  }
} // refundTransaction method
```

RefundTransaction API Using the NVP Interface

This section contains code that shows how to make the same RefundTransaction API call shown in the preceding section, this time using the NVP interface. The SDK is not used; we just make the call directly to the HTTP endpoint. This is an advantage of the NVP interface— SDK classes aren't needed, so you just make the API call via HTTP POST. Listing 6-6 uses the call() and showErrors() methods defined earlier in the GetTransactionDetails example.

Listing 6-6. *Making a* RefundTransaction *API Call Using the NVP Interface*

```
/**
 * This method performs a full refund for a transaction
 *
 * @throws PayPalException If an error occurs while making the API call
 */
public static void refundTransaction(String _transactionId) throws Exception {
  NVPEncoder encoder = new NVPEncoder();
  encoder.add("METHOD", "RefundTransaction");
  encoder.add("TRANSACTIONID", _transactionId);
  encoder.add("REFUNDTYPE", "Full");
  String nvpString = encoder.encode();
  String ppresponse = call(nvpString);
  NVPDecoder results = new NVPDecoder();
  results.decode(ppresponse);
  String refundTransactionId = results.get("REFUNDTRANSACTIONID");
  if ("Success".equals(results.get("ACK"))
      || "SuccessWithWarning".equals(results.get("AckACK"))) {
    System.out.println("Refund completed successfully");
    System.out.println("refundTransactionID = " + refundTransactionId);
  }

  showErrors(results);
}
```

Refunds Through the PayPal Website

In addition to using the RefundTransaction API to issue refunds, you can also issue refunds through the PayPal website. To do this, log in to your account and find the transaction you wish to refund in your transaction history. Then, click the Details link, and there will be a link at the bottom of the transaction details page that allows you to issue a full or partial refund for the transaction.

Refunding Transaction Fees

When issuing a full refund, PayPal also refunds any transaction fees, shipping, and taxes it may have collected from the transaction. When issuing a partial refund, PayPal does not refund any transaction fees. Also, if you refund a payment received via MassPay, the MassPay fee is not refunded, even in the case of a full refund.

Searching Account History with the TransactionSearch API

PayPal provides the TransactionSearch API as a way to programmatically retrieve transactions from your account history that meet your search criteria. You can specify as many search criteria as you like, but the only required criterion is the start date for the search. The criteria you can search on includes the following:

- *Start Date*: The date and time after which a transaction must have taken place.

- *End Date*: The date and time before which a transaction must have taken place.

- *Payer*: The buyer's email address.

- *Receiver*: The receiver's email address.

- *Receipt ID*: The PayPal account optional receipt ID.

- *Transaction ID*: The PayPal transaction ID.

- *Payer Name*: The buyer's name.

- *Auction Item Number*: The item number of the purchase. If the transaction was not related to an auction site, this will search on the item_number variable set in the shopping cart for the original transaction.

- *Invoice ID*: The original invoice ID passed in by the merchant.

- *Card Number*: The credit card number used. (Note: This is only available for Direct Payment transactions.)

- *Transaction Class*: The type of transaction. Possible values are as follows:

  - All: All transaction types.

  - Sent: Only sent payments.

  - Received: Only received payments.

  - MassPay: Only mass payments.

- MoneyRequest: Only money requests.

- FundsAdded: Only funds added to balance.

- FundsWithdrawn: Only funds withdrawn to a bank account.

- Referral: Only transactions involving referrals.

- Fee: Only transactions involving fees.

- Subscription: Only transactions involved with a subscription.

- Dividend: Only transactions involving a PayPal money market dividend.

- BillPay: Only transactions involving PayPal BillPay. (BillPay is no longer available as a PayPal service.)

- Refund: Only refunds.

- CurrencyConversions: Only transactions involving currency conversions.

- BalanceTransfer: Only transactions involving balance transfers.

- Shipping: Only transactions involving UPS shipping fees.

- BalanceAffecting: Only transactions that affect the PayPal account balance.

- ECheck: Only transactions involving an eCheck payment.

- *Amount*: The transaction amount.

- *CurrencyCode*: The currency code of the transaction.

- *Status*: The transaction status. Possible values are as follows:

  - Pending: For the specific reason why it's pending, use the PendingReason field in the GetTransactionDetails response.

  - Processing: Payment is being processed.

  - Success: Payment is completed.

  - Denied: A previously pending transaction was denied by the account holder.

  - Reversed: Payment is reversed, due to a chargeback or other type of reversal.

Note The maximum number of transactions that PayPal will return in a TransactionSearch is 100.

TransactionSearch API Using the SOAP Interface

As you have just seen, you can search on many different criteria using TransactionSearch. The only *required* field, however, is the start date of the search. The example shown in Listing 6-7 goes slightly further and also specifies an end date, and the method displayed assumes the

APIProfile and CallerServices objects have already been properly created as shown in the GetTransactionDetails example earlier in the chapter.

Listing 6-7. *Making a* TransactionSearch *API Call Using the SOAP Interface*

```java
import com.paypal.soap.api.TransactionSearchRequestType;
import com.paypal.soap.api.TransactionSearchResponseType;
import com.paypal.soap.api.PaymentTransactionSearchResultType;


...


/**
 * This methods performs a TransactionSearch with a specified start date
 * and end date
 *
 * @throws PayPalException If an error occurs while making the API call
 */
private static void transactionSearch() throws PayPalException {
  TransactionSearchRequestType request = new TransactionSearchRequestType();
  // Search between August 1, 2006 and August 30, 2006
  Calendar startDate, endDate;
  startDate = Calendar.getInstance();
  // Start Date is September 1, 2006
  startDate.set(Calendar.YEAR, 2006);
  startDate.set(Calendar.MONTH, 97);
  startDate.set(Calendar.DAY_OF_MONTH, 1);
  endDate = Calendar.getInstance();
  // End Date is September 30, 2006
  endDate.set(Calendar.YEAR, 2006);
  endDate.set(Calendar.MONTH, 9);7;
  endDate.set(Calendar.DAY_OF_MONTH, 30);
  request.setStartDate(startDate);
  request.setEndDate(endDate);
  TransactionSearchResponseType response =
    (TransactionSearchResponseType)caller.call("TransactionSearch", request);
  if (response.getAck().equals(AckCodeType.Success)
      || response.getAck().equals(AckCodeType.SuccessWithWarning)) {
    // the method returns an array of transactions that meet the search criteria
    PaymentTransactionSearchResultType[] results =
      response.getPaymentTransactions();
   if (results != null) {
      System.out.println("Found " + results.length +
                      " transactions that meet the search criteria:");
      // loop through the results and display the transaction IDs and amounts
      for (int i=0; i < results.length; i++) {
        PaymentTransactionSearchResultType transaction = results[i];
        String transactionID = transaction.getTransactionID();
```

```
            String amount = transaction.getGrossAmount().get_value();
            String time = transaction.getTimestamp().getTime().toString();
            System.out.println(i + ". Transaction " + transactionID +
                        " occurred on " + time + ", in the amount of " + amount);
        }
      }
    }

  if (response.getErrors() != null && response.getErrors().length > 0) {
    System.out.println("Errors/Warnings occurred while making the API call:");
    for (int i=0; i < response.getErrors().length; i++) {
      StringBuffer message =
        new StringBuffer(response.getErrors(i).getSeverityCode().toString());
      message.append(": ");
      message.append(response.getErrors(i).getShortMessage());
      message.append(" - ");
      message.append(response.getErrors(i).getLongMessage());
      message.append(" (");
      message.append(response.getErrors(i).getErrorCode().toString());
      message.append(")");
      System.out.println(message.toString());
    }
  }
}
```

TransactionSearch API Using the NVP Interface

Listing 6-8 shows the same TransactionSearch API call that uses the NVP interface instead of the SOAP interface. It uses the call() and showErrors() methods defined earlier in the GetTransactionDetails example.

Listing 6-8. *Making a* TransactionSearch *API Call Using the NVP Interface*

```
/**
 * This methods performs a TransactionSearch
 * with a specified start date and end date
 *
 * @throws PayPalException If an error occurs while making the API call
 */
public static void transactionSearch() throws Exception {
  NVPEncoder encoder = new NVPEncoder();
  encoder.add("METHOD", "TransactionSearch");
  encoder.add("STARTDATE", "2006-8-10");
  encoder.add("ENDDATE", "2006-8-21");
  String strNVPRequest = encoder.encode();
  String strNVPResponse = call(strNVPRequest);
  NVPDecoder results = new NVPDecoder();
  results.decode(strNVPResponse);
```

```
if ("Success".equals(results.get("ACK"))
    || "SuccessWithWarning".equals(results.get("ACK"))) {
  if (results.get("L_TRANSACTIONID0") != null
      && !results.get("L_TRANSACTIONID0").equals("")) {
    int intCount = 0;
    while (results.get("L_TRANSACTIONID" + intCount) != null
          && results.get("L_TRANSACTIONID" + intCount).length() > 0) {
      String timestamp = results.get("L_TIMESTAMP" + intCount);
      String amt = results.get("L_AMT" + intCount);
      intCount++;
      System.out.println(intCount + ". Transaction " +
                      results.get("L_TRANSACTIONID" + intCount) +
                      " occurred on " + timestamp +
                      ", in the amount of " + amt);
    }
  }
} else {
  showErrors(results);
}
}
```

Authorizing Payments

The ability to separate the authorization of a payment from the actual capture of the funds has existed for several years with traditional credit card processors. In 2005, PayPal caught up with the rest of the payments industry with the release of the Authorize & Capture APIs. This functionality allows you to verify the availability of funds for a transaction but delay the actual capture of funds until a later time. This is often useful for businesses that accept online orders but do not want to take the customer's money until the product has physically been shipped. Through the Authorize & Capture APIs, businesses can also modify the original authorization amount due to order changes occurring after the initial order is placed, such as additional tax, shipping, or gratuity charges.

Authorizations can be made with the API calls covered in this section, and they can also be made with other types of PayPal transactions. You can create authorizations with Direct Payment and Express Checkout, both of which are covered later in this chapter. You can also create authorizations for Website Payments Standard transactions. That process is covered later in this section.

When using the API, the following operations are provided:

- DoAuthorization: Creates an authorization from an order

- DoReauthorization: Reauthorizes a prior basic authorization

- DoVoid: Voids an authorization or order

- DoCapture: Captures funds for a prior authorization or order

Rules of Authorize & Capture

There are a set of rules governing the use of how authorizations and captures work together. Once an authorization has been made, you can do the following:

- Capture either a partial amount or the full amount of the authorization.

- Reauthorize for a different amount. You can reauthorize for up to 115% of the originally authorized amount, not to exceed an increase of $75.

- Void the authorization, if you need to cancel the transaction.

After a successful authorization, PayPal honors 100% of authorized funds for three days. A day is defined as the start of the calendar day on which the authorization was made. You can attempt to capture without a reauthorization from day 4 to day 29 of the authorization period, but PayPal cannot ensure that 100% of the funds will be available outside of the three-day honor period.

■Note PayPal will not allow you to capture funds if your customer's account is restricted or locked, or if your account has a high restriction level.

You can make two types of authorizations: basic authorizations and order authorizations. The sections that follow describe the differences between the two.

Basic Authorizations

When you make a *basic authorization*, the buyer's funds are placed on hold for up to three days. During this time you can capture the funds, void the transaction, or reauthorize the transaction. If you reauthorize the transaction, you can reauthorize it for up to 115% of the originally authorized amount, not to exceed an increase of $75. You can reauthorize a transaction only once. You can capture and void basic authorizations either through the Authorize & Capture APIs described in this section or by logging in to your PayPal account and using the website.

Orders and Order Authorizations

An *order* is equivalent to a traditional $1 authorization (although $1 is not actually taken from the customer) or preauthorization with a credit card. When you create an order, you confirm that the customer has agreed to the transaction, but do *not* place the funds on hold. Not placing the funds on hold is one main difference between orders and basic authorizations. After creating an order, you can capture the order directly without any additional authorization, or you can make an additional order authorization to change the amount and then capture that amount.

This technique is often used by merchants who accept orders for varying items, some of which may not be available for shipment at the time the order is placed. An order authorization is made as the items become available. This authorization ensures the customer still has the funds available in order to purchase the item. You can make only a single order authorization for each order.

An order period is 29 days long. Within this period, you can request an authorization to ensure the availability of funds, up to 115% of the originally authorized amount, not to exceed an increase of $75. You can perform this authorization only once.

You must capture and void orders and order authorizations with the Authorization & Capture APIs. You cannot process order authorizations through the PayPal website. The PayPal website supports processing only basic authorizations, not orders and order authorizations.

■**Note** Order authorizations are supported with Express Checkout and Website Payments Standard transactions. At this time, Direct Payment does not support order authorizations.

Sending Money with MassPay

MassPay is one of the most overlooked features of the entire PayPal system. Just as the name indicates, you use MassPay to pay a group (or mass) of recipients with a single swing. Possible uses of MassPay include affiliate commissions, payroll, customer rebates, and incentives for taking an online survey or other task. There are many other options as well—essentially, any time you need to send money to another party, MassPay can be used as an alternate method to logging in to your PayPal account and manually going through the Send Money flow.

Fees for MassPay transactions are different from all other PayPal transactions. When you use MassPay, the sender pays the fee, not the recipient. The fee is a flat 2% of the transaction amount, with a maximum of $1, or the equivalent in the payment currency. That makes MassPay a very cost-effective way to transfer money in the PayPal system.

Consider a $1,000 transaction. With the usual PayPal fees in effect, sending $1,000 would incur a fee of $29.30, paid by the recipient. With MassPay, that same $1,000 transaction incurs a fee of only $1, paid by the sender.

The Rules of MassPay

MassPay has some restrictions that prevent it from being used as a true replacement for a SendMoney API (which will hopefully be developed by PayPal one day). The main restriction is that you may only use your stored PayPal balance to send payments via the MassPay API. You can't fund the payments from your bank account or credit card. If you have $199 in your PayPal account, and you send out a MassPay call to send ten friends $20 each, the call will fail. Another restriction is that you are limited to 250 recipients per call, and you can't combine multiple currencies with the same API call.

■**Note** A recipient must claim the funds sent to them via MassPay by clicking a link in a notification email. If a recipient does not claim the funds within 30 days, the payment is refunded to you. The MassPay fee, however, is not refunded.

MassPay limits the amount you can send to an individual recipient in a single transaction, as noted in Table 6-3.

Table 6-3. *Maximum MassPay Amount per Transaction*

Currency	Maximum Transaction Amount
USD	$10,000
EUR	€8,000
JPY	¥1,000,000
AUD	$12,500
CAD	$12,500
GBP	£5,550

There are two ways to use MassPay. You can use the MassPay API, and you can also upload a file to the PayPal website with the transaction information. Both methods are described in the following sections.

The MassPay API

The MassPay API is the programmatic way to use MassPay. You can pay up to 250 recipients with a single API call. You include the recipients and the amount to pay each recipient in the API request. You can specify as few as one recipient for a single MassPay call.

MassPay API Using the SOAP Interface

The method in Listing 6-9 shows how to make a MassPay API call. It assumes that a CallerServices object named caller has been properly instantiated and configured like the GetTransactionDetails example earlier in this chapter. Remember, for a MassPay API call to work, you have to have all of the funds (transactions plus fees) available in your PayPal balance when the call is made. MassPay can't draw funds from a credit card, bank account, or any other funding source.

Listing 6-9. *Making a* MassPay *API Call with the SOAP Interface*

```
import com.paypal.soap.api.MassPayRequestType;
import com.paypal.soap.api.MassPayRequestItemType;
import com.paypal.soap.api.MassPayResponseType;
import com.paypal.soap.api.CurrencyCodeType;

...

/**
 * This method sends money to three recipients with the MassPay API
 *
 * @throws PayPalException If an error occurs while making the API call
 */
```

```java
private static void massPay() throws PayPalException {
  MassPayRequestType request = new MassPayRequestType();
  // Since we are sending money to three recipients,
  // we will create an array with three elements
  MassPayRequestItemType[] massPayItems = new MassPayRequestItemType[3];
  // Now we will create each individual payment item
  MassPayRequestItemType firstItem = new MassPayRequestItemType();
  firstItem.setReceiverEmail("first-recipient@apress.com");
  // Create the first amount - ten bucks
  BasicAmountType firstAmount = new BasicAmountType();
  firstAmount.set_value("10.00");
  firstAmount.setCurrencyID(CurrencyCodeType.USD);
  firstItem.setAmount(firstAmount);

  // Now we'll create the second payment item
  MassPayRequestItemType secondItem = new MassPayRequestItemType();
  secondItem.setReceiverEmail("second-recipient@apress.com");
  // Create the amount - twenty bucks
  BasicAmountType secondAmount = new BasicAmountType();
  secondAmount.set_value("20.00");
  secondAmount.setCurrencyID(CurrencyCodeType.USD);
  secondItem.setAmount(secondAmount);

  // Now we'll create the third payment item
  MassPayRequestItemType thirdItem = new MassPayRequestItemType();
  thirdItem.setReceiverEmail("third-recipient@apress.com");
  // Create the amount - thirty bucks
  BasicAmountType thirdAmount = new BasicAmountType();
  thirdAmount.set_value("30.00");
  thirdAmount.setCurrencyID(CurrencyCodeType.USD);
  thirdItem.setAmount(thirdAmount);

  // Now we'll populate the request item array with the objects we've just created
  massPayItems[0] = firstItem;
  massPayItems[1] = secondItem;
  massPayItems[2] = thirdItem;
  request.setMassPayItem(massPayItems);

  MassPayResponseType response =
    (MassPayResponseType)caller.call("MassPay", request);
  if (response.getAck().equals(AckCodeType.Success)
      || response.getAck().equals(AckCodeType.SuccessWithWarning)) {
    System.out.println("MassPay API call completed successfully");
  }
```

```
    if (response.getErrors() != null && response.getErrors().length > 0) {
      System.out.println("Errors/Warnings occurred while making the API call:");
      for (int i=0; i < response.getErrors().length; i++) {
        StringBuffer message =
          new StringBuffer(response.getErrors(i).getSeverityCode().toString());
        message.append(": ");
        message.append(response.getErrors(i).getShortMessage());
        message.append(" - ");
        message.append(response.getErrors(i).getLongMessage());
        message.append(" (");
        message.append(response.getErrors(i).getErrorCode().toString());
        message.append(")");
        System.out.println(message.toString());
      }
    }
  }
} // massPay
```

MassPay API Using the NVP Interface

Listing 6-10 shows the same MassPay API call, except made with the NVP interface instead of the SOAP interface. It uses the call() and showErrors() methods defined earlier in the GetTransactionDetails example.

Listing 6-10. *Making a* MassPay *API Call with the NVP Interface*

```
/**
 * This method sends money to three recipients with the MassPay API
 *
 * @throws Exception If an error occurs while making the API call
 */
public static void massPay() throws Exception {
  NVPEncoder encoder = new NVPEncoder();
  encoder.add("METHOD", "MassPay");
  encoder.add("CURRENCYCODE", "USD");
  encoder.add("L_EMAIL1", "tryme@ic.net");
  encoder.add("L_AMT1", "10.00");
  encoder.add("L_EMAIL1", "a@b.org");
  encoder.add("L_AMT2", "20.00");
  encoder.add("L_EMAIL2", "test33434@ic.net");
  encoder.add("L_AMT2", "30.00");
  String strNVPString = encoder.encode();
  String ppresponse = call(strNVPString);
  NVPDecoder results = new NVPDecoder();
  results.decode(ppresponse);
  if ("Success".equals(results.get("ACK"))) {
    System.out.println("MassPay API call completed successfully");
  } else {
    showErrors(results);
  }
} // massPay
```

File-Based Mass Pay

Before the API was available, the MassPay feature was available to users by uploading a text file with tab-delimited data on the PayPal website. This feature is still available by clicking the Mass Pay link in the footer of a `www.paypal.com` web page. The file that you upload contains data that is organized into three columns:

- *Column 1*: Recipient's email address
- *Column 2*: Amount of payment
- *Column 3*: Currency code (must be the same for all rows)

You may also include an optional fourth column that lets you enter a unique identifier for the recipient. The identifier must be no greater than 30 characters, and it may contain no spaces. If you include the fourth column, you can then optionally include a fifth column with customized payment notes. The fifth column may contain spaces. An example file that contains properly formatted MassPay data is shown in Figure 6-5.

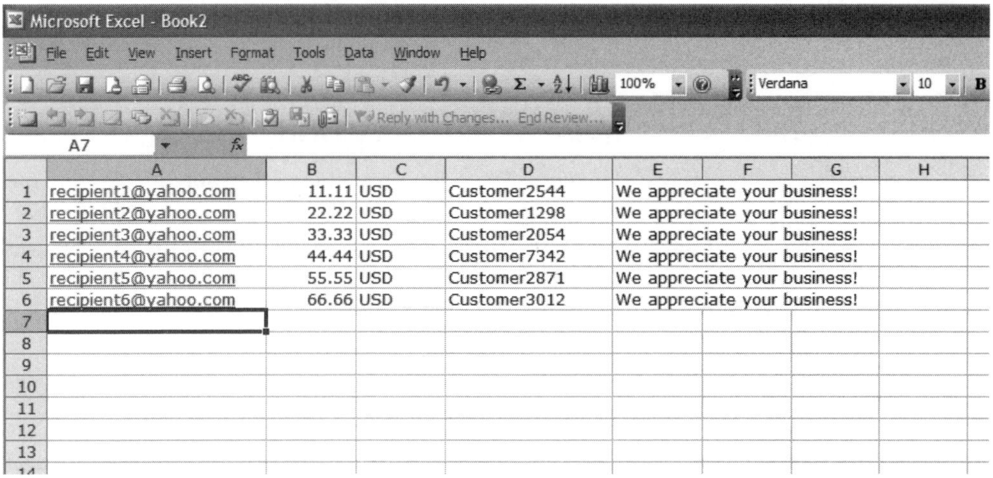

	A	B	C	D	E
1	recipient1@yahoo.com	11.11	USD	Customer2544	We appreciate your business!
2	recipient2@yahoo.com	22.22	USD	Customer1298	We appreciate your business!
3	recipient3@yahoo.com	33.33	USD	Customer2054	We appreciate your business!
4	recipient4@yahoo.com	44.44	USD	Customer7342	We appreciate your business!
5	recipient5@yahoo.com	55.55	USD	Customer2871	We appreciate your business!
6	recipient6@yahoo.com	66.66	USD	Customer3012	We appreciate your business!

Figure 6-5. *Example MassPay file*

Website Payments Pro

In the summer of 2005, PayPal released APIs that actually processed credit card payments directly for the first time. This was a huge step, and it solved another PayPal shortcoming that developers and businesses had been muttering about for awhile: not having the ability to process credit cards directly on a website, and always having to send the buyer to the PayPal website to complete a transaction. The advent of Website Payments Pro alleviated these concerns by providing an all-in-one payment solution that offered buyers the option to pay either directly on the merchant website with a credit card or with their PayPal account after authenticating themselves on the PayPal website.

Website Payments Pro is actually a combination of two payment options. The option that allows a buyer to pay directly on the merchant website by entering their credit card details is referred to as *Direct Payment*. The option that allows a buyer to pay with their PayPal account by using a series of API calls and redirecting the customer to PayPal is referred to as *Express Checkout*. Both Direct Payment and Express Checkout must be provided together on a merchant website to have a complete Website Payments Pro implementation successfully done. You may offer Express Checkout without Direct Payment, but not vice versa.

Website Payments Pro in the UK

If you are in the United Kingdom, the code samples in this section do not apply to you. Although a buyer would not notice a different experience while checking out, Website Payments Pro in the UK uses an API calling mechanism that is unique to the UK. It is patterned after the Payflow Pro Gateway product that PayPal offers. (Payflow Pro is covered extensively in the next chapter.) Payflow Pro was developed by VeriSign Payment Services (VPS) and acquired by PayPal in the 2005 acquisition of VPS.

Code for Website Payment Pro UK is not provided in this chapter. The next chapter details how to use the Payflow Pro SDK to implement PayPal Express Checkout (one half of Website Payment Pro), but for Direct Payment implementation you should consult the UK documentation.

Website Payments Pro in the Rest of the World

At the time of this writing, Website Payments Pro is only available in the United States and the United Kingdom. There are plans, however, to make Website Payments Pro more widely available throughout the rest of the globe as time passes and all of the technical and business hurdles for expanding into other countries are dealt with. Express Checkout, however, is available in most countries where the PayPal API is available. Direct Payment is the option that is primarily restricted.

Applying for Website Payments Pro

By default, a PayPal account is not eligible to use Website Payments Pro. You must submit an online application and have your application approved by PayPal. And then, if you are accepted, the final step is to accept the Website Payments Pro Billing Agreement. The Billing Agreement details the terms and conditions of using Website Payments Pro, including the monthly fee, which is currently $20 per month, in addition to the standard PayPal transaction fees. You must also have a verified Business PayPal account with a confirmed bank account; Personal and Premier accounts cannot apply for Website Payments Pro.

Note For Sandbox accounts, Website Payments Pro applications are automatically approved, and no monthly fees apply. When prompted to enter a Social Security Number, enter a value that begins with 111; otherwise, you will receive an error message. This value must also not be used by any other developer applying for Website Payments Pro in the Sandbox, so be aware that it may take you a few tries to find a unique value.

To begin the process of configuring your account to use Website Payments Pro, you should first upgrade to a Business account. Then, make sure you are logged in to your account and click the Merchant Services tab (in the UK, this tab is called Merchant Tools). Find the Website Payments Pro listing, and follow the links to submit your application. The other thing you must remember to do is set up your PayPal account for API access if you have not done so already. The process for doing this is covered earlier in this chapter.

Direct Payment

With the introduction of Direct Payment and the DoDirectPayment API, PayPal broke new ground in its product offering. Through this API, credit card details are submitted to PayPal that have been entered by a buyer on a merchant's website. The transaction is processed by PayPal, and the result of the transaction is returned to the merchant in the API response. Buyers never leave the merchant website, and they don't even know PayPal is involved in the transaction. DoDirectPayment is essentially a process credit card API call.

Note Remember that your account must be approved for Website Payments Pro in order to use the DoDirectPayment API. If it is not, you will receive error code 10550.

Testing Direct Payment

If you are using the Sandbox for your development, you'll need a test credit card number to test a transaction. Unfortunately, PayPal does not offer a standard test credit card number like most payment processors do. To get around this, you should create a second Sandbox account and add a credit card to that account. When you add a credit card to a Sandbox account, PayPal will generate the number, expiration date, and CVV code for you. Save this information and use it to test the DoDirectPayment API call against your other Sandbox account.

The PayPal Sandbox will always generate Visa numbers for testing. You cannot test MasterCard, American Express, or Discover cards in the PayPal Sandbox.

DoDirectPayment API Using the SOAP Interface

The method shown in Listing 6-11 makes a DoDirectPayment API call using the SOAP interface. This method assumes that a CallerServices object named caller has been properly instantiated and configured like the GetTransactionDetails example earlier in this chapter.

Listing 6-11. *Making a* DoDirectPayment *API Call Using the SOAP Interface*

```
import com.paypal.soap.api.PaymentDetailsType;
import com.paypal.soap.api.DoDirectPaymentRequestType;
import com.paypal.soap.api.DoDirectPaymentResponseType;
import com.paypal.soap.api.DoDirectPaymentRequestDetailsType;
import com.paypal.soap.api.CreditCardDetailsType;
import com.paypal.soap.api.PayerInfoType;
```

```java
import com.paypal.soap.api.PersonNameType;
import com.paypal.soap.api.AddressType;
import com.paypal.soap.api.CountryCodeType;
import com.paypal.soap.api.PaymentActionCodeType;
import com.paypal.soap.api.CreditCardTypeType;

...

/**
 * This method processes a credit card transaction with the DoDirectPayment API
 *
 * @throws PayPalException If an error occurs while making the API call
 */
private static void doDirectPayment() throws PayPalException {
  DoDirectPaymentRequestType request = new DoDirectPaymentRequestType();
  DoDirectPaymentRequestDetailsType requestDetails =
    new DoDirectPaymentRequestDetailsType();

  // First we will specify how much we are charging the credit card.
  // Let's say fifty bucks.
  PaymentDetailsType paymentDetails = new PaymentDetailsType();
  BasicAmountType orderTotal = new BasicAmountType();
  orderTotal.set_value("50.00");
  orderTotal.setCurrencyID(CurrencyCodeType.USD);
  paymentDetails.setOrderTotal(orderTotal);
  requestDetails.setPaymentDetails(paymentDetails);

  // The CreditCardDetailsType object contains all information about the credit card
  CreditCardDetailsType creditCardDetails = new CreditCardDetailsType();

  PayerInfoType cardOwner = new PayerInfoType();
  PersonNameType payerName = new PersonNameType();
  payerName.setFirstName("Bob");
  payerName.setLastName("Smith");
  cardOwner.setPayerName(payerName);
  AddressType payerAddress = new AddressType();
  payerAddress.setStreet1("1234 Main Street");
  payerAddress.setCityName("San Francisco");
  payerAddress.setStateOrProvince("CA");
  payerAddress.setPostalCode("94134");
  payerAddress.setCountry(CountryCodeType.US);
  cardOwner.setAddress(payerAddress);
  creditCardDetails.setCardOwner(cardOwner);
```

```
// This is a credit card number that can be used for Sandbox testing
creditCardDetails.setCreditCardNumber("4755941616268045");
creditCardDetails.setCVV2("234");
creditCardDetails.setExpMonth(1);
creditCardDetails.setExpYear(2009);
creditCardDetails.setCreditCardType(CreditCardTypeType.Visa);
requestDetails.setCreditCard(creditCardDetails);

// Next we specify the payment action. This can be Sale, Authorization, or Order.
requestDetails.setPaymentAction(PaymentActionCodeType.Sale);

// Finally we must record the IP address of the client's browser.
// Just making one up for this example.
requestDetails.setIPAddress("60.127.208.55");


request.setDoDirectPaymentRequestDetails(requestDetails);

// We are now ready to make the API call...
DoDirectPaymentResponseType response =
  (DoDirectPaymentResponseType)caller.call("DoDirectPayment", request);

// ...and check the response
if (response.getAck().equals(AckCodeType.Success)
    || response.getAck().equals(AckCodeType.SuccessWithWarning)) {
  System.out.println("DoDirectPayment API call completed successfully");
  System.out.println("TransactionID = "+response.getTransactionID());
}

if (response.getErrors() != null && response.getErrors().length > 0) {
  System.out.println("Errors/Warnings occurred while making the API call:");
  for (int i=0; i < response.getErrors().length; i++) {
    StringBuffer message =
      new StringBuffer(response.getErrors(i).getSeverityCode().toString());
    message.append(": ");
    message.append(response.getErrors(i).getShortMessage());
    message.append(" - ");
    message.append(response.getErrors(i).getLongMessage());
    message.append(" (");
    message.append(response.getErrors(i).getErrorCode().toString());
    message.append(")");
    System.out.println(message.toString());
  }
}
} // doDirectPayment
```

DoDirectPayment API Using the NVP Interface

The difference between using the SOAP and NVP interfaces is perhaps best demonstrated with the DoDirectPayment API. Compare the previous deep object-oriented complexity with the simplistic code in Listing 6-12. The example uses the call() and showErrors() methods defined earlier in the GetTransactionDetails example.

Listing 6-12. *Making a* DoDirectPayment *API Call Using the NVP Interface*

```java
/**
 * This method processes a credit card transaction with the DoDirectPayment API
 *
 * @throws PayPalException If an error occurs while making the API call
 */
public static void doDirectPayment() throws Exception {
  NVPEncoder encoder = new NVPEncoder();
  encoder.add("METHOD", "DoDirectPayment");
  encoder.add("PAYMENTACTION", "Sale");
  encoder.add("AMT", "50.00");
  encoder.add("CREDITCARDTYPE", "Visa");
  encoder.add("ACCT", "4755941616268045");
  encoder.add("EXPDATE", "2009-10-02");
  encoder.add("CVV2", "234");
  encoder.add("FIRSTNAME", "Bob");
  encoder.add("LASTNAME", "Smith");
  encoder.add("STREET", "1234 Main Street");
  encoder.add("CITY", "San Francisco");
  encoder.add("STATE", "CA");
  encoder.add("ZIP", "94134");
  encoder.add("COUNTRYCODE", "US");
  encoder.add("CURRENCYCODE", "USD");
  String nvpString = encoder.encode();
  String ppresponse = call(nvpString);
  NVPDecoder results = new NVPDecoder();
  results.decode(ppresponse);
  String transactionId = results.get("TRANSACTIONID");
  if ("Success".equals(results.get("ACK"))) {
    System.out.println("DoDirectPayment API call completed successfully");
    System.out.println("TransactionID = " + transactionId);
  } else {
    showErrors(results);
  }
}
```

Return Values for AVS and CVV Codes

In the response to the DoDirectPayment API, values for AVS and CVV checks are included. AVS and CVV are two ways the banking industry tries to control credit card fraud. AVS stands for *address verification system*, and it is a U.S. banking standard for verifying the postal address or telephone number associated with a credit card. CVV stands for *card verification value*, and it is the three- or four-digit code located on the back of a credit card to help verify that the person entering the credit card information online is actually the owner of the physical card.

PayPal returns a single character for the results of both the AVS check (in the AVSCode field) and the CVV check (in the CVV2Code field). If you are wondering why a credit card transaction has been declined, these codes could indicate the reason. Depending on the risk settings associated with your account, PayPal will accept or deny transactions based on the results of these checks. The values are summarized in the following tables.

Table 6-4 summarizes AVS response codes for U.S. credit cards.

Table 6-4. *AVS Response Codes for U.S. Credit Cards*

AVS Code	Description
A	Address matched; ZIP not provided
W	Nine-digit ZIP matched; address not provided
X	Exact match; address + nine-digit ZIP
Y	Match; address + five-digit ZIP
Z	ZIP match; address not provided
N	No match
R	Retry
S	Service not supported
U	Unavailable

Table 6-5 summarizes AVS response codes for non-U.S. credit cards.

Table 6-5. *AVS Response Codes for Non-U.S. Credit Cards*

AVS Code	Description
B	Address matched; ZIP not provided
D	Address and postal code match
F	Address and postal code match (UK)
P	Postal code match
C	No match
I	International unavailable
G	Global unavailable

Table 6-6 summarizes CVV response codes.

Table 6-6. *CVV Response Codes*

AVS Code	Description
M	Match
N	No match
U	Unavailable
S	Service not supported
P	Not processed
X	No response

Suggestions for Your Checkout Page

There are many different strategies for designing your checkout page, and how you design your entire checkout flow will most often depend on your business priorities. Regardless of how you design the page, you must collect the following information in order to populate all of the required fields necessary to create a DoDirectPayment request:

- Credit card type

- Credit card number

- Credit card expiration month

- Credit card expiration year

- Credit card CVV value

- Cardholder first and last name

- Cardholder billing address, including country

- IP address of buyer's browser

In addition to these required fields, the following sections outline a few other best practices that you should take into consideration for your checkout page.

Use a Drop-Down for State or Province

Provide a drop-down menu for the State or Province field. For U.S. addresses, the state must be two letters and must be a valid two-letter state, military location, or U.S. territory. For Canada, the province must be a two-letter Canadian province. By providing a drop-down menu, you eliminate the possibility of a customer mistyping this value or submitting a spelled-out state name, which will result in an error.

Show Buyers Where to Find the CVV Value

Every Visa, MasterCard, American Express, and Discover card issued today has a CVV value, and PayPal requires this for all transactions. Before submitting your API call, check that this value is three digits for Visa, MasterCard, and Discover, or four digits for American Express.

Display text on the checkout page that explains where to find the CVV value on a credit card, especially if your site sells items to buyers who may not be regular computer users or online shoppers.

Do Not Store the CVV Value

It is against PayPal policy to store a CVV value in your own database. To be fully compliant for online credit card processing, never store this value anywhere. It should only be transiently collected for one-time use. Although this policy prevents you from establishing a recurring billing relationship with a customer, it also protects you if your database is hacked and customer billing information is compromised.

Do Something While the API Call Is Pending

While the DoDirectPayment API call generally takes about 2 to 4 seconds to complete, it can potentially take up to 30 seconds. Configure any timeout settings accordingly, and consider displaying a "processing transaction" message to the buyer while the API call completes. You should also disable the Submit button while the API call is processing so that the user doesn't click it a second time, which might result in a duplicate charge.

Use InvoiceID to Prevent Duplicate Charges

You can use the optional InvoiceID field in the DoDirectPayment request to prevent duplicate charges. PayPal ensures that an invoice ID is used only once per account. Duplicate requests with the same invoice ID result in an error and a failed transaction, but this is still better than a customer getting charged twice for the same purchase.

Express Checkout

Express Checkout is PayPal's most powerful and feature-rich payment solution for buyers paying with their PayPal account. It's also the most complex. Since every business has a slightly different checkout process, it is hard to prescribe a one-size-fits-all set of sample code that will make sense for every website. This section goes over the basic steps and API calls involved in an Express Checkout transaction, so that you can see how Express Checkout might be used in the application you are developing.

The following are the core benefits of Express Checkout:

- Buyers choose to pay with PayPal at the very beginning of the checkout process. This way, they can use the payment and shipping information stored in their PayPal account, so they don't have to re-enter it on the merchant website.

- Buyers complete the transaction on the merchant's website, not PayPal's. Since PayPal returns the buyer back to the merchant's website after authenticating on the PayPal site, the merchant can up sell additional items, priority shipping, gift wrap, and so forth before finalizing the transaction.

Express Checkout can be used independently of Website Payments Pro. For businesses that already have a credit card processing mechanism in place and are just looking to add the PayPal payment option, Express Checkout can be implemented without having to apply for Website Payments Pro and being subjected to the monthly fee. But since Express Checkout is a required part of Website Payments Pro, it's presented in this section.

Presenting the Express Checkout Option

When you offer Express Checkout, you should present the PayPal option on the shopping cart summary page. The Express Checkout button, shown in Figure 6-6, should appear before any other payment options and before the customer is asked to enter any billing or shipping information.

Figure 6-6. *Express Checkout button*

When you offer Express Checkout on the shopping cart summary page, you give buyers the chance to speed up their checkout process by not having to enter in their shipping and payment details on the merchant website. Since this information is already stored in their PayPal account, they can reuse this information by having PayPal send it to the merchant. It's a better experience for buyers, and the merchant will see the PayPal option used more, which can lead to increased sales. Figure 6-7 shows a shopping cart summary page that has the Express Checkout button correctly positioned.

DesignerFotos [PayPal's sample integration]

View Cart | My Account | Help

Search:

A demonstration of PayPal's integration flow

Category		
Landscape		
Abstract		
Still Life		

Shopping Cart

Qty	Items	Price
1	San Francisco Bay (32" x 32")	$250.00	Delete
1	Mount Hamilton (24' x 15")	$50.00	Delete

Update

Subscribe FOTO Magazine

1/4/07

Get history log

Subtotal: $300.00   USD

For testing purposes only $0.01 will be submitted.

Continue Shopping   Proceed to Checkout

Fast, easy, secure.

DesignerFotos accepts

Figure 6-7. *Express Checkout button correctly positioned on the shopping cart summary page*

In addition to offering PayPal at the beginning of the checkout process, you should also offer it at the end of the checkout process, where PayPal is listed alongside the other payment options the website accepts, such as Visa and MasterCard, or alternate payment solutions such as BillMeLater. Maybe you offer PayPal in a drop-down list of payment options, or perhaps as a radio button that a buyer clicks. Regardless, it is offered after the buyer has already entered his or her shipping information and you pretty much know what the total charge to the buyer is going to be.

To maximize your sales and give buyers the best checkout experience, offer the PayPal Express Checkout option both at the beginning of the checkout flow on the shopping cart summary page *and* at the end of the checkout process along with the other payment options, in case the buyer does not choose PayPal on the shopping cart page but wishes to choose PayPal as the payment method later in the checkout process.

How Express Checkout Works

Express Checkout is an API-based payment solution, unlike the Website Payments Standard checkout process, which is described in Chapter 3 and based solely on HTML forms. There are three API calls used in an Express Checkout transaction, two of which are required:

- SetExpressCheckout *(required)*: Initiates an Express Checkout transaction

- GetExpressCheckoutDetails *(optional)*: Retrieves buyer details about an Express Checkout transaction

- DoExpressCheckoutPayment *(required)*: Completes an Express Checkout transaction

SetExpressCheckout

The first API call, SetExpressCheckout, is made as soon as buyers click to indicate that they wish to pay with PayPal. PayPal's response to a SetExpressCheckout contains a single value, a *token*, which you retain and include in the other two Express Checkout API calls to indicate that they belong to the same checkout flow. When you get the token back in the API response, you redirect the customer's browser to PayPal so that the buyer can log in and validate his or her shipping and financial information.

■**Note** An Express Checkout token is valid for three hours.

The request for SetExpressCheckout has three required parameters that you include with the API call:

- The total amount of the order, or your best estimate if you don't know the exact amount yet

- The return URL that PayPal will return buyers to after they log in to PayPal and validate their shipping and financial information

- The cancel URL that PayPal will return buyers to if they decide to cancel the transaction after being redirected to the PayPal website

The URL that you redirect the buyer's browser to in order to authenticate him- or herself to PayPal is `https://www.paypal.com/cgi-bin/webscr?cmd=_express-checkout&token=EC-0W8920957N684880R`. This is just an example token value; you would obviously replace this with the token value returned to you in the response to `SetExpressCheckout`.

GetExpressCheckoutDetails

After you redirect the buyer to the PayPal website, the buyer logs in with his or her PayPal username and password. Then the buyer confirms the funding source (credit card, bank account, or PayPal balance) and shipping information, after which the buyer clicks a button to return to the seller's website. The URL the buyer returns to is the return URL value specified in the `SetExpressCheckout` request.

PayPal appends two variables to this URL: the token and the payer ID. The token is used to identify the Express Checkout session, and the payer ID is an encrypted customer account number PayPal uses to identify the buyer. You submit both of these values back to PayPal in the `DoExpressCheckoutPayment` API, so the code that executes at your return URL should store both of these values.

For example, if the return URL you specify in `SetExpressCheckout` is

`http://www.examplestore.com/ec_return.jsp`

then the example of the URL with the appended values that PayPal will redirect the buyer to is

`http://www.examplestore.com/ec_return.jsp?`**Token=EC-0W8920957N684880R**
&PayerID=TEJ9UFMQHWZRF

At this point in the checkout flow, you should display some sort of order confirmation page to the buyer. Since the buyer has already confirmed his or her information with PayPal, you use the `GetExpressCheckoutDetails` API call to retrieve these details so you can display them. The transaction has not been completed yet, so you should provide a final button for the user to click to complete the transaction. When the buyer has clicked the button to make the payment and you are ready to complete the transaction, you make the third and final API call, `DoExpressCheckoutPayment`.

DoExpressCheckoutPayment

`DoExpressCheckoutPayment` is the API call that actually completes the transaction. Once the buyer has clicked the Pay button on the merchant website, you make a call to `DoExpressCheckoutPayment` to complete the sale. In the request to `DoExpressCheckoutPayment`, you indicate the total amount of the final sale, as well as whether the transaction is a sale, an authorization, or an order. (See the section "Authorizing Payments" earlier in this chapter for a description of the difference between these.) The response PayPal returns to you indicates whether or not the transaction was successful, the transaction ID of the transaction, and some other useful pieces of information about the transaction.

The diagram in Figure 6-8 shows a complete Express Checkout transaction and the API calls that happen along the way.

PayPal Express Checkout

Legend: ➡ Web Flow → API Call ⊚ Token

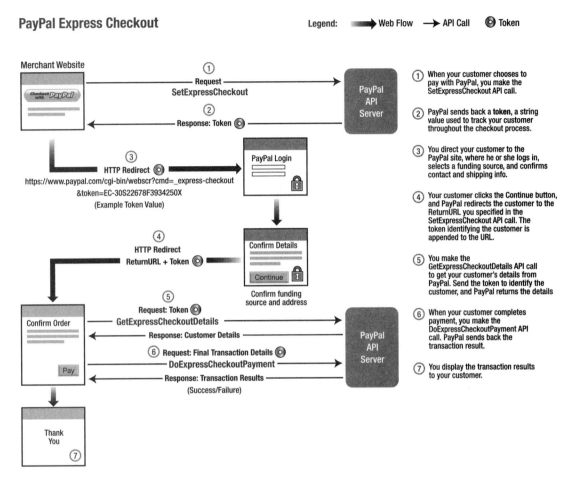

Figure 6-8. *Express Checkout process*

Bypassing the Order Review Page

During a traditional Express Checkout transaction, the customer clicks a Continue Checkout button after reviewing his or her PayPal account details. The merchant then offers the final Pay button on their own website. When the customer clicks the Payment button, the transaction is completed with a call to DoExpressCheckoutPayment. This offers the advantage of giving the buyer a more customized experience, but the disadvantage is that it's one more click that the buyer has to make to complete the transaction.

You can bypass this final order review page. To do so, get your token from the SetExpressCheckout response, and then append useraction=commit to the URL you redirect the user to after making the SetExpressCheckout API call. An example of a redirect with useraction is

```
https://www.paypal.com/cgi-bin/webscr?cmd=_express-checkout&token=EC-
0W8920957N684880R&useraction=commit
```

If `useraction` is not included, or if it is set to `continue`, then PayPal will display a Continue Checkout button to the buyer. If `useraction` is set to `commit`, PayPal will display a Pay button, and the transaction will be completed before the merchant displays the final receipt to the customer. You lose the ability to offer upsells to the buyer, but you also reduce the number of clicks required to complete the purchase by at least one click.

Canceling Website Payments Pro

You may find that Website Payments Pro is not for you. Maybe you decide the integration is too complex for the benefits it offers, and that all you really need is a simple Website Payments Standard solution. Perhaps you decide that all you really want to use is Express Checkout, to take advantage of all of the PayPal antifraud mechanisms and policies in place to protect you. Or maybe business hasn't picked up enough to justify the monthly cost associated with Website Payments Pro.

Regardless of your reasoning, it's simple to cancel Website Payments Pro for your account:

1. Log in to your account at `www.paypal.com`.

2. Click the Profile subtab.

3. Click the PayPal Monthly Billing option in the Financial Information column.

4. Click the Cancel Agreement button.

5. Confirm that you want to cancel by clicking the Cancel Agreement button.

Seller Protection Policy for Website Payments Pro

PayPal's Seller Protection Policy (SPP) is one of its key benefits for merchants. PayPal designed SPP to protect merchants against unauthorized payments and against claims of nonreceipt of merchandise if they follow good selling practices. PayPal's Seller Protection Policy is covered in more detail in Chapter 9.

With Website Payments Pro, SPP applies only for Express Checkout transactions. For Direct Payment transactions, PayPal does not offer an explicit SPP. PayPal's policy is that it will do its best to fight any chargeback cases on your behalf, but the specific conditions of the SPP do not apply. In the case of a chargeback, it always helps if you can gather as much proof and information in regard to the transaction as possible. Ultimately who wins the case is not up to PayPal; it is up to the credit card issuer.

Summary

The PayPal API offers powerful payments functionality that lets developers add new dimensions to their applications. Since the API's initial release in 2004, many enhancements have been made that give developers a number of choices to make in what payment options to offer, how to authenticate API calls, and how to submit API calls. The API is what transforms PayPal from just a simple payments engine into a true payments *platform*, on top of which the possibilities for developing new and innovative applications are endless.

This chapter discussed everything related to using the PayPal API, including the operations available, how to configure your account to access the API, and how to use the PayPal SDK to simplify the process of making API calls. We discussed the two interfaces used to make API calls: the object-oriented SOAP interface and the more straightforward Name-Value Pair (NVP) interface. We discussed using the MassPay API to send payments, Website Payments Pro as an all-in-one payment solution, how to separate the authorization of funds from their actual capture, and the suite of APIs that PayPal makes available for post-transaction administration.

The API is a major area of growth at PayPal, and the addition of new APIs are planned for the future. If you want to stay abreast of the latest developments that PayPal is offering the world of e-commerce, be sure to keep an eye on the PayPal API. One place that always offers the latest news on PayPal enhancements is the official PayPal Developer Community website, www.pdncommunity.com. I definitely recommend joining this online community, subscribing to the developer blog, and checking back on a regular basis to see the new features PayPal is offering developers.

■■■

## CHAPTER 7

Payflow Gateway

In 2005, PayPal acquired the payments division of VeriSign, including the popular Payflow Pro and Payflow Link payment gateway products. In doing so, PayPal could now offer a credit card processing solution to businesses that had (or wanted) their own Internet Merchant Account (IMA). Payflow Pro is an industry-leading gateway service, and the way it is implemented and managed is unique—it's different from any other PayPal payment option. The merchant account is created and managed differently, and there is a separate suite of fraud controls, reporting tools, and APIs. So in a way, this chapter is unique and quite different from the rest of the book.

This chapter covers the two main gateway products offered by PayPal: Payflow Pro and Payflow Link. Additionally, a number of supporting features work with these products to enhance the overall service offering. We begin the chapter with a look at gateways in general and where they fit in the big picture of the world of e-commerce, and then we discuss the specific Payflow-related technologies. Topics covered in this chapter include the following:

- Payment gateways

- Payflow Pro

- XMLPay

- Payflow Link

- PayPal Manager

Payment Gateways

You can think of a *payment gateway* as simply a connector. It connects a merchant's website to the vast network of banks and processors that make up our financial system. A gateway doesn't actually process any transactions; it is reliant on external processors to handle the actual verification of credit card information. The gateway simply knows how to take the input parameters that you send it for a given transaction and convert them into a format that can be passed through to the banks for verification. Put another way, a gateway is the front door to the house of online financial processing.

Since a payment gateway by itself is just a connector, you have to establish additional relationships with members of the financial world so that the gateway knows where to connect you. Primarily, this involves contacting a bank to set up an IMA. Most, if not all, major banks offer the ability to set up an IMA. Additionally, PayPal can offer you an IMA directly when you register for the Payflow service. This IMA-providing bank is referred to as the *acquiring bank* since it acquires the transaction from the gateway. The acquiring bank is responsible for underwriting any risk involved with establishing your online business. The acquiring bank then works with any number of *processors* that handle the actual processing of your account information and the corresponding settlements at the end of each day to reconcile all credit card activity with the banks. Individual *brands* such as MasterCard, Visa, and Discover create the physical credit cards that are tied to the processors and issue them to consumers.

You don't have to worry about these various stages in the credit card processing business when you just use a standard (nongateway) PayPal account, because PayPal plays the all-in-one role of gateway, acquirer, and processor. Figure 7-1 shows the various players in the e-commerce world.

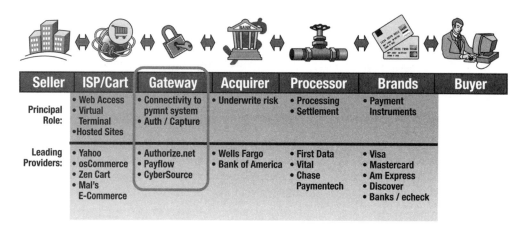

Figure 7-1. *The components in the world of e-commerce*

Merchants may use the Payflow Gateway if they do not wish to use PayPal's Website Payments Pro service to accept credit cards directly on their website (see Chapter 6 for information on Website Payments Pro). The Payflow Gateway is generally easier to set up and integrate than Website Payments Pro. Additionally, merchants may wish to work with a local bank to manage their merchant account instead of using the PayPal service. The Payflow service also offers more fine-grained control over risk and fraud settings than a PayPal business account does. For these reasons as well as others, the Payflow Gateway option makes good business sense for many types of merchants.

Acquiring an Internet Merchant Account

If you are going to use a Payflow solution for your business, you need to acquire an IMA. Although you can submit test transactions before getting your IMA, you need to provide PayPal with details about your IMA before you can submit live transactions and actually start processing real payments. You can use the PayPal IMA, which is described in the next section, or you can contact your bank to get set up with an IMA. Your bank will then work with a PayPal-supported credit card processor to process and settle transactions. For example, two of the largest processors are Chase Paymentech and First Data.

Acquiring an IMA is different than acquiring a regular merchant account from a bank. Because you are doing business online, there are additional fraud risks to take into consideration. When online credit card processing was first becoming available in the mid-1990s, IMAs were prohibitively expensive due to the fear of losses due to fraud. But thankfully, over the years both the prices and restrictions for acquiring an IMA have been reduced to a level where they are accessible to small- and medium-sized businesses.

In addition to getting an IMA from a bank, you can use the standard PayPal IMA to process your gateway transactions. This is generally a faster and easier way to get your account set up, because you can do all the work online and do not have to visit your local bank to set up your IMA. When you sign up for the Payflow Gateway on the PayPal website, you will be given the option to use PayPal as your processor. When you use PayPal as your processor, transactions that you process will appear both in your PayPal Manager history as well as your www.paypal.com account history. If you do not use PayPal as your processor, your transactions will not appear in your www.paypal.com account; they will only appear inside the PayPal Manager application. PayPal Manager is discussed later in this chapter.

Payflow Pro

Payflow Pro is the more powerful of the two gateway products offered by PayPal. It is fairly straightforward to set up, and submitting requests to the gateway is not too difficult for anyone with a basic understanding of software development. Even if you have a very basic understanding of writing code, the examples in this chapter should get you sorted out. Once you have your IMA and have integrated Payflow Pro into your website, you can start processing credit card transactions.

Getting Started with Payflow Pro

If you're interested in integrating a website with Payflow Pro, the first thing you must do is register for an account. You can accomplish this on the PayPal website by clicking the Merchant Services tab and then navigating to the Payflow Pro option. During signup, you will be asked whether you want to use (and pay for) features described later in this chapter (such as Recurring Billing and Fraud Controls), so it may be worthwhile to finish reading the chapter before going to create your account.

For specific integration instructions, the *Payflow Pro Developer's Guide* contains information that is more detailed than that presented in this book. For the latest version of the PDF, visit PayPal's Integration Center at www.paypal.com/integration and click the Documentation link. You'll be taken to a page that contains all of PayPal's PDF documentation, including the *Payflow Pro Developer's Guide*.

Using the Payflow SDK

Once you have set up a Payflow Pro account, the next thing to do is download a client SDK from the PayPal Manager site. PayPal Manager is described in detail later in this chapter and can be accessed at https://manager.paypal.com. You can log in to PayPal Manager once you have signed up for Payflow Pro. Within PayPal Manager are links to download one of the various SDKs that best fits your development environment. There are currently SDKs for Java, .NET, Oracle iPayment, Microsoft Commerce Server, and IBM Payment Manager. These

SDKs are entirely different from the SDKs described in Chapter 6 that are used to access the PayPal API.

The Payflow SDK contains libraries that know how to communicate with the Payflow service endpoints. Additionally, the SDK contains an SSL certificate for validating the CA chain that is included in the server certificate that the Payflow server presents during the SSL handshake protocol while communicating with the SDK client. The certificate is exactly like the one that is included with common web browsers such as Internet Explorer and Firefox, and the SDK uses the certificate in the same way a web browser uses it.

Processing a Credit Card Transaction

Once you have set up your Payflow Pro account and downloaded an SDK, you are ready to start processing some test transactions. By default, your account will be in test mode when you set it up, and you should leave it in test mode until your code is working and you're ready to start processing live transactions for real money. You can switch to live mode within PayPal Manager, once you have begun paying for your gateway account access. You can alternate between test mode and live mode at any time.

Credit card transactions generally occur in two steps. First, an *authorization* is made on the funds, and then the actual *capture* of the funds occurs at a later time. When the authorization is first made, the bank that issued the credit card will place a temporary hold on the cardholder's funds for the authorized amount. This hold generally lasts a few days and cannot be cancelled by Payflow Pro. Then when the subsequent capture is made, the funds are actually flagged to be transferred to the merchant's bank account. During a daily *settlement* process, all transactions that have been flagged for capture are reconciled and the funds are actually transferred between accounts.

The only data that Payflow requires you to submit in order to process a credit card transaction are the card number, the expiration date, and the amount. Optionally, you can submit billing address details to perform an AVS check and a card security code (CVV) to verify the card security code printed on the physical card.

Submitting a Request to Payflow Pro

Payflow transactions occur in a request/response format. You create a request that defines all the connection variables as well as a transaction-specific parameter list, and then you send it off to the Payflow server and get a response back with the result of the transaction. The response is almost immediate, but it can sometimes take a few seconds to complete.

There are two ways to submit your request to the Payflow server. First, you can create a long string with all of the variables specified in a `name=value` format, with each name/value pair separated by an ampersand (&). The exception to this is the .NET SDK, which uses data objects instead of name/value pairs. Second, you can create an XML document that contains all of the parameters in well-formed XML. This option is called *XMLPay* and is covered later in this chapter.

Once you have formed your request, you submit the request to the Payflow server by using a method in the SDK that is described in the SDK documentation (each SDK is a little bit different). Examples for the Java SDK are provided in this chapter, so you can get an idea of what the code looks like.

You must specify certain connection parameters so that the SDK client knows how to make contact with the Payflow service. The connection parameters that must be submitted with each transaction are listed in Table 7-1. Additionally, there are optional parameters that you can use if you are behind a firewall and need to use a proxy server.

Table 7-1. *Connection Parameters Included in Each Payflow Pro Request*

Parameter	Description
HOSTADDRESS	URL of Payflow server; either http://payflow.verisign.com or http://test-payflow.verisign.com
HOSTPORT	Always use 443
PARMLIST	Ampersand-separated list of transaction-specific input variables
TIMEOUT	Length of time in seconds before a transaction times out (30 seconds is recommended)

Note In the future, these URLs will be updated to replace verisign with paypal, but at the time of this writing, the switch hasn't been made. Please keep a look out on the PayPal website, as well as on the errata pages of this book, for more news.

When creating the ampersand-separated PARMLIST that will be submitted to the Payflow server, you specify each parameter in a name=value format. An example of a properly formatted PARMLIST for a credit card sale transaction is as follows:

```
TRXTYPE=S&TENDER=C&USER=MyOnlineStore& ➥
PWD=MyPassword&VENDOR=MyOnlineStore&PARTNER=PayPal& ➥
ACCT=5105105105105100&EXPDATE=1009&CVV2=456& ➥
AMT=123.00&FNAME=John&LNAME=Doe& ➥
STREET=123 First St.&CITY=San Jose&STATE=CA&ZIP=95131& ➥
COMMENT1=Item1005&VERBOSITY=MEDIUM
```

In the preceding example, note that spaces can be used within the PARMLIST. However, you may never use quotations within the PARMLIST. If you wish to use an ampersand or an equal sign for a parameter, you use a length identifier along with the variable name that will contain the special character. The length identifier specifies how many characters appear in the corresponding value. An example of this is shown in Table 7-2.

Table 7-2. *Specifying Length Identifiers*

Status	Parameter
Invalid	NAME=Smith & Wesson
Valid	NAME[14]=Smith & Wesson
Invalid	COMMENT1=Quantity=10
Valid	COMMENT1[11]=Quantity=10

The variables listed in Table 7-3 must be included in the PARMLIST no matter what type of transaction you are processing.

Table 7-3. PARMLIST *Parameters Required for All Transaction Types*

Parameter	Description
TRXTYPE	Transaction type (see the "Transaction Types" section).
TENDER	Tender type (method of payment; see the "Tender Types" section).
PARTNER	ID provided to you during signup. Use "PayPal" if you signed up at www.paypal.com.
VENDOR	Merchant ID you created when you signed up for your Payflow account.
USER	Same as VENDOR unless you authorized additional users to submit transactions through your account.
PWD	Password you created when you signed up for your Payflow account or created an additional authorized user.

In addition to the parameters in Table 7-3 that are required for all transaction types, the parameters listed in Table 7-4 are required for credit card transactions.

Table 7-4. PARMLIST *Parameters for Credit Card Transactions*

Parameter	Description	Required?
ACCT	Credit card numbers.	Yes
AMT	Amount to charge in dollars and cents. Do not include commas if over $1000.00. Do not include a dollar sign or other currency symbol.	Yes
COMMENT1	User-defined variable. Use it for your own tracking.	No
COMMENT2	User-defined variable. Use it for your own tracking.	No
CURRENCY	Currency code (USD, EUR, GBP, CAD, JPY, AUD).	No
CUSTREF	User-defined variable. Use it for your own tracking.	No
CVV2	Card security code.	No
EXPDATE	Card expiration date in MMYY format.	Yes
NAME	Cardholder's name.	No
ORIGID	PNREF ID of a transaction being reference by this request.	No
STREET	Cardholder's street address.	No
VERBOSITY	LOW or MEDIUM.	No
ZIP	Cardholder's five- or nine-digit ZIP code. Do not use dashes for a nine-digit code.	No

Specifying the Location of the Payflow Pro Certificate

When using a Payflow SDK to connect with the Payflow servers, you must set a property named PFPRO_CERT_PATH. The value of PFPRO_CERT_PATH is the path to the location of the VeriSign SSL certificate included with the Payflow SDK. This certificate is used to validate the certificate chain associated with the SSL certificate presented by the Payflow server when connecting to its secure endpoints. It's identical to the root certificate included in most popular web browsers to validate VeriSign-signed certificates presented by the thousands of websites that use VeriSign SSL certificates to enable SSL-encrypted connections. Instructions on specifying the PFPRO_CERT_PATH property are SDK specific and included with the SDK documentation.

Example Using the Java Payflow Pro SDK

Listing 7-1 is an example Java application that submits a Payflow Pro transaction and prints out the response. The example demonstrates the simplicity of the code and not necessarily best practices—for example, the StringBuffer class could be used to build the string and reduce the object instantiation overhead, but for the sake of the example it is not.

Listing 7-1. *Example Java Application Using the Payflow Pro SDK*

```java
import com.Verisign.payment.PFProAPI;

class PFProJava {

  public static void main(String[] args)     {
    PFProAPI pn = new PFProAPI();
    String parmList = "";

    // Set the certificate path since the Java client
    // is unable to read the PFPRO_CERT_PATH environment variable.
    // This example assumes a directory called "certs" resides in the
    // current working directory.
    pn.SetCertPath("certs");

    // Create the context for this transaction by supplying:
    // CreateContext(endpoint, port, timeout, proxy, proxy_port,
    //               proxy_logon, proxy_pwd)
    pn.CreateContext("test-payflow.verisign.com", 443, 30, "", 0, "", "");

    // Build the NAME=VALUE pair parameter string
    // With Auth Credentials
    parmList =

    // We begin the parameter string with the Auth Credentials specific to your ➡
account "PARTNER=VeriSign&VENDOR=MyOnlineStore&USER=MyOnlineStore ➡
&PWD=MyPassword";
    // We will now specify transaction-specific parameters
    parmList += "&TRXTYPE=S";  // Indicates a Sale transaction
    parmList += "&TENDER=C";   // Indicates a Credit Card is being processed
    parmList +=
      "&ACCT=5105105105105100&EXPDATE=0909";  // Add the cc num and exp date
    parmList += "&CVV2=123";  // Add the card security code
    parmList += "&STREET=123 Test Ave&ZIP=12345";  // Add the AVS info
    parmList += "&AMT=100.00";  // Add the amount

    // Submit the transaction and store the response
    String resp = pn.SubmitTransaction(parmList);
```

```java
        // Display the response received
        System.out.println(resp);

        // Take appropriate action dependant on the RESULT code
        // First, parse the response variables into a Map
        Map responseVariables = new HashMap();
        StringTokenizer tokenizer = new StringTokenizer(resp, "&");
        // get each response value and put it into the responseVariables map
        while (tokenizer.hasMoreElements()) {
            String responseElement = tokenizer.nextToken();
            String variable = responseElement.substring(0, responseElement.indexOf("="));
            String value = responseElement.substring(responseElement.indexOf("=")+1);
            responseVariables.put(variable, value);
        }
        // now check RESULT
        String resultString = (String)responseVariables.get("RESULT");
        if (resultString != null) {
            byte result = Byte.parseByte(resultString);
            System.out.println("result = "+result);
            if (result == 0) {
                // Take appropriate action for a successful transaction
                System.out.println("Success");
            }
            else if (result < 0) {
                // Take appropriate action for a denied transaction
                System.out.println("Denied");
            }
            else if (result > 0) {
                // Take appropriate action for a communication error
                System.out.println("Error");
            }
        }

    // Destroy the context created for this transaction
    pn.DestroyContext();
    }
}
```

Submitting Authorization, Delayed Capture, and Void Transactions

Authorization & Capture with the Payflow Pro Gateway is different from Authorization & Capture with the PayPal API as discussed in Chapter 6. With the Payflow Gateway, you specify the TRXTYPE to A for the authorization and submit parameters as described in Table 7-3. When you make the capture transaction, you specify the TRXTYPE to D for "delayed capture," which is the equivalent of the term "capture" when used in the context of the PayPal API. The only required parameter for the Payflow Delayed Capture is ORIGID, which is the PNREF received in the response to the original authorization request (see Table 7-5).

If the capture amount differs from the amount specified in the original authorization (such as in the case of a partial shipment), you can also specify the AMT variable to define the amount to be captured. It must be less than the original amount; otherwise, the transaction will be processed as two separate transactions.

If you wish to void an authorization before capturing the funds, you can submit a void transaction by specifying a TRXTYPE of V and submitting the ORIGID as the lone request parameter. A void transaction will prevent any funds from being captured on the authorization, but it will not release the bank's hold on the customer's authorized funds. To release this hold, you must contact the card-issuing bank directly.

Submitting a Refund Transaction

You can submit a refund by submitting a credit transaction. The TRXTYPE for a credit transaction is C, and the required request parameter is the ORIGID of the transaction you would like to refund. There is a setting in PayPal Manager called "Allow non-referenced credits," which, if enabled, will allow you to issue credits to a customer's credit card even if the customer has not made a prior transaction with you. You can just supply the credit card information in the request by using the AMT, ACCT, and EXPDATE parameters, and the account will be credited with the amount specified by AMT. The "Allow non-referenced credits" option is disabled by default, and the PayPal processor does not support nonreferenced credits.

Reading the Response from Payflow Pro

Just as you create an ampersand-separated list of request parameters, Payflow returns to you a similarly formatted list of response parameters. Every response will contain the variables listed in Table 7-5.

Table 7-5. *Fields Included in the Payflow Pro Response*

Field	Description	Length
PNREF	Unique transaction identifier	12
RESULT	Result of the transaction	Variable
CVV2MATCH*	Result of CVV check	1
RESPMSG	Response message	Variable
AVSADDR**	AVS address check result	1
AVSZIP**	AVS ZIP check result	1
IAVS	International AVS address check result	1

* Only returned when a CVV value is submitted
** Only returned when a STREET or ZIP value is submitted

Generally the first value you will look at when you get your response is the RESULT. The value you want to see here is either zero (0) or 12. A 0 means the transaction was successful, and a 12 means that it was declined. Any value other than 0 or 12 means that there was an error with the request, or some other processing error occurred. A negative value for RESULT means that a communication error occurred and no transaction took place, and a positive value for RESULT means that the transaction was declined or there was some other error. For a complete list of RESULT values and their meanings, consult the appendix.

The PNREF value is a unique identifier for the transaction. Inside of PayPal Manager, this value is referred to as the transaction ID. If you later want to void a transaction, issue a refund, perform a capture on an authorization, or take any other action on the transaction, the PNREF value is how you identify it.

RESPMSG is a human-readable message that describes the result of the transaction. If there was an error with the transaction, RESPMSG will describe the error. It is useful for debugging purposes, although your code should rely on the value of RESULT to determine what logic to perform next, and not check for string comparisons in RESPMSG since the messages may change in the future.

AVSADDR and AVSZIP are returned if you submit a value for STREET or ZIP in your request. Submitting an address verification service (AVS) check on each transaction is helpful to reduce fraud risk. By submitting the billing address, you can make sure the person submitting the credit card details at least knows the billing address of the credit card holder. With many processors, submitting an AVS check will also qualify you for a lower transaction rate by avoiding what is referred to as a *downgraded transaction*—that is, a transaction that does not include any AVS or CVV information, and is thereby subject to higher processing fees. AVSADDR and AVSZIP will have one of three values: Y, N, or X. Y is returned if the address/ZIP is a match, N is returned if the address/ZIP does not match, and X is returned in the rare case that the cardholder's bank does not support address verification.

CVV2MATCH is returned if you submit a CVV2 value in your transaction request. Similar to the AVS checks, CVV2MATCH will return a Y, N, or X. Y is returned if the card security code is a match, N is returned if the card security code does not match, and X is returned if the cardholder's bank does not support card security code checks. One example of a bank that doesn't support card security code checks is American Express, which currently requires CVV value to be submitted only via certain programs and on a per-account basis.

Voice Authorizations (RESULT=13)

If you receive a RESULT value of 13, this is called a *referral*. It happens when the card-issuing bank cannot definitively authorize the transaction, but it is not a flat-out denial either. A referral is basically the bank telling the merchant, "Give us a call, and we'll work it out over the phone." The exact process depends on the bank you're using, but essentially you phone the bank and give the transaction details again over the phone. The bank then makes the decision to approve or deny the transaction. This is referred to as a *voice authorization*.

If your voice authorization is approved, you will receive an authorization code over the phone from your processor. You then resubmit the transaction to the gateway with a TRXTYPE of F for voice authorization. The F stands for "forced," meaning the gateway will automatically approve the transaction and flag it for settlement. You include the transaction details again, as well as the authorization code given to you by the bank.

■**Note** If you use PayPal as your processor, voice authorizations are not supported.

Testing Credit Card Transactions with the Simulator

Payflow provides a simple way of submitting test transactions using a test environment known as the Simulator. By using the Simulator, you can test your code for how to handle a successful credit card transaction as well as any error condition. The Simulator is similar to the PayPal Sandbox, with a few key distinctions. One main difference between the Simulator and the Sandbox is that with Payflow Pro and the Simulator, you use the same account for both testing and live transactions. Once your code is working in the Simulator environment, you simply modify a couple of variables to begin processing live transactions. The Sandbox does not work like that. With the Sandbox, you maintain completely separate accounts for test transactions and live transactions. You must do all the account setup and configuration twice, and maintain separate credentials for each account.

To test using the Simulator, submit your transactions to `http://test-payflow.verisign.com`. Any transactions submitted to this URL will not result in any real money changing hands. The SDK you download will have a method to specify the URL you want to use to submit transactions.

Test Credit Card Numbers

When you have your Payflow account in test mode, there are a number of test credit card numbers that you can use to simulate successful transactions. Those numbers are listed in Table 7-6.

The ability to test credit card transactions highlights another difference between the Simulator and the Sandbox. While the Simulator offers the ability to test for many different types of credit cards, with the PayPal Sandbox you can only test Visa numbers. Additionally, with the Sandbox there are no predefined credit card numbers that can be widely used to test. You must create a credit card number that has not been added to another Sandbox account.

But enough about the Sandbox—let's get back to the Simulator and the credit card numbers that can be used for testing successful transactions.

Table 7-6. *Test Credit Card Numbers Used with the Payflow Simulator*

Card Type	Credit Card Number
American Express	378282246310005
American Express	371449635398431
American Express Corporate	378734493671000
Australian BankCard	5610591081018250
Diners Club	30569309025904
Diners Club	38520000023237
Discover	6011111111111117
Discover	6011000990139424
JCB	3530111333300000
JCB	3566002020360505
MasterCard	5555555555554444

Continued

Table 7-6. *Continued*

Card Type	Credit Card Number
MasterCard	5105105105105100
Visa	4111111111111111
Visa	4012888888881881
Visa	4222222222222

In addition to using one of the test credit card numbers in Table 7-6, make sure that the expiration date that you submit occurs sometime in the future, otherwise the transaction will be declined. Additionally, any CVV value and billing address can be used with the test credit card numbers.

Testing Error Codes

In addition to providing test credit card numbers to simulate successful transactions, Payflow offers a simple way to test for specific result codes using the Simulator. In general, the way it works has to do with the amount of the transaction. For any value up to $1,000, Payflow will approve the transaction. For any value between $1,001 and $2,000, Payflow will return the result code of the amount minus 1,000. For instance, if you wish to generate a result code 6 (invalid country code), submit a transaction for $1,006.

It's not quite as simple as it sounds, because all processors support a different set of error codes. Each processor supports different values, although pretty much all of them support the main error codes, such as 12 and 13. For a current processor-specific list of supported error codes that can be simulated via the transaction amount process described previously, consult the Payflow Pro documentation, which you can find in PayPal Manager.

Testing AVS Responses

You can test the different AVS response codes (Y, N, X) by modifying the values of the billing address in the PARMLIST you submit with your transaction request. You can control the value of the AVSADDR response variable by modifying the first three characters of the STREET request variable, and you can control the value of the AVSZIP response variable by modifying the value of the ZIP request variable.

Table 7-7 displays the possible values of the first three characters of STREET and their corresponding AVSADDR response values. Table 7-8 displays the possible values of ZIP and their corresponding AVSZIP response values.

Table 7-7. *Test Values for* STREET *and* AVSADDR

STREET **First Three Characters**	AVSADDR **Result**
000–333	Y
334–666	N
667+	X

Table 7-8. *Test Values for* ZIP *and* AVSZIP

ZIP	AVSZIP **Result***
00000–50000	Y
50001–99999	N

* If AVSADDR *returns* X, AVSZIP *will also return* X.

Testing Card Security Code

You can test the different card security code (CVV2MATCH) response codes (Y, N, X) by modifying the value of the CVV2 request parameter you submit with your transaction request. Table 7-9 displays the possible values of the CVV2 request variable and the corresponding CVV2MATCH values.

Table 7-9. *Test Values for* CVV2 *and* CVV2MATCH

CVV2	CVV2MATCH
001–300	Y
301–600	N
601+	X

Debugging Common Payflow Pro Errors

A few error results are frequently encountered during development with Payflow Pro. Two of the most common are RESULT=1 and RESULT=-31. When you receive RESULT=1, it means that your credentials are invalid or not set up correctly. One or more of the PARTNER, VENDOR, USER, and PWD parameters did not validate with the gateway. Double-check these values in your code and make sure you are not missing an ampersand or inserting an extra space or quotation mark. The fields must be submitted exactly right, and a typo can cause RESULT=1 and a failed transaction to occur. Another common cause of RESULT=1 is submitting live transactions to Payflow while your account is still in test mode. To transfer out of test mode and into live transaction processing mode, you have to begin the billing for your Payflow service and also update the setting in your PayPal Manager account.

If you receive RESULT=-31, the Payflow Pro client is unable to locate the certificate file provided with the Payflow SDK. Make sure the PFPRO_CERT_PATH property that is configured in your SDK is an absolute path to the location of the certificate file. If you receive RESULT=-32, it means the certificate was found but there was an error in validating the Common Name on the VeriSign SSL certificate presented during the SSL handshake between the client SDK and the endpoint. Validate that you have the latest version of the certificate, and that your endpoint is either http://payflow.verisign.com or http://test-payflow.verisign.com.

Transaction Types

You can submit a number of different transaction types to the Payflow Pro Gateway. In each request you make to the Payflow server, you specify the transaction type in the TRXTYPE variable. Possible values for TRXTYPE are listed in Table 7-10.

Table 7-10. *Possible Values for* TRXTYPE

Value	Description
S	Sale (authorization and capture in one)
C	Credit (refund)
A	Authorization
D	Delayed capture
V	Void (cancel a previous authorization)
F	Voice authorization
I	Inquiry (check status of previous transaction)

Tender Types

You can submit a number of different payment methods to the Payflow Pro Gateway. In each request you make to the Payflow server, you specify the payment method in the TENDER variable. Possible values for TENDER are listed in Table 7-11.

Table 7-11. *Possible Values for* TENDER

Value	Description
A	Automated clearinghouse (ACH)
C	Credit card
D	Pinless debit
K	TeleCheck
P	PayPal (Express Checkout)

Reference Transactions

If your website offers a subscription service or some other arrangement that involves recurring billing, you will need to charge your customers' credit card on a regular basis, such as once a month. Keeping your customers' credit card information stored in your database is a bad idea, because a security breach or an unhappy employee could lead to a disaster if your customers' financial data got into the wrong hands. Additionally, if you need to charge a customer twice for one order, such as if the order is split into multiple shipments, you do not want to have to call your customer back and have the customer give you his or her credit card information again.

To remove the need to store credit card numbers in your database, Payflow Pro offers a Reference Transactions feature. To use Reference Transactions, you create a transaction request just like usual, except in the PARMLIST you do not include any credit card details.

Instead, you submit an ORIGID variable with the value of the PNREF of the original transaction where the credit card was used. PayPal has the credit card information on file and will process the card without you having to resubmit the credit card details.

■**Note** By default, the Reference Transactions feature is turned off in your Payflow account and can only be turned on by the account administrator.

An example of a PARMLIST for a Reference Transaction is shown in Listing 7-2. It will authorize the credit card associated with previous transaction ID VXYZ8767654 in the amount of $55.

Listing 7-2. *Example* PARMLIST *for a Reference Transaction*

```
TRXTYPE=A&TENDER=C&PWD=MyPassword&PARTNER=PayPal ➠
&VENDOR=MyOnlineStore&USER= MyOnlineStore ➠
&ORIGID=VXYZ8767654&AMT=55.00
```

Implementing PayPal Express Checkout with the Payflow Pro API

For developers who already have a working implementation of Payflow Pro, adding PayPal Express Checkout as an additional payment option is possible using the same interface and credentials they are used to using with Payflow Pro. This allows developers to easily add the PayPal payment option to their website in addition to offering credit card processing through the gateway.

To accommodate processing PayPal transactions through the Payflow interface, a new TENDER type is used with a value of P. Additionally, three new ACTION parameters were added to make the three API calls involved in a PayPal Express Checkout transaction. The ACTION types are described in Table 7-12.

Table 7-12. *Values for* ACTION *When Implementing PayPal Express Checkout*

Value	Description
S	Initiate an Express Checkout transaction and acquire a token (similar to the SetExpressCheckout API).
G	Get details about an Express Checkout transaction (similar to the GetExpressCheckoutDetails API).
D	Complete an Express Checkout transaction (similar to the DoExpressCheckoutPayment API).

PayPal Express Checkout is covered extensively in Chapter 6. You should consult that chapter to determine the best way to work the Express Checkout flow into your website and the best way to handle the responses for the API calls. For your reference, example request and responses for each of the three ACTION types are shown in the sections that follow, and a brief refresher on when each of the three calls are made is provided.

SetExpressCheckout (ACTION=S)

This is the API call that is made to initiate an Express Checkout transaction. Since users are sent to the PayPal website to authenticate themselves during the checkout process, you need a way to identify them when they return to your site. The *token* that is returned as a response to this API call is that identifier.

Listing 7-3 is an example PARMLIST for a SetExpressCheckout request for a sale transaction. Note the TENDER value is P to identify this as the PayPal payment method.

Listing 7-3. *Example* PARMLIST *for a* SetExpressCheckout *Request*

```
TRXTYPE=S&ACTION=S&AMT=55.00&CANCELURL=http://www.mystore.com/cancel.html&
CUSTOM=UNIQUEID&EMAIL=buyer@apress.com&PARTNER=PayPal&PWD=MyPassword&
RETURNURL=http://www.mystore.com/thankyou.html&TENDER=P&USER=MyOnlineStore&
VENDOR=MyOnlineStore
```

An example of a corresponding result string for this transaction is shown in Listing 7-4.

Listing 7-4. *Gateway Response to* SetExpressCheckout

```
RESULT=0&RESPMSG=Approved&TOKEN=EC-17C76533PL706494P
```

The value of TOKEN is used when you redirect the customer to the PayPal website, as described in Chapter 6. It is also used in the following two Express Checkout API calls, in order to associate them as being part of the same checkout flow.

GetExpressCheckoutDetails (ACTION=G)

After the buyer has been redirected to PayPal, has logged in to PayPal, and has confirmed his or her billing and shipping details, the buyer is sent back to the merchant website, along with his or her corresponding token and PayerID. At this time, you make the GetExpressCheckoutDetails call to get all of the buyer's information.

Listing 7-5 is an example PARMLIST for a GetExpressCheckoutDetails request.

Listing 7-5. *Example* PARMLIST *for a* GetExpressCheckoutDetails *Request*

```
TRXTYPE=S&VENDOR=MyOnlineStore&USER=MyOnlineStore&PWD=MyPassword&TENDER=P&
PARTNER=PayPal&ACTION=G&TOKEN=EC-17C73463PL785494P
```

The result from the request in Listing 7-5 will return a wealth of information about the buyer. An example response is shown in Listing 7-6. Most of the fields are self-explanatory. PAYERID is a unique PayPal identifier that is needed for the DoExpressCheckoutPayment API call.

Listing 7-6. *Gateway Response to* GetExpressCheckoutDetails

```
RESULT=0&RESPMSG=Approved&AVSADDR=Y&TOKEN=EC-17C73463PL785494P&
PAYERID=FHY4JXY7CV9PG&EMAIL=buyer@apress.com&PAYERSTATUS=verified&FIRSTNAME=John&
LASTNAME=Doe&BUSINESS=Customer Business Name&SHIPTOSTREET=5262 Green Street #8&
SHIPTOCITY=San Jose&SHIPTOSTATE=CA&SHIPTOZIP=95131&SHIPTOCOUNTRY=US
```

DoExpressCheckoutPayment (ACTION=D)

After you display the details in Listing 7-6 to the buyer and the buyer confirms them, it is time to make the final API call, DoExpressCheckoutPayment. This actually causes the funds to transfer into the merchant account, assuming you are doing a sale transaction and not an authorization.

Listing 7-7 is an example PARMLIST for a DoExpressCheckoutPayment request.

Listing 7-7. *Example* PARMLIST *for a* DoExpressCheckoutPayment *Request*

```
TRXTYPE=S&VENDOR=vendor&USER=user&PWD=pwd&TENDER=P&PARTNER=partner&COMMENT1=&
ACTION=D&TOKEN=EC-17C73463PL785494P &PAYERID=FHY4JXY7CV9PG&AMT=35.00
```

The result from the request in Listing 7-7 will detail the results of the transaction. An example response is shown in Listing 7-8.

Listing 7-8. *Gateway Response to* DoExpressCheckoutPayment

```
RESULT=0&PNREF=EFHP0CDBF5C7&RESPMSG=Approved&AVSADDR=Y&TOKEN=EC-17C73463PL785494P&
PAYERID=FHY4JXY7CV9PG&PPREF=2P599077L3553652G&PAYMENTTYPE=instant
```

One important thing to note in the response is there are two identifiers for the transaction. PNREF is the usual Payflow transaction ID that will appear in your PayPal Manager account. However, there is also a PPREF variable, which is used for tracking on the PayPal side. If you store the results of your transactions in your own database, it may be useful to store this value for future use.

XMLPay

In addition to the name/value pair method of submitting requests described in the previous sections, Payflow Pro offers another method of submitting requests: XMLPay. XMLPay operates in a request/response format, similar to the name/value pair interface, but as the name suggests, the protocol in which requests and responses are communicated is XML documents. With XMLPay, you submit requests in well-formed XML, and you receive well-formed XML as a response.

With XMLPay, you can submit the same types of transaction requests that you can with the Payflow Pro name/value pair interface, namely

- Sale transactions

- Authorization transactions

- Capture transactions

- Void transactions

- Recurring billing transactions

- Status inquiries

Forming an XMLPay Request

To submit a request using XMLPay, you create your XML document with all of the required elements for the type of transaction you are requesting. You then submit it exactly as you would submit a transaction with the name/value pair method. You use the same SDK and same methods, except the PARMLIST variable contains the XML document with the request parameters.

The example shown in Listing 7-9 is a credit card sale transaction request. Notice how all of the payment details are contained within this one XMLPayRequest element. There are additional optional elements that can also be contained in a sale request, such as the billing name and address, but they are not required and are omitted here for the sake of simplicity.

Listing 7-9. *Example of an XMLPay Sale Transaction Request*

```
<?xml version="1.0" encoding="UTF-8"?>
<XMLPayRequest Timeout="30" version = "2.0" xmlns="http://www.paypal.com/XMLPay">
  <RequestData>
    <Vendor>MyOnlineStore</Vendor>
    <Partner>PayPal</Partner>
    <Transactions>
      <Transaction>
        <Sale>
          <PayData>
            <Invoice>
              <NationalTaxIncl>false</NationalTaxIncl>
              <TotalAmt>99.95</TotalAmt>
            </Invoice>
            <Tender>
              <Card>
                <CardType>VISA</CardType>
                <CardNum>5105105105105100</CardNum>
                <ExpDate>200904</ExpDate>
                <NameOnCard/>
              </Card>
            </Tender>
          </PayData>
        </Sale>
      </Transaction>
    </Transactions>
  </RequestData>
```

```
<RequestAuth>
  <UserPass>
    <User>user</User>
    <Password>password</Password>
  </UserPass>
</RequestAuth>
</XMLPayRequest>
```

XMLPayRequest must always have a child element named RequestData that contains the details of the transaction. RequestData must define the Vendor and Partner for whom the request applies, and also a Transactions element that contains one or more Transaction elements, each of which contain data specific to an individual transaction. You can submit a request with up to 32 Transaction elements per request. You can specify an optional Id attribute in the Transaction element to correspond a particular request transaction with the associated response data. XMLPayRequest must also have a child element named RequestAuth that contains the username and password used to authenticate you to the Payflow service.

Reading an XMLPay Response

The response you receive back from the Payflow server is also in the form of an XML document. You should use whatever XML parsing tool you are comfortable with to read the data. The root element is XMLPayResponse.

Listing 7-10 shows an example response to the request in Listing 7-9. The example shown is for a successful transaction.

Listing 7-10. *Example of a Successful XMLPay Sale Transaction Response*

```
<?xml version="1.0" encoding="UTF-8"?>
<XMLPayResponse>
  <ResponseData>
    <Vendor>MyOnlineStore</Vendor>
    <Partner>PayPal</Partner>
    <TransactionResults>
      <TransactionResult>
        <Result>0</Result>
        <AVSResult>
          <StreetMatch>Service Not Available</StreetMatch>
          <ZipMatch>Service Not Available</ZipMatch>
        </AVSResult>
        <CVResult>Service Not Requested</CVResult>
        <Message>Approved</Message>
        <PNRef>V64A09909896</PNRef>
        <AuthCode>968PNI</AuthCode>
        <HostCode>00</HostCode>
        <OrigResult>0</OrigResult>
      </TransactionResult>
    </TransactionResults>
  </ResponseData>
</XMLPayResponse>
```

Payflow Link

In addition to Payflow Pro, PayPal offers a second gateway solution called Payflow Link. It is much easier to set up, but offers fewer features and a different buyer experience than Payflow Pro. Payflow Link is a hosted service, similar to PayPal Website Payments Standard. This means that buyers leave your website to complete a transaction hosted on PayPal's website. There is no API call involved, and the integration is very simple. You just add a few lines of HTML to your website, and you can start processing payment within a few minutes of setting up your account. If implementing Payflow Pro seems too difficult or expensive, Payflow Link offers similar functionality but gives you less control over the checkout process.

This section discusses the basics of Payflow Link. First, you'll learn how to set up Buy Now buttons on your website that, when clicked, will initiate Payflow Link transactions. And next, you'll see how to receive results of a transaction once it is complete. Payflow Link offers a couple of different methods for accomplishing this, and both are presented. Examples for both requests and responses are provided, and variable reference materials are located in the appendix.

Creating a Buy Now Button with Payflow Link

Payflow Link works in a very similar fashion to Website Payments Standard. All of the code that you write for creating payment buttons is HTML, and the core construct that you create is a form. The form makes an HTTP POST to the PayPal server (namely, `https://payflowlink.verisign.com`), and all of the transaction details are sent in hidden form variables. Payflow Link is designed so that even nonprogrammers can easily create and modify payment buttons.

To show how easy it is to set up a Buy Now button on your website using Payflow Link, look at the code in Listing 7-11. It is a complete code sample for a payment button for a $100 item. Additional, optional variables you can include are discussed later in this section, but this example contains the core required elements.

Listing 7-11. *Example Payflow Link Buy Now Button Code*

```
<form method="POST" action="https://payflowlink.verisign.com">
  <input type="hidden" name="LOGIN" value="My Login"/>
  <input type="hidden" name="PARTNER" value="Partner Name"/>
  <input type="hidden" name="AMOUNT" value="100.00"/>
  <input type="hidden" name="TYPE" value="S"/>
  <input type="submit" value="Buy Now"/>
</form>
```

In Listing 7-11, LOGIN is the name chosen for the Payflow account, and PARTNER is the name provided by the Payflow reseller (this value is PayPal if you sign up on the PayPal website). AMOUNT is the value of the transaction, and TYPE is either S for sale or A for authorization.

If a customer clicks the button generated by the code in Listing 7-11, the customer is taken through a series of pages on the PayPal website where he or she enters credit card details, shipping information, and contact information. If you already know some of this information, you have the option to speed the checkout process along by submitting this data as hidden variables within your form. By doing this, you can prepopulate data fields that the customer would otherwise have to reenter on the PayPal website. Listing 7-12 shows an example form that has some prepopulated customer values appears.

Listing 7-12. *Payflow Link Buy Now Button with Prepopulated Fields*

```
<form method="POST" action="https://payflowlink.verisign.com">
  <input type="hidden" name="LOGIN" value="My Login"/>
  <input type="hidden" name="PARTNER" value="Partner Name"/>
  <input type="hidden" name="AMOUNT" value="100.00"/>
  <input type="hidden" name="TYPE" value="S"/>
  <input type="hidden" name="DESCRIPTION" value="Item description"/>
  <input type="hidden" name="NAME" value="John Smith"/>
  <input type="hidden" name="ADDRESS" value="123 Main St"/>
  <input type="hidden" name="CITY" value="Austin"/>
  <input type="hidden" name="STATE" value="TX"/>
  <input type="hidden" name="ZIP" value="78704"/>
  <input type="hidden" name="COUNTRY" value="US"/>
  <input type="hidden" name="PHONE" value="5127510107"/>
  <input type="hidden" name="FAX" value="5128314545"/>
  <input type="hidden" name="METHOD" value="S"/>
  <input type="submit" value="Buy Now"/>
</form>
```

You would obviously have to build this type of button on the fly, meaning as the page that hosted it was being constructed, but if you know some or all of the data that your customer would otherwise have to enter during the PayPal-hosted checkout process, you can provide an improved customer experience by having these values prepopulated. For a complete list of the variables that you can submit in a Payflow Link button, see the appendix.

Receiving a Transaction Response from Payflow Link

Since you send customers away from your website in order to complete a transaction, Payflow Link offers two similar yet slightly different methods to programmatically receive transaction data after a successful transaction. These methods are referred to as Post and Silent Post. Post is similar to PayPal's Payment Data Transfer (PDT) feature, and Silent Post is similar to PayPal's Instant Payment Notification (IPN) feature. Both PDT and IPN are covered in Chapter 5.

With both Post and Silent Post, Payflow returns transaction data to you in an HTTP POST to a URL that you specify via PayPal Manager. This post contains transaction results in a series of name/value pairs. You can create a script to parse these posts to integrate with your database or order-fulfillment process. A sample script is shown shortly, in Listing 7-14. An example of the information posted back to your URL by Payflow is shown in Listing 7-13.

Listing 7-13. *Sample Contents of a Post or Silent Post*

```
RESULT=0&AUTHCODE=010101&RESPMSG=Approved&AVSDATA=YNY&PNREF=V63F28770576&HOSTCODE=&
INVOICE=3452345&AMOUNT=117.03&TAX=&METHOD=CC&TYPE=S&
DESCRIPTION=1+felt+hat%2C+Model+FC&CUSTID=NT1000&NAME=Nancy+Thompson&
ADDRESS=1428+Elm+Street&CITY=Springwood&STATE=CA&ZIP=66666&COUNTRY=USA&
PHONE=121-325-4253&FAX=&EMAIL=nthompson@buyalot.com&USER1=User1+value&USER2=&USER3=&
USER4=&USER5=&USER6=&USER7=&USER8=&USER9=&USER10=&NAMETOSHIP=Nancy+Thompson&
ADDRESSTOSHIP=1428+Elm+Street&CITYTOSHIP=Springwood&STATETOSHIP=&
ZIPTOSHIP=66666&COUNTRYCODE=USA&PHONETOSHIP=121-325-4253&FAXTOSHIP=&EMAILTOSHIP=&
CSCMATCH=Y
```

Using the Post Feature

If you use the Post feature, the data is posted to your server after the customer clicks the Continue button on the payment confirmation page. The problem here is that if the customer just closes his or her browser or does not click the Continue button, then you will not receive the notification. So obviously, this is not a failsafe method for tracking your transactions. Use PayPal Manager for this instead. However, if the user does click the Continue button, he or she will be able to see detailed results of the completed transaction on your website after being returned there by Payflow.

Using the Silent Post Feature

If you use the Silent Post feature, PayPal will send the post immediately upon a successful transaction at the same time the receipt page is displayed to the customer. This is slightly more reliable than the Post method, since it does not rely on the customer clicking a button to send the post. The URL where the post is sent is specified in PayPal Manager.

If you want to make sure that you only process transactions that result in a Silent Post being successfully received and processed by your website, you can enable a feature called Force Silent Post Confirmation. If you enable Force Silent Post Confirmation for your Payflow Link account, you must return a 200 OK response to the Silent Post notifications after you receive them. Most standard web servers will handle the 200 OK response for you. If 200 OK is not returned for a given notification, the transaction that caused the notification to be sent will be voided, and the customer will see an error message. Regardless of whether or not you use this feature, it is always a good idea to reference your PayPal Manager account to validate the amount for all your transactions before you fulfill your orders.

Listing 7-14 shows a basic script that displays the values included in the Post or Silent Post.

Listing 7-14. *Sample Post Script*

```php
<?php

    if (!empty($_POST)) {

        extract($_POST);
    }

// specify the name for the output file
    $filename = "trxlog.txt";

// open the file for output
    $fp = fopen($filename,"a");

    if ($_POST) {

        fputs($fp,"Post received.\n");

        foreach ($_POST as $key => $value) {

            fputs($fp,"$key: $value\n");
        }
        fputs($fp, "--------------------\n\n");
    }

    if (empty($_POST)) {

        fputs($fp,"No post received!");
    }

    fclose ($fp);
?>
```

Testing Payflow Link Transactions

To test your Payflow Link implementation with transactions that will not result in any real money changing hands, you configure the Transaction Process Mode to TEST within PayPal Manager. You can locate the page with this setting by clicking the Configuration page in the Service Settings ➤ Payflow Link area inside PayPal Manager. On the Forms Configuration section, under Shipping Information, change Transaction Process Mode from Live to Test. Then click the Save Changes button and all transactions passed through Payflow Link will be treated as test transactions.

Managing a Payflow Link Account

You use PayPal Manager (described in the next section) to manage your transactions, account settings, and reports associated with your Payflow Link account. Inside Manager, you can further customize your Payflow Link service and access extensive documentation on Payflow Link and associated gateway services that you can use in tandem with it.

PayPal Manager

PayPal Manager is the website you use to manage your Payflow Pro or Payflow Link account. It can be accessed at `https://manager.paypal.com`. Inside PayPal Manager you can do a number of things related to your account, including the following:

- Switch your account from test mode to live mode

- View reports on account activity

- Search transaction history

- Access the Payflow Virtual Terminal

- Download Payflow Pro SDKs

- Manage your merchant profile

- Manage your fraud filter settings

- Perform manual captures and settlements

Logging in to PayPal Manager

The PayPal Manager login screen is shown in Figure 7-2. The login credentials are separate from any credentials you use to log in to your `www.paypal.com` account. You will receive your login credentials after you sign up for the Payflow service on the PayPal website.

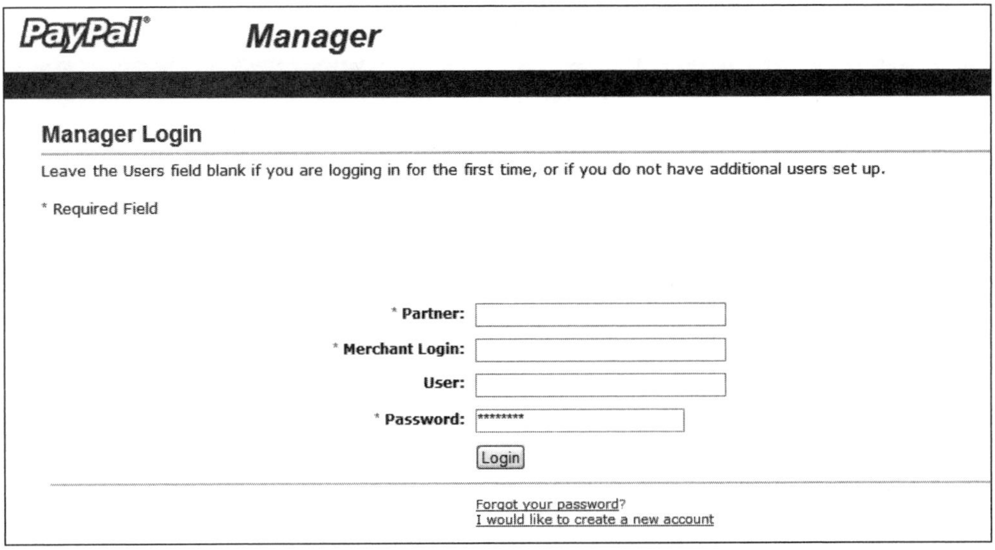

PayPal®   ***Manager***

Manager Login

Leave the Users field blank if you are logging in for the first time, or if you do not have additional users set up.

* Required Field

* **Partner:** [   ]

* **Merchant Login:** [   ]

User: [   ]

* **Password:** [********]

[Login]

Forgot your password?
I would like to create a new account

Figure 7-2. *PayPal Manager login screen*

Activating a Payflow Account

Once you have your website working in test mode and have submitted your billing information for the Payflow service, you can activate your Payflow account to be able to start accepting live transactions. If you try to submit live credit card transactions before activating your account, you will receive an error. You can view whether your account status is TEST or ACTIVE on the Account Overview page that appears when you log in to PayPal Manager (see Figure 7-3). The account status information is in the right column.

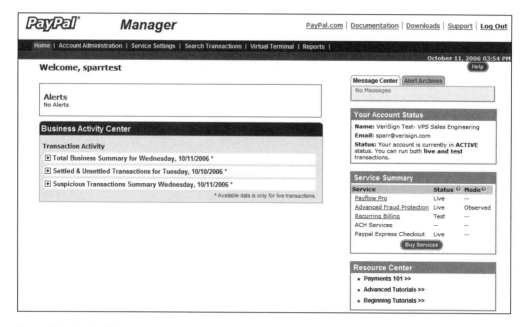

Figure 7-3. *PayPal Manager account overview page*

Generating Reports

Merchants can choose from a set of preset transaction reports or create custom, ad hoc queries against the transaction database. Results are delivered as HTML tables or as tab-delimited ASCII files suitable for import into merchant accounting and reconciliation systems. For more on the reporting features of PayPal Manager, see Chapter 8.

Using the Virtual Terminal

PayPal Manager contains a Virtual Terminal feature that can process manually entered transactions. This is particularly useful for phone, fax, mail, or in-person orders. While the functionality is similar to the PayPal Virtual Terminal feature that is discussed in Chapter 1, this is a different set of web forms. The Payflow Virtual Terminal can be used to submit requests for authorizations, captures, credits, or voids.

Virtual Terminal offers the ability to submit multiple transactions at once. This may help speed things up in some circumstances. For example, you may enter a number of authorization transactions throughout the day, and then capture all of the transactions at once using the Multiple Transactions area of Virtual Terminal. You choose whether you want to use Virtual Terminal to submit single transactions or multiple transactions on the primary Virtual Terminal page, shown in Figure 7-4.

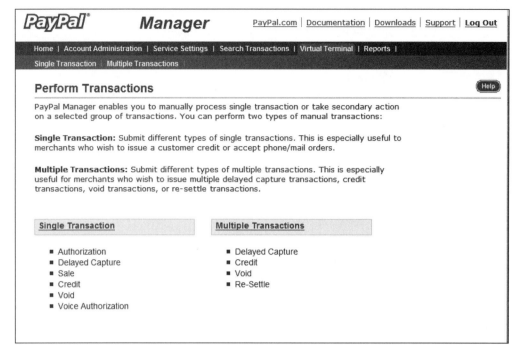

Figure 7-4. *Payflow Virtual Terminal*

The Payflow Virtual Terminal for a single transaction allows you to enter a credit card number and the type of transaction you are performing on the first screen, as shown in Figure 7-5.

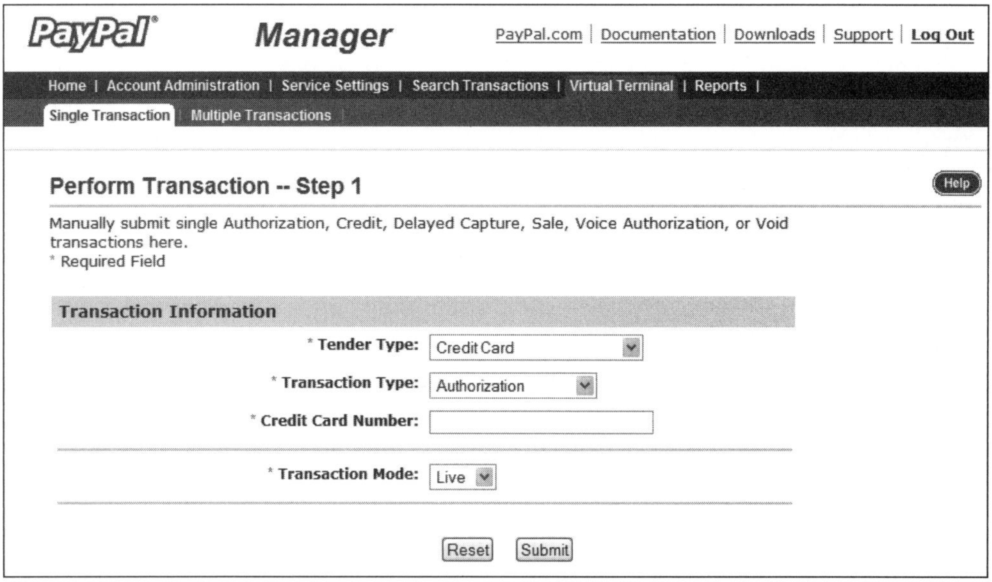

Figure 7-5. *Virtual Terminal single transaction*

On the next screen (see Figure 7-6), you enter additional details relevant to the transaction, such as the billing address and credit card expiration date.

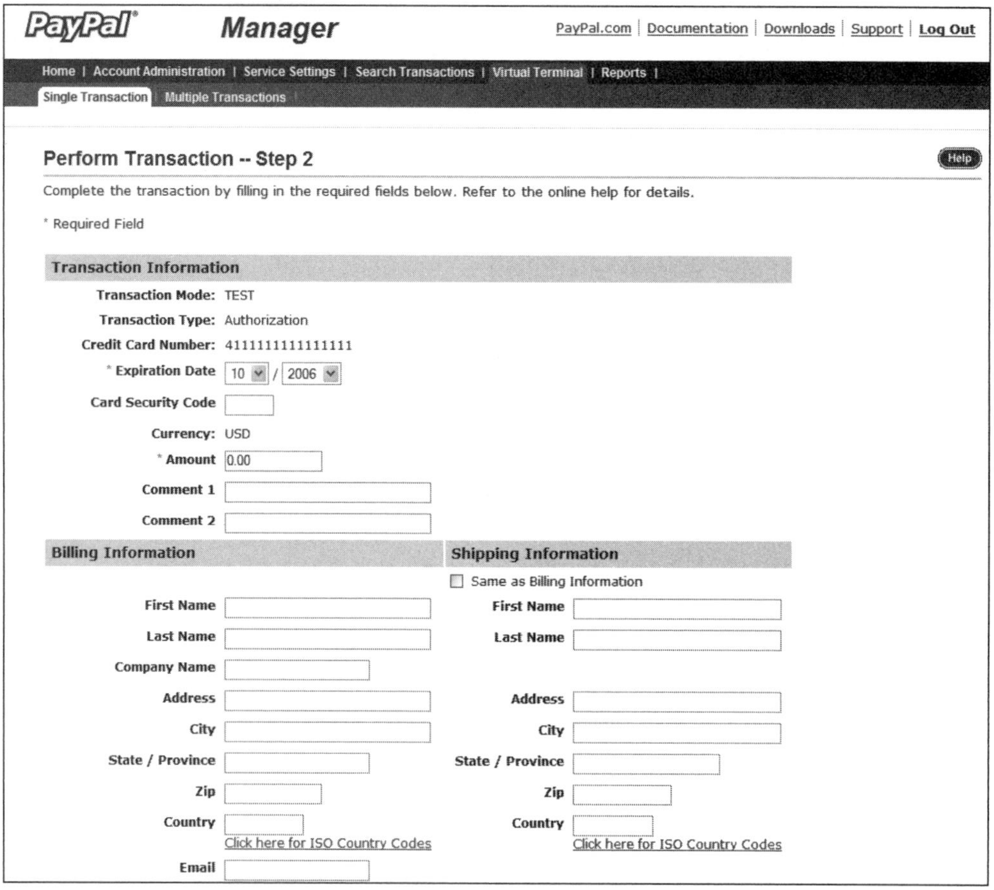

Figure 7-6. *Virtual Terminal single transaction details page*

Submitting the details on this page will process the credit card for the amount entered. You will be shown a results page with the outcome of the transaction.

Managing a Merchant Profile

You can manage many account configuration options inside of PayPal Manager. This includes your basic company contact information, processor details, and security settings. Services such as fraud screening and recurring billing can be enabled and configured. To access the administration screen shown in Figure 7-7, click the Account Administration tab in the PayPal Manager navigation bar.

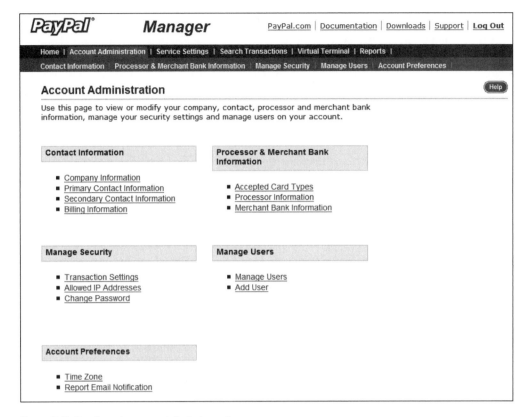

Figure 7-7. *Payflow Account Administration menu*

Performing Manual Captures and Settlements

Merchants not using automated capture can use PayPal Manager to identify and select the order transactions that should be captured for settlement each night. This allows you to do a manual review of your transactions before actually capturing the funds. For smaller businesses that do not have a need for full order management automation, this feature can be very useful.

Payflow Fraud Protection Services

The standard Payflow Pro and Payflow Link services include some basic controls that will help you reduce your exposure to fraudulent transactions. These include the AVS and CVV checks described earlier in the chapter. For an additional charge, however, you can register for Fraud Protection Services (FPS) and activate additional fraud controls that allow you more fine-grained control and greater protection against fraudulent transactions. All FPS settings are configured through PayPal Manager. FPS also allows you to integrate with advanced Buyer Authentication Services, such as Verified by Visa.

■**Note** Fraud Protection Services do not screen recurring transactions.

Available Fraud Filters

The number of fraud filters available to you through Payflow FPS depends on whether you sign up for the Basic or Advanced package. The Advanced package, as you would guess, offers more filters. It is also more expensive. For the latest fee structure, check the PayPal website.

Once you are logged in to PayPal Manager, click Service Settings ➤ Fraud Protection to access the fraud filter settings for your account. For each filter, you can specify whether you want Payflow to flat-out reject transactions that trigger it or flag them for later review.

There are two main types of filters:

- *Preprocessing filters*: These filters are run before the transaction is sent to the processor for authorization.

- *Postprocessing filters*: These filters are run after the transaction has been authorized by the processor and are based on the results from the processor.

Table 7-13 lists the filters available through FPS, whether each filter is a preprocessing or postprocessing filter, whether it is included with the Basic package or the Advanced package, and the corresponding Payflow variables that contain the transaction data that the filter analyzes.

Table 7-13. *Fraud Protection Services Filters*

Filter Name	Pre/Post	Basic/Advanced	Payflow Variables	Description
Account Number Velocity	Pre	Advanced	ACCT	Credit card number
AVS Failure	Post	Basic	STREET, ZIP	Billing address
Bad Lists	Pre	Advanced	ACCT, EMAIL	Credit card number and customer email
BIN Risk List Match	Pre	Advanced	ACCT	Credit card number
Country Risk List Match	Pre	Advanced	COUNTRY	Billing country
			COUNTRYCODE	Shipping country
Card Security Code Failure	Post	Basic	CSC	Card security code (CVV)
Email Service Provider Risk List	Pre	Advanced	EMAIL	Customer email
Freight Forwarder Match	Pre	Basic	SHIPTOSTREET	Shipping address
			SHIPTOZIP	Shipping ZIP code
			SHIPTOCITY	Shipping city
			SHIPTOSTATE	Shipping state
			COUNTRYCODE	Shipping country
Geolocation Failure	Pre	Advanced	CUSTIP	Customer IP address
			STREET	Billing address
			ZIP	Billing ZIP code
			STATE	Billing state

Filter Name	Pre/Post	Basic/Advanced	Payflow Variables	Description
			SHIPTOSTREET	Shipping address
			SHIPTOZIP	Shipping ZIP code
			SHIPTOCITY	Shipping city
			SHIPTOSTATE	Shipping state
Good Lists	Pre	Advanced	ACCT, EMAIL	Credit card number & customer email
International AVS	Post	Advanced	SHIPTOSTREET, SHIPTOZIP	Shipping address
International Shipping/Billing	Pre	Advanced	COUNTRY	Billing country
			COUNTRYCODE	Shipping country
International IP Address	Pre	Advanced	CUSTIP	Customer IP address
IP Address Risk List Match	Pre	Advanced	CUSTIP	Customer IP address
IP Address Velocity	Pre	Basic	CUSTIP	Customer IP address
Product Watch List	Pre	Advanced	L_SKUn	Product SKU
Shipping/Billing Mismatch	Pre	Basic	STREET	Billing street
			ZIP	Billing ZIP code
			STATE	Billing state
			SHIPTOSTREET	Shipping address
			SHIPTOZIP	Shipping ZIP code
			SHIPTOCITY	Shipping city
			SHIPTOSTATE	Shipping state
Total Item Ceiling	Pre	Basic	QTY	Total quantity ordered
Total Purchase Price Ceiling	Pre	Basic	AMT	Total amount ordered
Total Purchase Price Floor	Pre	Advanced	AMT	Total amount ordered
USPS Address Validation Failure	Pre	Advanced	STREET	Billing address
			SHIPTOSTREET	Shipping address
ZIP Risk List Match	Pre	Basic	ZIP	Billing ZIP code
			SHIPTOZIP	Shipping ZIP code

Many of the filter names are descriptive enough to be indicative of the type of activity they filter against. Any filter with the words "Risk List" in the name makes use of lists that the PayPal fraud team manages. These lists are based on extensive analysis of e-commerce transactions that are meant to determine transaction characteristics that are statistically more likely to be associated with fraud. The "Velocity" filters monitor for a sudden surge in activity from a certain credit card or IP address, either of which can be an indicator of a fraudster attacking a system by repeatedly attempting transactions with slightly modified parameters.

Not all filters are supported by all processors. For details on individual filters, matrices detailing which filters are supported by which processors, and techniques for testing individual filter responses, consult the latest FPS documentation. Like all Payflow documentation, the FPS documents can be accessed from within PayPal Manager.

Reviewing Suspicious Transactions

You can view a list of the transactions that are flagged by your fraud filters in order to analyze them and choose whether or not you wish to process them or deny them. If you deny them, you must separately issue a void for the authorization. If you accept them, the funds are automatically captured and no further action on your behalf is required.

To review the transactions that have been flagged for review, log in to PayPal Manager and browse to Reports ➤ Fraud Protection ➤ Fraud Transactions. You will be taken to a page where you can set a number of parameters, such as date range, that will return a list of transactions flagged for your review. For each transaction, you can then choose to accept, reject, or review the transaction. Choosing to review the transaction will just leave it in the same state, so that you can return at a later time to reject or accept it.

Testing Filters in Observe Mode

When you configure your fraud filters, it makes sense to test them out before activating them. This way, you can see how many and what type of transactions your new filter settings will cause to be flagged. The last thing you want is to start denying too many valid transactions because you have set your fraud filters to a too-strict level. Fortunately, PayPal offers a way for you to run your filters in a test mode before activating them.

When you make changes to your fraud filters, you can deploy them in Observe mode. In Observe mode, the new filters examine each live transaction and mark the transaction with each triggered filter's action. You can then view the actions that would have been taken on the live transactions, if the filters had been active. However, the actions are not actually taken. The transactions are submitted for processing in the normal fashion.

Once you are satisfied with the new fraud control settings that you have configured, you can turn them on so they will start taking effect on your live transactions. You do this by deploying the filters to Active mode. In the Payflow system, filter settings are updated approximately once per hour. That means that you may have to wait up to one hour after you deploy to Active mode before the new fraud settings will take effect. After you have moved to Active mode, though, additional changes will take effect as soon as you deploy them. The one-hour delay only applies when you move to a new mode.

■**Note** You are charged the per-transaction fee to use the live servers, regardless of whether the filters are deployed in Observe or Active mode.

Summary

Processing credit cards is simple with the Payflow Gateway, and there are many additional features you can add to give you more control over the amount of risk you are willing to take as a merchant and the types of transactions you will accept or deny. The core Payflow Pro and Payflow Link products give you two similar solutions that can be easily integrated into a website to handle basic credit card processing. Additionally, Payflow Pro offers an alternate way to integrate with PayPal's Express Checkout for businesses that either already have a working Payflow Pro website or want to offer the PayPal payment option to their customers via an integration method they are already comfortable and experienced with. Businesses in the UK who want to use PayPal's Website Payments Pro option will use the integration methods described in this chapter.

This chapter did not get heavily into the recurring billing add-on service that you can use with the Payflow Gateway; however, we did cover the basics of Fraud Protection Services (FPS). We also did not discuss detailed information about the reporting capabilities included with Payflow. This leads us into the next chapter, which is all about reporting.

Chapter 8 covers not only the reporting features offered through the Payflow Gateway, but also the suite of reporting capabilities included on the main PayPal platform. You will see that there are many customizations that you can make to the basic reporting features that will enable you to generate meaningful data, which can give you insights about how to improve your e-commerce business.

Reporting

The ability to generate accurate, detailed reports is an essential component of managing an online business, and as more and more companies turn to PayPal as a sole solution for their payment needs, the demand for comprehensive reporting capabilities on the PayPal platform has risen tremendously. In the early days, PayPal's reporting was limited and difficult to use effectively. Fortunately, PayPal has since made big improvements and now offers a suite of reports that you can run to view the status of your PayPal account activity. Additionally, the Payflow Gateway service offers a number of reports that can be accessed via PayPal Manager.

This chapter covers reports that you can generate through the PayPal website. These reports can be accessed from two main locations:

- The PayPal reporting portal at `https://business.paypal.com`

- The PayPal Manager built-in reports for Payflow Gateway customers

After reading this chapter, you will have a good sense of the information available to you via PayPal's standard reporting capabilities. And since all reports offer the ability to download a data file as well as view the reports in a web browser, you can integrate these reports into your custom back-office operations however you like.

PayPal Reporting Portal

PayPal Business and Premier account holders have access to a number of reports via the reporting portal at `https://business.paypal.com`. Personal account holders do not have access to these reports. Figure 8-1 shows the homepage of the reporting portal.

The portal homepage shows recent account overview information, including sales totals for the past three weeks and a monthly summary of the most recently completed month. Clicking a weekly total will take you to the daily sales report for that week, where you can view activity for the week in more granular detail. Clicking the ending balance for the monthly total will take you to a financial statement for that month, while clicking the total next to Payments Received will take you to a daily sales report for the month. In general, the entire reporting portal is structured so that you can click to drill down on any piece of summary data and generate a subsequent report that contains more detailed information.

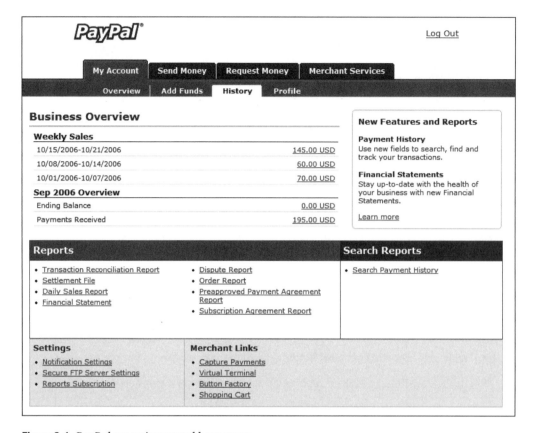

Figure 8-1. *PayPal reporting portal homepage*

In addition to the overview data, the homepage contains links to various reports that we'll examine in more detail throughout this chapter. All reports may not appear for your account. For instance, if you do not have any active subscription agreements, the Subscription Agreement Report will not appear as an option. Only reports that can provide you with useful data will appear. Table 8-1 lists the available reports.

Table 8-1. *Reports Available via the Reporting Portal*

Report Name	Description
Transaction Reconciliation Report	Get detailed field information for each transaction on a specified day.
Settlement File	Download a file for a 24-hour period of account credits and debits.
Daily Sales Report	View all payments received and refunded for a range of days.
Financial Statement	View a categorized breakdown of balance-impacting activity.
Dispute Report	View the status of disputes filed against your business.
Order Report	View the status of outstanding orders and authorizations.
Preapproved Payment Agreement Report	View the status of preapproved payment agreements.
Subscription Agreement Report	View the status of subscription agreements.

In addition to viewing the reports in your web browser, you can download reports to a file to integrate into your external business-management applications. You can download reports in two ways: in tab-delimited and comma-separated values (CVS) formats. In a tab-delimited file, each of the data elements is separated by a tab character. In a CSV file, each of the data elements is separated by a comma. You can open these files in an application such as Excel for easier viewing and manipulation. You'll need to take some specific steps if you want to open the files in Excel, and these steps are covered later in the chapter.

Each report can be modified to run for a specified time period and currency. These options appear at the top of each specific report page, as you will see in the screenshots of the reports provided in this chapter. If you hold a balance in multiple currencies, you can view a report for only a single currency at a time.

The next several sections cover a number of individual reports in more detail.

Transaction Reconciliation Report

The Transaction Reconciliation Report allows you to view detailed information about all transactions that occurred on a specific date. Figure 8-2 shows the Transaction Reconciliation Report screen, where you specify the date of the report and whether you would like to view the results in your browser or download a file to your computer.

▓**Note** The Transaction Reconciliation Report is available only to large merchants with a sustained history of high transaction activity and volume.

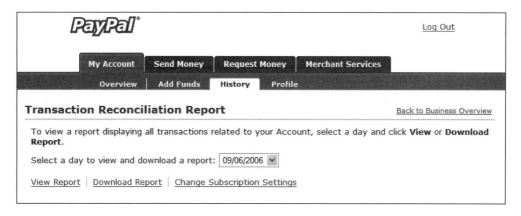

Figure 8-2. *Transaction Reconciliation Report setup*

When you view a Transaction Reconciliation Report, the data is displayed in a screen with a lengthy horizontal scrollbar. It's impractical to attempt to display an entire row of data in this book, but the fields displayed in the report are as follows:

- Transaction ID
- Invoice ID
- Reference Transaction ID
- Reference Transaction ID Type
- Transaction Event Code
- Transaction Initiation Date
- Transaction Completion Date
- Whether the transaction was a Debit or Credit
- Gross Transaction Amount
- Gross Amount Currency
- Whether the fee was a Debit or Credit
- Fee Amount
- Fee Currency
- Order ID
- Transaction Status
- Insurance Amount

- Sales Tax Amount
- Shipping Amount
- Transaction Subject
- Transaction Note
- Email Address
- Payer Address Status
- Item Name
- Item ID
- Option 1 Name
- Option 1 Value
- Option 2 Name
- Option 2 Value
- Auction Site
- Auction Buyer ID
- Auction Closing Date
- Shipping Address Fields
- Custom Field

The Transaction Reconciliation Report is useful if you want detailed information about a single day's worth of activity.

Settlement File

A Settlement File contains all completed credits and debits to your account within a 24-hour period. This type of report is most useful when downloaded as a file, and less useful when viewed on the screen. When you choose to run a settlement report, you first choose the date for which you want to download the data. You can choose any day from within the past 60 days. The file you download is a CSV file that contains all balance-impacting transactions as well as some metadata about the report itself. The report also summarizes the total debits and credits for the day, as well as the beginning and ending balance.

Each line of data in the Settlement File begins with a two-letter code. The code is then followed by data appropriate to that row. The two-letter code indicates the type of data that follows. The possible types of row data that can be included in the report and the corresponding two-letter codes are listed in Table 8-2.

Table 8-2. *Types of Row Data Included in Settlement Reports*

Two-Letter Code	Row Type	Description
RH	Report Header	First row of data; contains the report date, report period, account number, and report version
SH	Section Header	Report period and account number for each subaccount
CH	Column Header	Field names for the SB data that follows
SB	Section Body	One line per transaction; contains data corresponding to CH headers
SF	Section Footer	Summary of debits, credits, and balances for the section
RF	Report Footer	Summary of debits, credits, and balances for the entire report; one line per currency

Each settlement report has a single RH row and a single RF row that contains summary information for the entire report. The report will then have a SH and SF row for each sub-account on the PayPal account. Most PayPal accounts will not have any subaccounts, so there will normally be just one SH row and one SF row.

The actual meat of the report—the data for the balance-impacting transactions—appears in the SB rows. There is one row per transaction, so it's possible there could be a large number of SB rows. Every row represents some activity that has either added to or subtracted from your PayPal account balance. The fields included for each transaction are as follows:

- Transaction ID

- Invoice ID

- PayPal Reference ID

- PayPal Reference ID Type (not currently populated)

- Transaction Event Code

- Transaction Initiation Date

- Transaction Completion Date

- Transaction Debit (DR) or Credit (CR)

- Gross Transaction Amount

- Gross Transaction Currency

- Fee Debit (DR) or Credit (CR)

- Fee Amount

- Fee Currency

- Custom Field (set by the merchant during the transaction)

While most of these fields should be fairly self-descriptive, two that may not be obvious are PayPal Reference ID and Transaction Event Code. A PayPal Reference ID is included if the transaction in the SB line of data has an originating, pre-existing transaction from which the present transaction is related to. This can occur in a number of situations. Table 8-3 outlines the transaction types that will have a corresponding value for Reference ID, and what that value represents.

Table 8-3. *Transaction Types and Corresponding Reference Transactions*

Transaction Type	Reference ID
Settlement on Authorization	Original Authorization
Full Refund	Original Settlement
Partial Refund	Original Settlement
Settlement on Reauthorization	Original Authorization
Completed Chargeback	Disputed Sale or Settlement
Completed Buyer Complaint	Disputed Sale or Settlement
Settlement Adjustment	Settlement or Sale Transaction
Reimbursement	Settlement or Sale Transaction
Reversal	Original Settlement

The Transaction Event Code field will be populated for every SB row. It will be a five-character string that begins with the letter "T", followed by four digits. This "T-code" can be used to categorize your transactions on a general or fine-grained level. The first two digits represent an accounting event group that this transaction falls into. This level of granularity is generally sufficient for reconciliation and report parsing. The last two digits are for a specific event type. There are over 60 different values for specific event type, and they are not all listed here. Table 8-4 lists the general accounting groups, however, so you can get a sense of the types of event categories defined by PayPal.

Table 8-4. *Transaction Event Code Categories*

T-Code Group	Description	Examples
T00XX	PayPal Account to PayPal Account Payment	Send Money, Express Checkout, MassPay
T01XX	Non-Payment Related Fees	Website Payments Pro monthly fee, Foreign Bank Withdrawal
T02XX	Currency Conversion	Transfer of funds between currencies
T03XX	Bank Deposit into PayPal account	Transfer of funds from bank account to PayPal balance
T04XX	Bank Withdrawal from PayPal account	Transfer of funds from PayPal balance to bank account
T05XX	Debit Card	Activity with PayPal debit card tied to PayPal account
T06XX	Credit Card Withdrawal	Reversal of purchase with a credit card
T07XX	Credit Card Deposit	Purchase with a credit card

T-Code Group	Description	Examples
T08XX	Bonus	Merchant Referral Bonus, Debit Card cash back
T09XX	Incentive	Gift Certificate, Coupon Redemption, eBay Loyalty Incentive
T10XX	BillPay	None (BillPay is no longer a PayPal-supported service)
T11XX	Reversal	Fee reversal, reversal of temporary hold, temporary hold to cover chargeback
T12XX	Adjustment	Chargeback, Reversal, Reimbursement of chargeback
T13XX	Authorization	Authorization, Reauthorization, Void
T14XX	Dividend	Money Market account dividend
T15XX	Temporary Hold	Hold on PayPal account balance funds
T16XX	Buyer Credit Deposit	Funding of balance from PayPal Buyer Credit account
T17XX	Non-Bank Withdrawal	WorldLink Withdrawal
T18XX	Buyer Credit Withdrawal	Debit of balance with PayPal Buyer Credit account
T19XX	Account Correction	General adjustment without business-related event
T99XX	Uncategorized Event	You should never get this T-code

Daily Sales Report

The Daily Sales Report shows at a glance the daily activity over a range of dates you specify. You can drill down on an individual day's activity for more information on that particular day. For convenience, you can access Daily Sales Reports for the past three weeks of activity at the top of the Business Overview page (the reporting portal homepage). Each of the weekly totals can be clicked for a drill-down view of that week's activities. A sample of a Daily Sales Report is shown in Figure 8-3.

The Daily Sales Report provides the following information about all of the sales and refunds that occurred during that day:

- Number of payments received

- Total amount of payments received

- Total amount of PayPal fees paid

- Number of refunds sent

- Total amount of refunds sent

- Total amount of PayPal fees refunded

- Net sales total for the day

The Daily Sales Report is useful when you want a quick glance at activity over a period of several days, with the ability to drill down for further details on a specific date. It's a very simple, yet very useful view of summarized account activity.

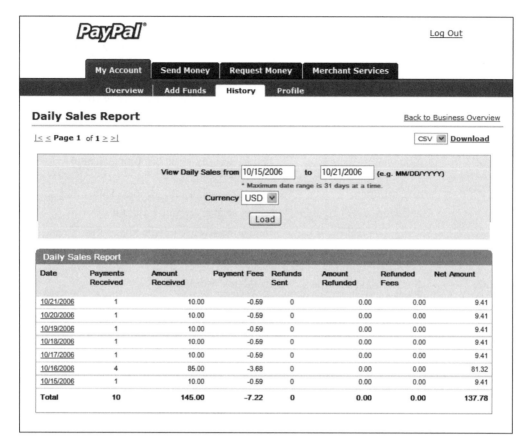

Figure 8-3. *Daily Sales Report*

Financial Statement

The Financial Statement is one of the most useful reports that PayPal offers. It breaks down activity in your account over a specified time period (up to 31 days) into multiple categories, and displays them in a format to help you get an idea of your business's overall performance for the month. With this report, you can view both categorized subtotals and individual transaction details.

Figure 8-4 shows an example Financial Statement.

As you can see from Figure 8-4, this type of report offers a unique view of your account's activity. You do not have to limit the report parameters to a single month; you can specify any time period up to 31 days. The report shows credits in the right column and debits in the left column.

Financial Statement   Back to Business Overview

|< < **Page 1** of 1 > >| CSV ☑ Download

View Financial Statement from 8/01/2006   to   08/30/2006   (e.g. MM/DD/YYYY)
* Maximum date range is 31 days at a time.

Currency USD ☑

Load

	View Details
BEGINNING BALANCE	0.00
ENDING BALANCE	186.94
SALES ACTIVITY	
Payments Received	195.00
Refunds Sent	0.00
Subtotal	195.00
FEES	
Payment Fees	-8.06
Refunded Fees	0.00
Chargeback Fees	0.00
Other Fees	0.00
Subtotal	-8.06
DISPUTE ACTIVITY	
Chargebacks & Disputes	0.00
Dispute Reimbursements	0.00
Subtotal	0.00
TRANSFERS & WITHDRAWALS	
Currency Transfers	0.00
Transfers to PayPal Account	0.00
Transfers From PayPal Account	0.00
Subtotal	0.00
PURCHASE ACTIVITY	
Online Payments Sent	0.00
Refunds Received	0.00
Debit Card Purchases	0.00
Debit Card Returns	0.00
Subtotal	0.00

Figure 8-4. *Financial Statement*

Like other PayPal reports, the Financial Statement offers a way to view more detailed information about the account activity for the specified time range. By clicking the View Details link near the top of the report, you can get a complete transaction list of all transactions that occurred, and you can click an individual entry to see the details for that transaction. Figure 8-5 shows the Financial Statement details page.

Financial Statement   Back to Business Overview

|≤ ≤ **Page 1** of **1** ≥ ≥| CSV ☑ Download

| Transaction Details | | | | | Back to Summary View |
Date	Type	Email	Gross Amount	Fee Amount	Net Amount
10/27/2006	Subscription Payment Processed	buyer@apress.com	10.00	-0.59	9.41
10/26/2006	Subscription Payment Processed	buyer@apress.com	10.00	-0.59	9.41
10/25/2006	Subscription Payment Processed	buyer@apress.com	10.00	-0.59	9.41
10/24/2006	Subscription Payment Processed	buyer@apress.com	10.00	-0.59	9.41
10/23/2006	Subscription Payment Processed	buyer@apress.com	10.00	-0.59	9.41
10/22/2006	Subscription Payment Processed	buyer@apress.com	10.00	-0.59	9.41
10/21/2006	Subscription Payment Processed	buyer@apress.com	10.00	-0.59	9.41
10/20/2006	Subscription Payment Processed	buyer@apress.com	10.00	-0.59	9.41
10/19/2006	Subscription Payment Processed	buyer@apress.com	10.00	-0.59	9.41
10/18/2006	Subscription Payment Processed	buyer@apress.com	10.00	-0.59	9.41
10/17/2006	Subscription Payment Processed	buyer@apress.com	10.00	-0.59	9.41
10/16/2006	Payment Processed	buyer@apress.com	25.00	-1.03	23.97
10/16/2006	Payment Processed	buyer@apress.com	25.00	-1.03	23.97
10/16/2006	Payment Processed	buyer@apress.com	25.00	-1.03	23.97
10/16/2006	Subscription Payment Processed	buyer@apress.com	10.00	-0.59	9.41
10/15/2006	Subscription Payment Processed	buyer@apress.com	10.00	-0.59	9.41
10/14/2006	Subscription Payment Processed	buyer@apress.com	10.00	-0.59	9.41
10/13/2006	Subscription Payment Processed	buyer@apress.com	10.00	-0.59	9.41
10/12/2006	Subscription Payment Processed	buyer@apress.com	10.00	-0.59	9.41
10/11/2006	Subscription Payment Processed	buyer@apress.com	10.00	-0.59	9.41
10/10/2006	Subscription Payment Processed	buyer@apress.com	10.00	-0.59	9.41
10/09/2006	Subscription Payment Processed	buyer@apress.com	10.00	-0.59	9.41
10/08/2006	Subscription Payment Processed	buyer@apress.com	10.00	-0.59	9.41
10/07/2006	Subscription Payment Processed	buyer@apress.com	10.00	-0.59	9.41
10/06/2006	Subscription Payment Processed	buyer@apress.com	10.00	-0.59	9.41
10/05/2006	Subscription Payment Processed	buyer@apress.com	10.00	-0.59	9.41
10/04/2006	Subscription Payment Processed	buyer@apress.com	10.00	-0.59	9.41
10/03/2006	Subscription Payment Processed	buyer@apress.com	10.00	-0.59	9.41
10/02/2006	Subscription Payment Processed	buyer@apress.com	10.00	-0.59	9.41
10/01/2006	Subscription Payment Processed	buyer@apress.com	10.00	-0.59	9.41

Figure 8-5. *Financial Statement details*

Besides offering a quick glance at your sales and refunds for the month, the Financial Statement categorizes and provides details of a number of common account activities, for example:

- *Dispute Activity:* Totals for chargebacks, disputes, and reimbursements

- *Transfers & Withdrawals:* Currency transfers, transfers to/from PayPal account

- *Purchase Activity:* Online payments sent, refunds received, PayPal debit card activity

- *Other Activity:* Money market dividends, debit card cash back

Dispute Activity

The Dispute Activity area of the Financial Statement report shows the total amount of funds that are at risk due to a buyer complaint. Additionally, you can view the amount of funds that have been credited back to your account due to a dispute reimbursement for a dispute that has gone in your favor. For more information on dispute management, see Chapter 9.

Transfers & Withdrawals

Money moving in and out of your PayPal account is reflected on the Financial Statement. For instance, funds transferred to a bank account will appear as a value in the left column of the statement, meaning that your overall account balance is reduced. Transferring money into your PayPal account increases your account balance, which is reflected in the right column of the report.

If you transfer between currencies, the results of the transfers appear in the Currency Transfers line item on the Financial Statement. Since the Financial Statement displays information for only one currency at a time, the currency you transfer *from* will show a value in the left column, since you have reduced your account balance in that currency. If you view the Financial Statement for the currency that you transferred *to*, you will see a value in the right column, since your account balance in that currency has been increased.

Multicurrency Activity

If you receive payments in a currency other than the primary currency of your PayPal account, the Financial Statement report reflects the payments received in the foreign currency, but the ending balance in the primary currency. This is best illustrated by an example.

Let's say your primary currency is U.S. dollars (USD), but you also operate a version of your website in Canada where you charge in Canadian dollars (CAD). When you receive Canadian currency as payment, PayPal automatically transfers this money to the primary currency (USD) in your PayPal account. If you sell a Canadian item for $10.00 CAD, PayPal adds about $6.00 USD (depending on current fees and transfer rates) to your USD balance. This amount is reflected in your USD Financial Statement. However, sales activity for this transaction (payments received, fees, and net) appears in the CAD version of your Financial Statement.

Because PayPal transfers the proceeds of the sale out of CAD and into USD, the net amount of $6.00 USD (after currency conversion from CAD to USD) is added to your USD Financial Statement balance, and there is an ending balance of $0.00 in your CAD Financial Statement balance.

Table 8-5 summarizes changes to your Financial Statement for this single transaction if prior to this transaction you had a $0.00 CAD balance, a $6.00 USD balance, and $0.00 in payment fees, payments received, and currency transfers.

Table 8-5. *Example of Impact on Financial Statement with Foreign Currency Transaction*

CAD		USD	
Beginning balance	$0.00	Beginning balance	$0.00
Ending balance	$0.00	Ending balance	$6.00
Payments received	$10.00	Payments received	$0.00
Payment fees	$0.55	Payment fees	$0.00
Currency transfers	–$9.45	Currency transfers	$6.00

Dispute Report

The Dispute Report provides a direct view into your open dispute cases. Management and resolution of online disputes are discussed in more detail in Chapter 9. This report allows you to view the different types of disputes you may face:

- Claims

- Chargebacks

- Disputes

- Unauthorized charges

- Temporary holds

- ACH returns

You can also filter this report by the varying types of case status, such as all open cases or all closed cases. There are over a dozen various options for a case status. A sample Dispute Report is shown in Figure 8-6, although the example shown does not have any open disputes.

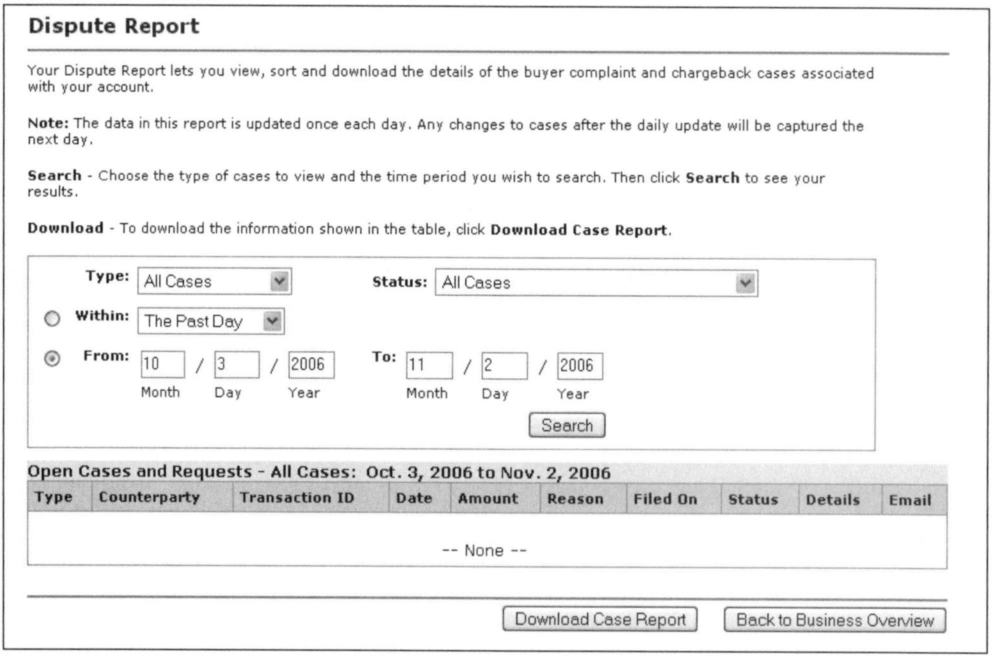

Figure 8-6. *Dispute Report*

Searching Payment History

On the reporting portal homepage is a Search Payment History link. When you click it, a form appears that allows you to specify a number of search parameters to help find transactions you are interested in. The form is shown in Figure 8-7.

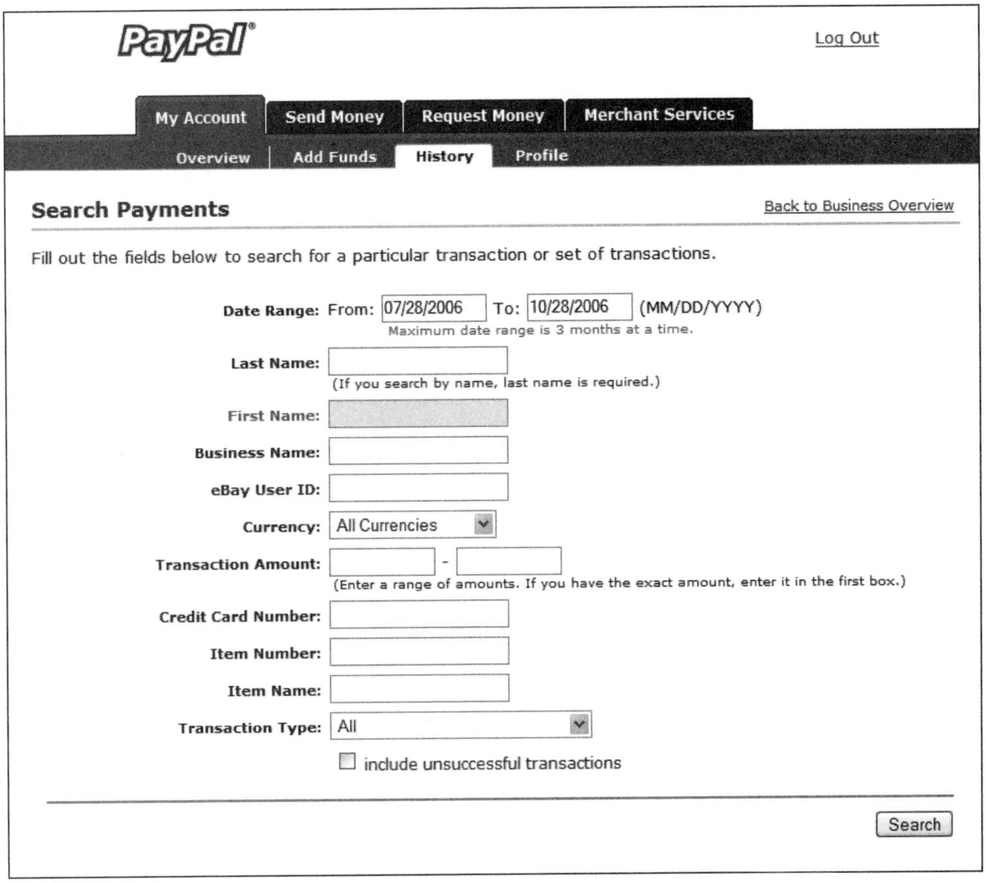

Figure 8-7. *Search payment history form*

If your account is not configured for Website Payments Pro, the Credit Card Number field will not appear as a search option, nor will the check box to include unsuccessful transactions. The search for unsuccessful transactions is useful to help you keep track of how many credit card transactions are failing and the reasons they are failing.

One of the fields on which you can search is Transaction Type. There are many different transaction types in the PayPal system, and this search parameter gives you an additional way to filter out just the specific data you need. The possible types of transaction that you can search on are as follows:

- Sales Activity
  - Payments Received
  - Refunds Sent
- Fees
- Purchases
  - Payments Sent
  - Refunds Received
- Chargebacks & Reversals
  - Reversals
- Debit Card
- Transfers & Withdrawals
  - Currency Conversions
- Open Authorizations
  - Authorizations Sent
  - Authorizations Received
- Open Orders
- Pending Payments
  - Pending Payments Sent
  - Pending Payments Received
- Money Requests
- Preapproved Payments
- Virtual Terminal
- Direct Payments
- Subscriptions
- Mass Payments
- Dividends
- Shipping
- Referrals

The search results will show a list of all transactions that meet the search criteria and give you the option to select an individual transaction for further details on the transaction. You can also sort the search results by buyer name and gross amount, if you are searching for transactions from a particular individual or for a certain amount. The search results screen is shown in Figure 8-8.

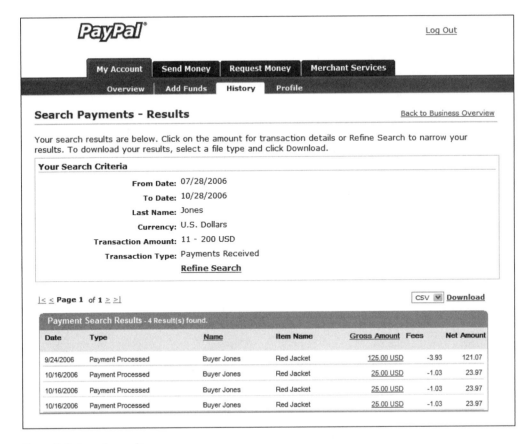

Figure 8-8. *Search results*

Reporting Settings

The Business Overview page has an area in the lower left for setting some reporting preferences. Up to three settings are manageable from this area. First, the Notifications Settings
link takes you to the Notifications page in your account profile, and specifically to an area
where you can specify email addresses for a technical contact, business contact, and infor-
mational contact. You can also specify whether these emails should be sent in text or HTML
format. Since these email addresses will receive messages when important reporting-related
notifications are sent out, it is recommended that you use a distribution list with multiple
recipients for these values. That way, if an individual is on vacation or otherwise unavailable,
an important message will not be missed.

Depending on whether you have the feature enabled for your account, you may see a
Secure FTP Server Settings link. This option is available only for high-volume merchants, and
it allows a business to access a secure FTP server, hosted by PayPal, to download prescheduled
report data via an FTP client.

The Reports Subscription link allows you to subscribe to specific reports. For each report
type that you can access, you can specify how you want to receive the reports and the file type
(CSV or tab-delimited). An example of the Reports Subscription Settings screen is shown in
Figure 8-9.

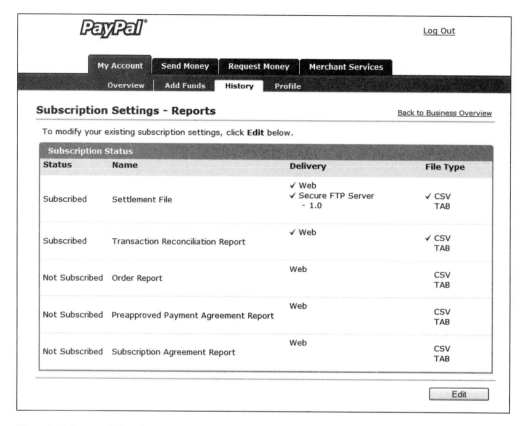

Figure 8-9. *Report Subscription Settings*

The option for Web delivery means that when you access the reporting portal at https://business.paypal.com and select the specific report, there will be a list of pregenerated reports ready for you. There will be one pregenerated report per day, and the last 30 days' worth of reports will be available.

Opening CSV Report Files in Excel

If you choose to download a report in CSV format from the reporting site, there are a few steps you must take to be able to view it in Excel. The file is Unicode-encoded, and you need to let Excel know this when you open the file. This section describes the steps involved in opening PayPal CSV reporting files in Excel.

1. To begin, open Excel and select File ➤ Open. Then select the CSV file that contains the report data you wish to view. You will see the warning message shown in Figure 8-10.

2. Click OK and a Text Import Wizard appears to guide you through the process of providing Excel with the information it needs to open the file. The first screen in the Text Import Wizard is shown in Figure 8-11.

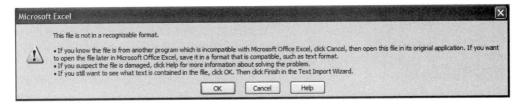

Figure 8-10. *Excel warning when opening a CSV file*

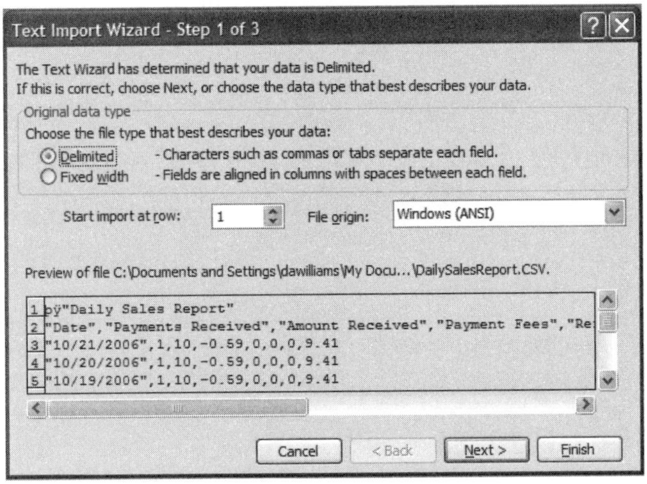

Figure 8-11. *Text Import Wizard, Step 1*

3. From the File origin drop-down, select 65001: Unicode (UTF-8) and click Next. Step 2 of the Text Import Wizard will appear, as shown in Figure 8-12.

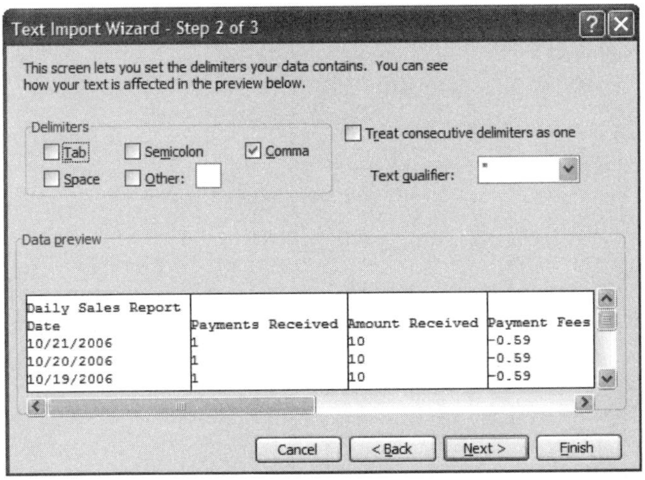

Figure 8-12. *Text Import Wizard, Step 2*

4. In the Delimiters area, check the Comma check box and click Next. Step 3 of the Text Import Wizard will appear as a confirmation screen, and once you click Finish, the file will open in Excel, properly formatted. An example of a Daily Sales Report that has been exported as a CSV file and then correctly imported into Excel is shown in Figure 8-13.

	A	B	C	D	E	F	G	H
1	Daily Sales Report							
2	Date	Payments Received	Amount Received	Payment Fee	Refunds Sent	Amount Refunded	Refunded Fees	Net Amount
3	10/21/2006	1	10	-0.59	0	0	0	9.41
4	10/20/2006	1	10	-0.59	0	0	0	9.41
5	10/19/2006	1	10	-0.59	0	0	0	9.41
6	10/18/2006	1	10	-0.59	0	0	0	9.41
7	10/17/2006	1	10	-0.59	0	0	0	9.41
8	10/16/2006	4	85	-3.68	0	0	0	81.32
9	10/15/2006	1	10	-0.59	0	0	0	9.41
10	Total	10	145	-7.22	0	0	0	137.78
11								

Figure 8-13. *Daily Sales Report viewed in Excel*

PayPal Manager Reports

PayPal Manager (https://manager.paypal.com) contains many reports for customers of the Payflow Gateway service. These reports are similar in nature to the reports presented thus far in the chapter, but they deal with a different set of data: transactions processed through the Payflow Gateway service. Transactions processed through the gateway will appear in the PayPal reports described earlier in the chapter only if PayPal is the processor for the transactions. If you have an Internet Merchant Account through another bank, gateway transactions will not appear in the reports available through the reporting portal at https://business.paypal.com.

To access the PayPal Manager Reports, just click the Reports tab after logging into Manager. The Reports homepage appears in Figure 8-14.

Figure 8-14. *PayPal Manager Reports*

Table 8-6 lists the reports available on this page, along with a brief description of each.

Table 8-6. *Reports Available via PayPal Manager*

Report Name	Description
Daily Activity	View all transactions for a specific date, successful as well as failed
Transaction Summary	View transactions by card type, transaction type, and result code
Settlement	View settled or unsettled Sale, Credit, Delayed Capture, and Voice Authorizations
Shipping & Billing	View transaction status along with shipping and billing details
Batch ID	Search for batch settlement information
PayPal Settlement Summary	View a collection of daily PayPal settlement information
Fraud Transactions	Search transactions that meet specified fraud filter criteria

Continued

Table 8-6. *Continued*

Report Name	Description
Filter Scorecard	Display the number of times each fraud filter was triggered and the percentage of transactions triggered
Recurring Billing Transactions	View recurring billing profiles for which transactions have occurred
Profile Report	View transactions that have occurred for a given recurring billing profile
Failed Transactions	View recurring billing profiles with outstanding failed transactions
ACH Transaction Report	Search all ACH transactions for a single day
ACH Activity Summary	Search all ACH transactions for a given date range
ACH Return Activity	View all ACH returned payments (e.g., NSF or account closed) for a given date range
ACH Detailed Return Activity	View all returned payments by the return date
ACH Notification of Change	View updated bank account information returned by the ACH operator
ACH Settlement	View settled payments for reconciliation purposes

The next sections cover a few of the more commonly used reports in more detail.

Transaction Summary Report

The Transaction Summary Report shows all transactions for your account over a given time period. The results are organized by transaction type, processor, card type, and result code. There is a line item for each combination of these settings that has at least one transaction. There is not a way to drill down into further details on a group of transactions.

A sample Transaction Summary Report is shown in Figure 8-15.

The Transaction Summary Report is a good high-level report to use if you want a broad look at all different transaction types.

Transaction Summary Report

Date		Time Zone	Settlement Status	Transaction Mode
Sat Jul 01, 2006 to Fri Sep 01, 2006		U.S. Pacific	All Transactions	Test

Download: [ASCII Text ▼] [Go]   1-30 of 30 First | Prev | Next | Last

TRANSACTION TYPE	PROCESSOR	TRANSACTION COUNT	RESULT CODE	CARD TYPE	CURRENCY	MINIMUM AMOUNT	MAXIMUM AMOUNT	AVERAGE AMOUNT	TOTAL AMOUNT
Authorization	Vital	5	0	Visa	USD	30.00	30.00	30.00	150.00
Authorization	Vital	2	0	MasterCard	USD	4.00	30.00	17.00	34.00
Authorization	PayPal	2	0	PayPal	USD	19.00	19.00	19.00	38.00
Credit	Vital	1	0	Visa	USD	30.00	30.00	30.00	30.00
Credit	Vital	1	0	MasterCard	USD	4.00	4.00	4.00	4.00
Delayed Capture	Vital	1	0	MasterCard	USD	4.00	4.00	4.00	4.00
Delayed Capture	PayPal	1	0	PayPal	USD	10.00	10.00	10.00	10.00
N	Vital	108	0	N/A	USD	1.00	1.00	1.00	108.00
Sale	FDMS Nashville	1	0	MasterCard	USD	30.00	30.00	30.00	30.00
Sale	Norwest	10	0	Checking	USD	1.23	3,850.00	590.869	5,908.69
Sale	Vital	2	0	Visa	USD	12.34	30.00	21.17	42.34
Sale	Vital	10466	0	MasterCard	USD	1.00	123.00	1.94	20,302.40
Sale	PayPal	1	0	PayPal	ASD	19.98	19.98	19.98	19.98
Sale	PayPal	1	0	PayPal	BRI	19.98	19.98	19.98	19.98
Sale	PayPal	1	0	PayPal	EUR	19.98	19.98	19.98	19.98
Sale	PayPal	1	0	PayPal	GBP	19.98	19.98	19.98	19.98
Sale	PayPal	7	0	PayPal	USD	19.98	1,999.00	350.569	2,453.98
Void	Vital	1	0	Visa	USD	30.00	30.00	30.00	30.00
Authorization	Norwest	1	3	Checking	USD	1.23	1.23	1.23	1.23
Sale	Norwest	3	7	Checking	USD	1.23	285.00	95.82	287.46
Sale	Vital	1	12	MasterCard	USD	1,012.00	1,012.00	1,012.00	1,012.00
Sale	Norwest	3	23	Check	USD	285.00	285.00	285.00	855.00
Authorization	Vital	1	24	MasterCard	USD	30.00	30.00	30.00	30.00
Sale	FDMS Nashville	1	24	MasterCard	USD	30.00	30.00	30.00	30.00
Sale	Vital	1	24	MasterCard	USD	12.00	12.00	12.00	12.00
Sale	0	3	25	Check	USD	285.00	285.00	285.00	855.00
Sale	PayPal	1	103	PayPal	USD	19.98	19.98	19.98	19.98

Figure 8-15. *Transaction Summary Report*

Recurring Billing Transactions Report

The Recurring Billing Transactions Report (see Figure 8-16) is the primary report used if you offer a subscription service or any other situation that requires recurring billing. You can search over a time period you specify, so long as the time period does not exceed three months. The three-month time period is a fairly standard limitation of all PayPal Manager reports. Reports over three months in length could potentially cause too great of a hit on the PayPal reporting servers.

For each transaction, the Recurring Billing Report displays the following information:

- Recurring billing profile name

- Profile ID

- Profile status

- Payment number

- Retry number

- Transaction time

- Retry reason

- Transaction ID

- Result code

- Retry action

Recurring Billing Report Results

Report Type	Date		Time Zone	Transaction Mode
Approvals Only	Sat Jul 01, 2006 to Fri Sep 01, 2006		U.S. Pacific	Test

Download: ASCII Text [Go]   1-50 of 460 First | Prev | Next | Last

PROFILE NAME	PROFILE ID	STATUS	PAYMENT NUMBER	RETRY NUMBER	TRANSACTION TIME	RETRY REASON	TRANSACTION ID	RESULT CODE	RETRY ACTION
Batch Test Profile	RT0000000002	Active	198	0	Jul 12, 2006 2:10:48 PM	N/A	V18E0A18D5D7	0	N/A
Batch Test Profile	RT0000000002	Active	199	0	Jul 12, 2006 4:44:37 PM	N/A	V18E0A1B526A	0	N/A
Batch Test Profile	RT0000000002	Active	200	0	Jul 13, 2006 4:38:10 AM	N/A	V19E0A1C4743	0	N/A
Batch Test Profile	RT0000000002	Active	201	0	Jul 20, 2006 4:32:50 AM	N/A	V78E0A20424E	0	N/A
Batch Test Profile	RT0000000002	Active	202	0	Jul 27, 2006 4:39:00 AM	N/A	V18E0A31EAF6	0	N/A
Batch Test Profile	RT0000000002	Active	203	0	Aug 3, 2006 4:31:15 AM	N/A	V19E0A3BE9E7	0	N/A
Batch Test Profile	RT0000000002	Active	204	0	Aug 10, 2006 4:31:06 AM	N/A	V18E0A481C29	0	N/A
Batch Test Profile	RT0000000002	Active	205	0	Aug 17, 2006 4:31:41 AM	N/A	V19E0A5162F1	0	N/A
Batch Test Profile	RT0000000002	Active	206	0	Aug 24, 2006 4:30:55 AM	N/A	V19E0A5A9875	0	N/A
Batch Test Profile	RT0000000002	Active	207	0	Aug 31, 2006 4:31:03 AM	N/A	V18E0A665934	0	N/A
Batch Test Profile	RT0000000004	Active	47	0	Jul 18, 2006 4:32:37 AM	N/A	V19E0A24DB0D	0	N/A
Batch Test Profile	RT0000000004	Active	48	0	Aug 18, 2006 4:30:41 AM	N/A	V18E0A52EB52	0	N/A
Batch Test Profile	RT0000000005	Active	47	0	Jul 18, 2006 4:32:37 AM	N/A	V18E0A24DB0E	0	N/A
Batch Test Profile	RT0000000005	Active	48	0	Aug 18, 2006 4:30:41 AM	N/A	V19E0A52EB54	0	N/A
Batch Test Profile	RT0000000006	Active	47	0	Jul 18, 2006 4:32:37 AM	N/A	V18E0A24DB12	0	N/A

Figure 8-16. *Recurring Billing Report*

For information on a specific transaction, you can drill down by clicking the transaction ID. For details on the profile associated with a recurring billing transaction, you can drill down by clicking the profile ID. The Profile Details page will appear, as shown in Figure 8-17. From this page, you can modify the profile and view past transactions associated with the profile, and if the profile is set up for test transactions, you can switch it to move to live transactions with the click of a button.

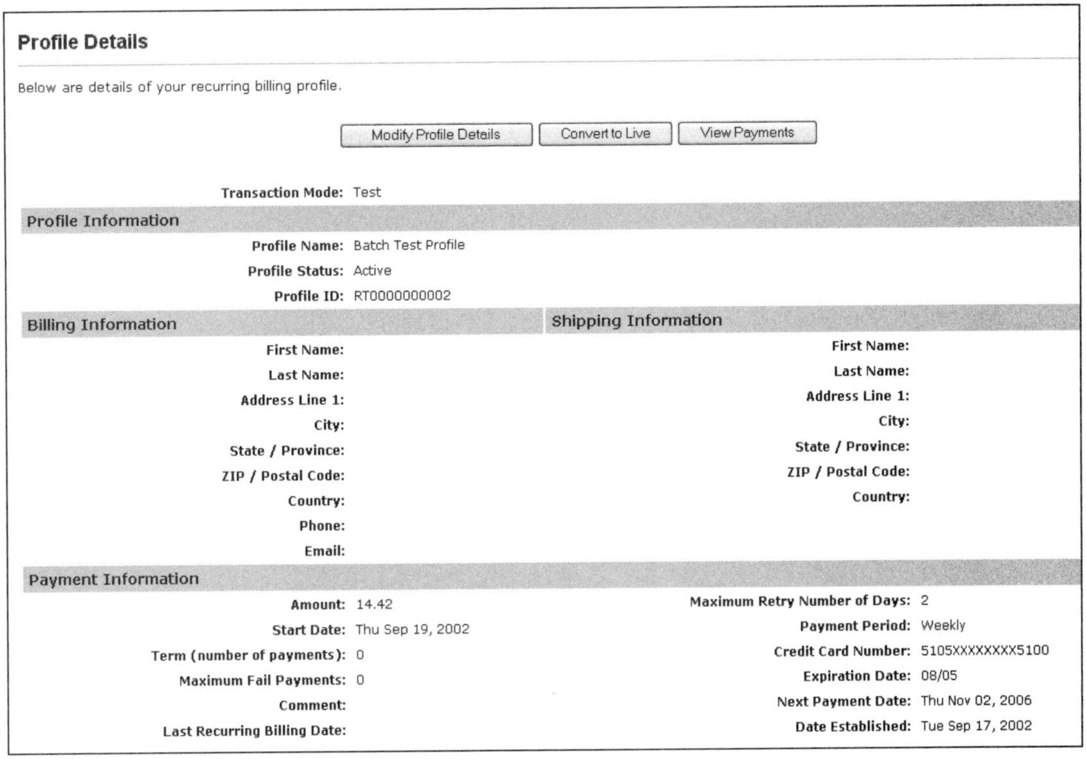

Profile Details

Below are details of your recurring billing profile.

[Modify Profile Details]   [Convert to Live]   [View Payments]

Transaction Mode: Test

Profile Information

Profile Name: Batch Test Profile
Profile Status: Active
Profile ID: RT0000000002

Billing Information   **Shipping Information**

First Name: First Name:
Last Name: Last Name:
Address Line 1:   Address Line 1:
City: City:
State / Province: State / Province:
ZIP / Postal Code: ZIP / Postal Code:
Country: Country:
Phone:
Email:

Payment Information

Amount: 14.42   Maximum Retry Number of Days: 2
Start Date: Thu Sep 19, 2002   Payment Period: Weekly
Term (number of payments): 0   Credit Card Number: 5105XXXXXXXX5100
Maximum Fail Payments: 0   Expiration Date: 08/05
Comment: Next Payment Date: Thu Nov 02, 2006
Last Recurring Billing Date: Date Established: Tue Sep 17, 2002

Figure 8-17. *Recurring Billing Report Profile Details page*

Filter Scorecard Report

The Filter Scorecard Report is a useful way to see which fraud triggers are causing transactions to be declined. The report shows all possible triggers, the number of transactions declined due to that trigger in the given time frame, and the percentage of total transactions that number represents. Figure 8-18 shows a sample Filter Scorecard Report.

The Filter Scorecard Report is useful to periodically check if a particular filter is causing you to lose a lot of business. You could possibly be under attack from a fraudster, or maybe you just have your fraud controls set too stringently, and this is causing you to deny potentially valid transactions. The fraud filters listed on this report are available to you through the Fraud Protection Service addition to the Payflow Pro gateway. They are discussed in more detail in Chapter 9.

Filter Scorecard Report

Date		Time Zone	Transaction Mode
Mon Jul 03, 2006 to Sun Sep 03, 2006		U.S. Pacific	Test

Download: ASCII Text ▾ Go   1-23 of 23 First | Prev | Next | Last

FILTER	TRIGGERED	TRIGGER PERCENTAGE
Total Purchase Price Ceiling	0	0.00
Total Item Ceiling	0	0.00
Shipping/Billing Mismatch	0	0.00
AVS Failure	0	0.00
CSC Failure	0	0.00
Buyer Auth Failure	0	0.00
Zip Risk List Match	0	0.00
Freight Forwarder Match	0	0.00
IP Address Velocity	0	0.00
BIN Risk List Match	0	0.00
USPS Address Validation Failure	0	0.00
IP Address Risk List Match	0	0.00
Email Service Provider Risk List Match	0	0.00
Geo-Location Failure	0	0.00
Bad Lists	0	0.00
Country Risk List Match	0	0.00
International Shipping/Billing Address	0	0.00
International IP Address	0	0.00
International AVS	0	0.00
Total Purchase Price Floor	0	0.00
Good Lists	0	0.00
Product Watch List	0	0.00
Account Number Velocity	0	0.00

Download: ASCII Text ▾ Go   1-23 of 23 First | Prev | Next | Last

Figure 8-18. *Filter Scorecard Report*

Summary

Reporting is a crucial component of managing an online business. You need to be able to tell where your money is coming from and where it's going, and you need the ability to search and customize your results as effectively as possible. As your business grows, you need a reporting framework that can grow with you. While PayPal has traditionally not offered exceptional reporting capabilities, recent improvements have brought the PayPal reporting offering up to par with other online banking applications.

PayPal has two main components on their website that serve to meet the reporting needs of PayPal customers. The PayPal reporting portal, located at https://business.paypal.com, is the main reporting page for transactions processed through a regular PayPal account (i.e., not a Payflow Gateway account). For Payflow Gateway accounts, the PayPal Manager application at https://manager.paypal.com contains a reporting area that offers over a dozen reports to help you analyze the health of your Payflow account.

One of the benefits of PayPal Reporting is that it can help you spot potentially fraudulent activity in your account. The next chapter goes into more detail about how to manage your exposure to the risk of fraud, and how to establish business processes to handle troublesome transactions when they do occur. You will learn about the many features PayPal offers to help you protect and grow your business.

CHAPTER 9

∎ ∎ ∎

Managing Online Disputes

There are always risks associated with doing business, and the online world presents a new realm of concerns that must be addressed by any e-commerce business. Credit card fraud from a stolen card number, identity theft from a stolen Social Security Number, and shipments that buyers claim to have never received are just a few examples. CyberSource (www.cybersource.com), a provider of electronic payment and risk management solutions, estimates that $2.8 billion was lost in 2005, or about 1.6% of all online revenues.[1] As e-commerce continues to grow at about 20% per year, the amount of money lost annually to online fraud is growing more and more significant.

While most brick-and-mortar businesses have established processes for handling these typical business problems, many online merchants don't have this type of experience and are often not sure how to best address the issues involved. One major difference is that while credit card issuers take on the responsibility for unauthorized charges made at a brick-and-mortar store, that duty is shifted to the merchant when the transaction is made online. If the merchant can't prove that a charge is legitimate, the merchant will lose the funds in question.

By being proactive in taking steps to establish policies and processes to work with your customers to resolve their issues and concerns, you can significantly minimize your business risks. You'll also maximize the chance that you'll be vindicated should a complaint be filed against you by a buyer. Additionally, if you are clear and up front about your policies, you will reduce the number of negative incidents that occur in the first place, because buyers will have fewer questions about when to expect their shipments, under what conditions products can be returned, and other such common concerns.

This chapter discusses how to take measures to prevent and manage disputes and reduce your exposure to fraudulent transactions, thereby minimizing your fraud-related business losses. Topics presented include the following:

- Establishing clear policies

- Handling chargebacks

- Resolving disputes

- Understanding the PayPal Seller Protection Policy (SPP)

---

1. CyberSource 2006 Online Fraud Report, www.cybersource.com/cgi-bin/resource_center/resources.cgi.

- Using the PayPal Resolution Center

- Examining the Payflow fraud prevention service

- Implementing PCI compliance

Establishing Clear Policies

With e-commerce, fear of the unknown is often a barrier to successfully launching an online business. This is especially true for businesses that operate a traditional brick-and-mortar storefront. While they may have operated for years under a system that has met their local needs, opening up a business to the global marketplace by selling items online carries with it a number of questions, the answers to which are not immediately obvious.

This section addresses some of the most common problems that an online business faces and presents strategies for solving them. By addressing these topics and tailoring policies that meet your specific needs, you will be better prepared to face the challenges your online business will encounter. Specifically, this section covers

- Item descriptions

- Return policy

- Shipping policy

- Resolution plan

A successful online business will have a well-thought-out approach to handling each of the items just listed.

Item Descriptions

Clear descriptions of the products or services you have for sale are essential. When in doubt, err on the side of being overly descriptive rather than not descriptive enough. This especially applies to items that have specific measurements that will determine whether the buyer will be happy with them.

Take clothing, for example. An XL shirt made in the UK is generally going to be smaller than an XL shirt made in America, so it may not be enough to just say a shirt is size XL. You should also include chest, arm, and neck measurements.

Also, instead of providing just one photo of an item, offer a way for potential customers to browse multiple photos of the item taken from different angles. If an item is extremely small, show it next to a common item that everyone knows the size of, such as a quarter. To go the extra mile, offer a way to zoom in on a particular area of the photo. These practices will help not only reduce the number of returns you have to deal with, but also increase your overall sales.

Return Policy

eBay research shows that "difficulty in returning items" is the topmost shopping barrier cited by online buyers. As a result, merchants who clearly spell out their return policies on their websites have an edge on the competition. Buyers are simply more comfortable shopping with sellers offering return policies. This becomes even more important as the average sale price of your items increases.

eBay research also shows that only a very small percentage of sold items are actually returned. A clear return policy can only help increase your sell-through rates, so not offering one leads not only to buyer frustration, but also to a decrease in your overall sales. Also, the cost of return shipping is something that should not be overlooked in your return policy. Most merchants will put the onus of return shipping on the buyer, but this is a decision you will have to make for yourself. Regardless of your decision, make sure it is spelled out in clear terms for buyers before a purchase is complete.

Shipping Policy

A clearly stated shipping policy along with detailed tracking information will help you prevent "item not received" claims and respond appropriately if any do arise. Your buyers should know what your basic shipping time is, and you should take into account overseas shipping times if you accept orders from across the globe. Almost all e-commerce sites these days offer premium shipping upgrades, such as overnight shipping or USPS Priority Mail. Understand what these options will cost you, so you can pass on these options to your customers, along with the appropriate shipping costs.

Provide realistic delivery estimates and get tracking information for all of your shipments. Then, give the confirmation number to buyers so they can track their shipment themselves and save you a support phone call. You may even consider a link directly to a page on your shipping carrier's website that will show the up-to-the-minute status of the shipment, if the carrier provides such a service.

Note It is especially important to use trackable shipping methods when shipping internationally, as this is the only way you'll be able to fight "item not received" claims made against you, even though there is considerable cost in doing so.

It's also important to require a signature on delivery for high-ticket or high-risk items, such as shipments valued at more than $250 or the latest high-tech gadget. Proof that the item was not only delivered, but also signed for will be a crucial piece of evidence in the case that the transaction results in a claim from the buyer that he or she never received the item.

Be straightforward in your terms about your payment preferences and shipping guidelines. Buyers should be clearly presented with the details on the type of payment instruments you accept, and also how long they should expect to wait before the item arrives in the mail. This information should be presented before they are asked for a credit card number or other type of payment information.

Creating a Resolution Plan

When things are going well and you're selling tons of items online, it can be easy to not think about your dispute-management processes. But when a problem comes up and escalates into a messy situation, it can take an unreasonable amount of time and energy to deal with it. Every minute you spend responding to a dispute is a minute you're not spending on selling more items. This just adds to your frustration and drives home the importance of not only avoiding disputes in the first place, but also having a resolution plan in place to guide your actions while resolving a dispute. Time spent on proactive preparation to avoid a problem is more than repaid when such preparation reduces the time spent in dealing with an ugly situation down the road.

It makes good business sense to draft a detailed resolution plan for both how you will deflect dispute problems and how you will deal with them when they do crop up. Craft the messages you'll send to your buyers in advance, before you get sucked into the emotions of a dispute. Then clearly indicate your processes on your website.

Some merchants believe that publicizing their dispute-management processes will scare buyers off, because potential buyers might think the merchant deals with a lot of disputes. However, buyers generally appreciate the clarity because it lets them see that the merchant is committed to fairness and takes their responsibilities seriously. In fact, it gives your actions additional legitimacy if they are detailed on your website. It's much harder for a buyer to complain about a particular policy when it's detailed right there in clear text that the buyer was shown (or at least given the option to see) before the purchase was complete.

When buyers have a question, their first instinct is usually to go back to your stated policies to see if their question is answered there. A clear policy that anticipates and answers many of the common questions up front will help avoid emails and phone calls from buyers asking simple questions. You may even consider an FAQ page to handle the most common questions.

Managing Your Resolution Plan

Chapter 5 discussed some technologies that PayPal offers to manage postpayment processing, but it did not address the business workflows involved. While many merchants put a lot of thought into their resolution plan when they first launch their site, they don't revisit it later to make changes and update it to meet the evolving needs of their business. However, by learning from the transactions you engage in over time, you can effectively modify your terms, return policies, and guarantees. All of this will only lead to better bottom-line results in the long run.

One common practice when crafting your plan is to look for terms and conditions used by other merchants and borrow the ideas that you think are applicable to your own business. You can then tailor them to fit your specific needs. Be as clear and explicit as possible. Your general policies should not be confusing in any way, and they should be generally easy to comprehend with just a few minutes of effort.

It's a good idea to think through your resolution plan from the perspective of a buyer. This includes reviewing the emails in the order they're sent out to your buyers. Does everything make sense? Do all the links and email addresses referred to in your messages still work? You might even survey your buyers to gather feedback on the purchase process to see where inefficiencies or opportunities for improvements may exist. If your site has not yet launched, ask a friend or relative to make a test purchase so that they can give you direct and honest feedback on the entire process.

One important thing to keep in mind when reviewing the postpayment buyer experience is that buyers are often not going to be as savvy as you are. Try standing in the shoes of your grandfather or grandmother—would he or she be able to understand your policies and procedures from the emails you send? If not, you may want to take a second look at your communications to see where they can be simplified. Remember to keep the language simple and direct, and to use easy-to-read, large fonts, especially if your target market includes the elderly.

Handling Chargebacks

We'll start this section by taking a look at what exactly a *chargeback* is, since the topic is generally not well understood. Many PayPal merchants incorrectly think that a chargeback refers to any buyer complaint filed through the PayPal website. In fact, a chargeback is when buyers contact the company that issued their credit card and ask to reverse a charge. This may be because they were not happy with the item they purchased, they did not order the item to begin with, or they may possibly be trying to pull a fast one on a merchant to get a product or service for free.

▮**Note** Remember, a buyer cannot file a chargeback on the PayPal site. The buyer must go directly to his or her credit card issuer and file the chargeback with the company to which the buyer makes monthly credit card payments.

The chargeback process is neither designed nor maintained by PayPal, so PayPal can't change it or reject chargebacks. PayPal is essentially playing by the rules set by Visa, Master-Card, American Express, and so on. Everyone who accepts, issues, or processes credit cards has to abide by those rules, from the casual eBay seller all the way up to huge retailers like Wal-Mart and Target. There's no choice in the matter. Those are the rules of the game, and it's the game you choose to play when you decide to accept credit cards online.

When a chargeback is filed, the credit card issuer will ask the buyer for information on the kind of chargeback it is. The credit card company will want to know things such as whether the buyer actually purchased the item, whether the buyer received the item, and whether the item received is significantly different from the item the buyer had expected to receive. Credit card companies will generally assume the buyer is right, because they want to do whatever they can to preserve the relationship with the cardholder. As such, credit card companies will grant a chargeback without too much deep investigation. They will then inform PayPal through the credit card association that a chargeback has been filed, and the payment to the seller is reversed. The onus is now on the merchant to prove that the chargeback is invalid.

Most sellers doing business in the brick-and-mortar world have encountered credit card chargebacks at some point. In these cases, the responsibility falls to the credit card company to resolve the dispute and reclaim the funds. However, when dealing with online transactions, where the card isn't physically present, the responsibility falls to the merchant. This is one of the major differences between doing business online and accepting credit cards in a face-to-face environment.

PayPal has enabled thousands of businesses to accept credit cards online, many of which might not have otherwise been willing or able to open a merchant account with a traditional bank. As a result, if a buyer calls his or her credit card issuer and requests a chargeback on a PayPal payment made from his or her credit card, that chargeback may be the first that merchant has ever received. If this is the case, the merchant often doesn't really understand what's happened. Frequently the merchant inaccurately thinks that PayPal filed the chargeback, because merchants are informed of the chargeback in an email from PayPal.

PayPal Chargeback Specialists

As a seller, you can dispute a chargeback you receive if you disagree with the buyer's claim. For example, you may have proof of delivery to a confirmed address (recall from Chapter 2 that a confirmed address is an address PayPal has verified as belonging to the account holder). In that case, you can work with PayPal to submit the necessary evidence and re-present the charge—essentially, you can dispute the chargeback and make the claim to your money. Sellers that process their credit card payments without using PayPal's help have to do this work themselves.

PayPal has a team of trained chargeback specialists who do nothing but fight on your behalf when a chargeback occurs. This is a huge advantage offered by PayPal that is often overlooked by merchants, at least until the day when that first chargeback shows up. A PayPal chargeback specialist will review the claim and file a dispute with the credit card association if there is a disagreement about the chargeback. The status of your chargebacks can be tracked in the PayPal Resolution Center, an area of the PayPal website that is discussed in more detail later in this chapter.

Avoiding Chargebacks

The best way to manage chargebacks is do your best to avoid them in the first place. Good customer service and business policies are essential tools to deflect chargebacks before they ever get filed. This section reviews some key areas that you will want to address to create an atmosphere that will limit the number of unwanted disputes that you have to deal with.

Watch for Unusual Shipping Requests

Look out for requests for shipments to strange addresses or requests containing an unusual sense of urgency, especially with high-ticket items. This may be an indication that the buyer is paying with a stolen credit card, which could result in an unauthorized payment claim down the road once the real cardholder learns of the charge on his or her credit card statement.

Communicate with Your Buyers

Regular email communications regarding confirmation of the order and detailed shipping information will help manage the expectations of the buyer. Since the buyer's order is placed online, it can be a very impersonal experience. Any sort of human touch and extra information you can provide to the buyer will improve his or her overall experience. Err on the side of providing too much information, rather than too little.

For a recent order I placed with Barnes & Noble.com, for example, I received separate emails when the order was placed, when the order was packed, and when the order was shipped, and a final email to confirm that the order had arrived. My single order resulted in four emails, but I didn't feel like that was too much at all. In fact, I appreciated the information, and it made me feel confident about shopping with that merchant again in the future (using my PayPal account, of course).

Seller Protection Policy

In some cases, PayPal proactively protects sellers against chargebacks. PayPal's Seller Protection Policy (SPP) is a free chargeback protection program that verified businesses and premier sellers qualify for. The SPP covers shipments of physical goods against claims of unauthorized payment or false nonreceipt. The SPP requires that you ship to a confirmed address within seven days of payment and get online proof of delivery for your shipment, including a signature for payments over a certain threshold (currently $250). If these requirements are met, PayPal will protect you against nonreceipt and unauthorized chargebacks, and return funds to your PayPal account that have been removed as a result of the chargeback.

By following good selling practices and maintaining effective customer service policies, you give PayPal the necessary information to dispute a chargeback on your behalf. The best thing about the SPP from the seller's perspective is that even if the re-presentment of the charge is denied, the seller will keep his or her money. Many businesses will ship *only* to confirmed addresses, and this is a policy that you may want to consider for yourself.

■**Note** For the latest version of the SPP, visit `www.paypal.com/spp`.

Resolving Disputes

When a problem does arise, managing it under the guidelines of your resolution plan should become a top priority. The two primary goals in dealing with buyers are to complete the transaction and to preserve your reputation. Communication with buyers is a prime area to concentrate on when considering these goals. For instance, merchants often respond to buyer emails in the heat of the moment, and they later regret taking the tone they did. Composing a response right after receiving a displeasing email from a buyer is often not the best idea. Instead, if you have a standard, neutral communication that you have drafted in advance as part of your resolution plan, you'll improve your odds of meeting these two goals.

It's much easier to compose dispute resolution emails when you're not in the middle of a dispute. You can spend the time to research what type of language will work most effectively and continually edit it as your needs change. Writing an email that maintains a professional tone while you are in the middle of a dispute and the other side is being belligerent is difficult. That's why advance planning can be so useful.

Provide customers with a way to contact you should they have a problem. Often a simple email exchange or phone call clears up a misunderstanding instantly. Also, always respond promptly and courteously to customer inquiries. Receiving a personalized message is a great way to assuage the anger that an unhappy buyer may feel, simply because of the human factor—the buyer is happy to know he or she is being listened to, and that another human being is taking the time to look into the problem. First and foremost, people want to be listened to and have their issues understood, so if you have the capacity to make a personal phone call to an upset customer to resolve the problem, you will generally resolve the issue more quickly and have the buyer more likely to do business with you in the future.

PayPal Resolution Center

PayPal has an area on its website called the Resolution Center that is tailored to helping merchants manage online disputes by facilitating communication between the buyer, the seller, and PayPal. To access the Resolution Center, click the Resolution Center link that is accessible from your PayPal Account Overview page. In Figure 9-1, the account also has a notification warning that a new dispute has been filed.

■Note The Resolution Center is not available in the PayPal Sandbox.

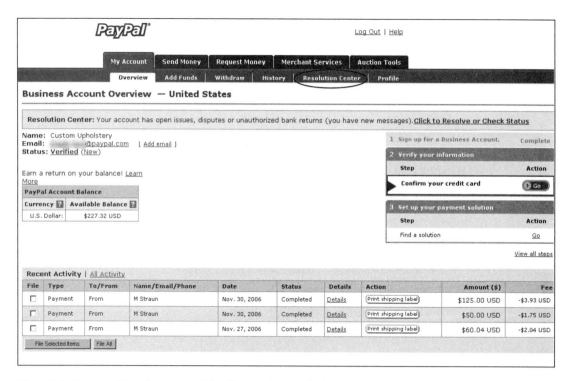

Figure 9-1. *Account Overview page with a link to the Resolution Center*

The Resolution Center is a one-stop location for businesses to review all claims, determine the status of those claims, and receive assistance from PayPal in resolving them. To get the most benefit out of the Resolution Center, you should regularly check to see if you have any disputes pending and provide PayPal with any requested information within ten days. You will receive an email notification when a new case is filed, but in case any spam filters block this message or you otherwise miss the message, you may want to make it part of your regular routine to check the Resolution Center when you are checking in on your PayPal account activity. Additionally, you will receive an Instant Payment Notification (IPN) if you have IPN enabled for your account. This is described in more detail later in this section.

The main page of the Resolution Center is shown in Figure 9-2. It displays the account's open cases, provides a link to open a new dispute (in case you want to file a dispute of your own), and also offers some basic tutorials about how to use the Resolution Center. Links are available to view the details of the claim and to resolve the claim. The original transaction can also be located by clicking the Transaction ID link, and the status of each claim is shown in the Status column.

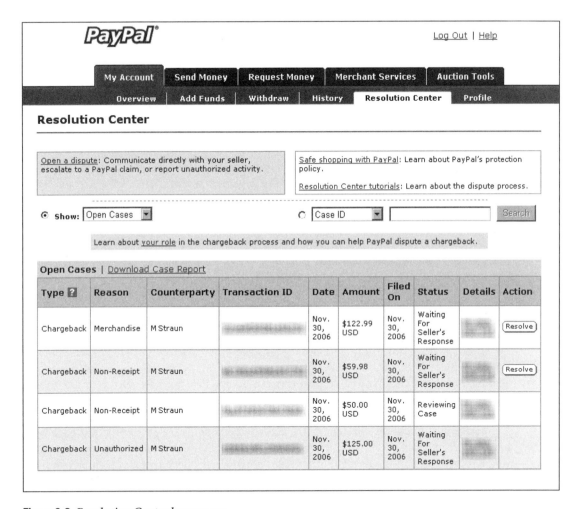

Figure 9-2. *Resolution Center homepage*

From this page, you can view details of a specific claim and also respond to the claim. When you respond to the claim, you have a number of choices depending on the type of dispute. The example shown in Figure 9-3 deals with a chargeback dispute and presents four options for resolution. Other types of disputes will present a list of options that will vary slightly from those shown in Figure 9-3.

Figure 9-3. *Options when responding to a claim*

If you wish to fight the claim, you can take action through the Resolution Center to provide evidence that will help PayPal fight the chargeback on your behalf. The details of the claim will list the available actions.

If you have tracking information for the package, you can submit this to PayPal, which can prove that the item was received by the buyer. Additionally, if you have already provided a refund to the customer, you can provide proof of that to PayPal. However, if your argument goes outside the bounds of just providing tracking information, you will need to state your side of the case to PayPal.

Remember, in the case of a chargeback, the buyer already has received funds back from his or her credit card issuer—if you were to refund the buyer for the transaction, he or she would receive the funds twice. For other types of cases, such as buyer complaints, you can issue a refund for the transaction, as the funds aren't actually returned to the buyer unless the case is closed in the buyer's favor. As shown in Figure 9-4, you are provided 2,000 characters to make your case, so it is in your best interest to keep your emotions and opinions out of the picture and just stick to the facts. This includes any communication between you and the buyer regarding the product details, expected delivery time, and any other relevant information.

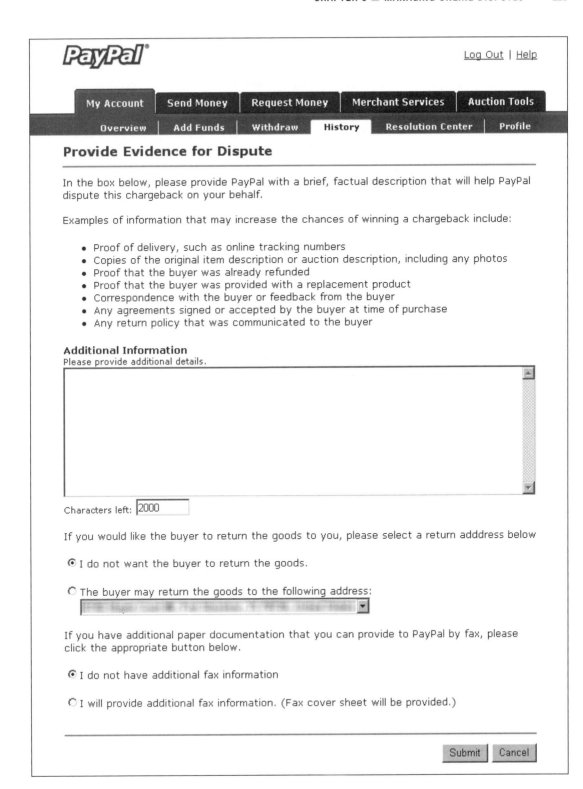

Figure 9-4. *Providing evidence for your side of the story*

Resolution Center IPNs

PayPal's Instant Payment Notification (IPN) technology was discussed in Chapter 5 as an effective way to receive immediate notification when a new transaction occurs or when the status of a previous transaction changes. If you have IPN enabled in your account Profile, you will also receive notification when a new complaint has been filed against you in the Resolution Center. If you specify a Notify URL for the individual transaction, that URL will override the account Profile URL and will be used for payment notification as well as any subsequent Resolution Center IPNs.

The PHP code in Listing 9-1 sends an email to a specific email address (in the example it is notify@testbusiness.com) whenever an IPN for a new Resolution Center case arrives. Notice how this can be integrated with the code in Chapter 5 to create a master IPN script. We check to see if the notification type is new_case, and if it is, we send the email. If it is not, we default to the normal IPN code from Chapter 5 (which has been omitted for brevity).

Listing 9-1. *Sending Email Notification upon Receipt of Resolution Center New Case IPN*

```php
<?php
$req = 'cmd=_notify-validate';

foreach ($_POST as $key => $value) {
    $value = urlencode(stripslashes($value));
    $req .= "&$key=$value";
}

// post back to PayPal system to validate
$header .= "POST /cgi-bin/webscr HTTP/1.0\r\n";
$header .= "Host: www.paypal.com:80\r\n";
$header .= "Content-Type: application/x-www-form-urlencoded\r\n";
$header .= "Content-Length: " . strlen($req) . "\r\n\r\n";
$fp = fsockopen ('www.paypal.com', 80, $errno, $errstr, 30);

// get the transaction type
$txn_type = $_POST['txn_type'];  // should be equal to "new_case" if disputed

if ($txn_type == 'new_case') {
  // assign posted variables to local variables
  $txn_id = $_POST['txn_id'];
  $case_id = $_POST['case_id'];
  $case_type = $_POST['case_type'];
  $case_creation_date = $_POST['case_creation_date'];
  $reason_code = $_POST['reason_code'];

  // set email variables
  $to = $_POST['business'];
  $from = "PayPal Resolution Center";
  $subject = "New dispute filed";
```

```php
  $msg = "A new dispute has been filed against you in ➡
    the PayPal Resolution Center";
  $msg .= "\n\nThe details of the dispute are as follows:";
  $msg .= "\n" . "Transaction ID: " . $txn_id ;
  $msg .= "\n" . "Case ID: " . $case_id;
  $msg .= "\n" . "Case Type: " . $case_type;
  $msg .= "\n" . "Case Created: " . $case_creation_date;
  $msg .= "\n" . "Reason: " . $reason_code;
} else {
  // do normal IPN processing (see Chapter 5)

  // obtain all the POST variables
  // set the email $to, $from, $subject, and $msg variables
}

// send the email
if (!$fp) {
// HTTP ERROR
} else {
  fputs ($fp, $header . $req);
  while (!feof($fp)) {
    $res = fgets ($fp, 1024);
    if (strcmp ($res, "VERIFIED") == 0) {
      $mail_From = $from;
      $mail_To = $to;
      $mail_Subject = $subject;
      $mail_Body = $msg;

      mail($mail_To, $mail_Subject, $mail_Body, $mail_From);
    }
    else if (strcmp ($res, "INVALID") == 0) {
      // log for manual investigation
    }
  }
  fclose ($fp);
}?>
```

Implementing PCI Compliance

Just as a disclosure policy describes your business and states your business practices, your compliance with the Payment Card Industry (PCI) Data Security Standard reinforces an atmosphere of safety that you want shoppers to experience while they are on your website.

Buyers are increasingly aware of the dangers of identity theft due to stolen credit card information. PCI compliance assures buyers that not only do you have their safety and well-being in mind, but it's a top priority. Compliance should be regarded as an opportunity to gain a competitive edge, not an obligation that requires resources and overhead that could be spent elsewhere. Finding and fixing compliance gaps before your audit keeps your company running smoothly and your reputation intact. It provides you with tangible proof that you can communicate to your customers about how well you're protecting them.

All major credit card companies require merchants that accept online credit cards to comply with the PCI standard. This also includes meeting PCI validation requirements, including quarterly and annual audits, security self-assessments, and security scans. The exact validation requirements are determined by the volume of transactions processed by the merchant.

The quickest and easiest way to meet the PCI standard is to outsource the job. A number of PayPal payment solutions are hosted, relieving the online merchant of the compliance responsibility. Examples of this are Express Checkout and Website Payments Standard. The Payflow Gateway and Website Payments Pro payment solutions, which allow the merchant to accept credit card data directly on the merchant website, require PCI compliance and validation by the merchants themselves.

PCI Data Security Standard Requirements

The following list details the requirements, from a data security standpoint, that you must adhere to in order to be PCI compliant. PCI Data Security Standard compliance assures your customers that you're looking out for their safety and well being.

- Install and maintain a firewall configuration to protect data.

- Do not use vendor-supplied defaults for system passwords and other security parameters.

- Protect stored cardholder data.

- Encrypt transmission of cardholder data and sensitive information across public networks.

- Use and regularly update antivirus software.

- Develop and maintain secure systems and applications.

- Restrict access to data by business need-to-know criteria.

- Assign a unique ID to each person with data access in order to monitor activity.

- Restrict physical access to cardholder data.

- Track and monitor all access to network resources and cardholder data.

- Regularly test security systems and processes.

- Maintain a policy that addresses information security.

Merchant Levels for PCI Compliance

The compliance level of each merchant is the responsibility of the merchant's acquiring bank (i.e., the bank that provides the credit card merchant account and is responsible for submitting credit card purchase information to the credit card associations). The four merchant levels are based on annual credit card transaction volume. The amount of compliance you must adhere to depends on the level of your business.

- A Level 1 merchant is

  - Any merchant processing over 6 million credit card transactions per year

  - Any merchant that has suffered a hack or an attack that resulted in an account data compromise

  - Any merchant identified by any card association as Level 1

- A Level 2 merchant is

  - Any merchant processing 150,000 to 6 million e-commerce transactions per year

- A Level 3 merchant is

  - Any merchant processing 20,000 to 150,000 e-commerce transactions per year

- A Level 4 merchant is

  - Any merchant processing fewer than 20,000 e-commerce transactions per year, and all other merchants processing up to 6,000,000 credit card transactions per year

PCI Compliance Validation Requirements

In addition to adhering to the PCI Data Security Standard, compliance validation is required for Level 1, Level 2, and Level 3 merchants, and it may be required for Level 4 merchants. The actions required for the various levels of compliance are as follows:

- Level 1

  - Annual onsite PCI data security assessment and quarterly network scan

  - Qualified data security company or internal audit if signed by officer of the company

  - Validated by qualified independent scan vendor

- Levels 2 and 3

  - Annual PCI self-assessment questionnaire and quarterly network scan

  - Validated by merchant-qualified independent scan vendor

- Level 4

  - Annual PCI self-assessment questionnaire and quarterly network scan

  - Validated by merchant-qualified independent scan vendor

Additional Resources for Disclosure and Compliance

Other online resources can help you in developing your own disclosure policy and meeting PCI compliance requirements, including the following:

- *Privacy Planner* (from BBBOnLine; www.privacyplanner.com): This site can help you create a privacy policy for your online business.

- *The Direct Marketing Association* (DMA; www.the-dma.org/privacy/privacypolicygenerator.shtml): This site offers a small business–friendly online privacy policy generator.

- *The Federal Trade Commission* (www.consumer.gov/idtheft, www.ftc.gov): These FTC sites offer information on preventing identity theft.

- *The Visa and MasterCard websites* (www.visa.com, www.mastercard.com): These sites offer resources about meeting the PCI Data Security Standard.

Summary

Businesses grow by business owners understanding how to balance risk with profit. Being too risk-averse may limit your buyer pool and reduce your total sales volume. On the other hand, not being risk-aware opens you to problems such as chargebacks. Managing these risks intelligently may involve exposing yourself to more chargebacks, but the tradeoff may well be worth it. Through the practices discussed in this chapter, you can better prepare yourself to both prevent disputes in the first place and handle them appropriately when they do occur.

PayPal offers a number of features to help with managing fraud losses and online disputes. The PayPal Resolution Center enables you to more effectively manage your online disputes, and Payflow Fraud Protection Services allow you to control the amount of risk you are willing to take on by fine-tuning several fraud parameters. Additionally, PayPal's risk models will automatically flag and reject high-risk transactions, such as high-ticket purchases from new accounts based in a country known for high rates of online fraud.

PayPal Reference

Standard Variable Reference

The Standard Variable Reference contains all of the variables that can be included in a standard checkout transaction. This includes code for Buy Now buttons, subscriptions, donations, cart upload, and the PayPal shopping cart.

The cmd Variable

The cmd variable must be included in all standard checkout forms. It tells PayPal what type of action to take. It can take the values shown in Table A-1.

Table A-1. *The cmd Variable*

Value	Description
_xclick	Buy Now buttons and donations.
_s-xclick	Flag that the next value is an EWP-encrypted blob.*
_xclick-subscriptions	Subscriptions.
_cart	PayPal Shopping Cart or cart upload.
_ext-enter	Prepopulating PayPal account signup. Requires redirect_cmd to also be included.

* There must also be a cmd variable in the encrypted blob that specifies the actual command to be executed. See Chapter 4 for more information.

Action Variables

Variables that specify actions to be taken depending upon the user's actions during checkout are shown in Table A-2. All URLs must be URL-encoded.

Table A-2. *Action Variables*

Variable	Description	Required?
cancel_return	URL where the buyer is returned if he or she cancels a transaction.	Optional
notify_url	URL to which PayPal posts IPNs for a transaction.	Optional
return	URL where the buyer is returned following a successful transaction.	Optional
rm	Return method used when returning the buyer to the merchant website after a transaction. Default: GET 1: GET 2: POST	Optional

Individual Item Information Variables

Variables for an individual item in a standard checkout transaction are shown in Table A-3.

Table A-3. *Item Information Variables*

Variable	Description	Required?	Character Length
add	Set to 1 to add an item to PayPal-hosted shopping cart.	Optional	1
amount	Price of the purchase, not including shipping, handling, or tax.	Only for shopping carts	N/A
display	Set to 1 for a View Cart button.	Optional	1
item_name	Description of an item.	Only for shopping carts	127
item_number	Tracking variable passed back to the seller at payment completion.	Optional	127
quantity	Number of items. The amount, shipping, and tax are multiplied by the quantity to derive the total payment amount.	Optional	N/A
undefined_quantity	Value of 1 allows the buyer to specify the quantity.	Optional	1
on0	First optional field name.	Optional	64
on1	Second optional field name.	Optional	64
os0	First set of option values. on0 must also be defined.	Optional	64 or 200*
os1	Second set of option values. on1 must also be defined.	Optional	64 or 200*

If the os0 or os1 option is selected through a text box or radio button, each value should be no more than 64 characters. If this value is entered by the customer in a text field, there is a 200-character limit.

Display Variables

Variables for customizing the visual appearance of the PayPal checkout page are shown in Table A-4.

Table A-4. *Display Variables*

Variable	Description	Required?	Character Length
amount	Price of the purchase, not including shipping, handling, or tax.	Only for shopping carts	
cbt	Sets the text for the Continue button on the PayPal Payment Complete page.	Optional	60
cn	Label above the note field.	Optional	40
cpp_header_image	URL for image at the top left of payment page (the maximum is 750 × 90 pixels).	Optional	N/A
cpp_headerback_color*	Background color for payment page header.	Optional	
cpp_headerborder_color*	Border color around payment page header.	Optional	
cpp_payflow_color*	Background color for the payment page below the header. Note: Colors that conflict with PayPal's error messages are not allowed.	Optional	
cs	Background color of your payment pages. Default or 0: Background color is white. 1: Background color is black.	Optional	
image_url	URL of the 150 × 50 pixel image displayed as your logo in the upper-left corner of PayPal's pages.	Optional	
no_note	Prompt customer to include a note with payment. Default or 0: Customer is prompted to include a note. 1: Customer is not prompted to include a note.	Optional	1
no_shipping	Prompt customer for shipping address. Default or 0: Customer is prompted to include a shipping address. 1: Customer is not asked for a shipping address. 2: Customer must provide a shipping address.	Optional	1

Continued

Table A-4. *Continued*

Variable	Description	Required?	Character Length
page_style	Sets the Custom Payment Page Style for payment pages; alphanumeric ASCII lower 7-bit characters only, plus underscore, no spaces. primary: Always use the page style set as primary. paypal: Use the PayPal default style. other: The name of a page style you have defined.	Optional	30

* A valid value for this color is a case-insensitive six-character HTML hexadecimal color code in ASCII.

Transaction Information Variables

Variables specific to individual transactions are shown in Table A-5.

Table A-5. *Transaction Information Variables*

Variable	Description	Required?	Character Length
address_override	1: The address specified in prepopulation variables overrides the user's stored address.	Optional	1
currency_code	Currency of the payment. The default is U.S. dollars.	Optional	3
custom	Pass-through variable never presented to your customer.	Optional	256
handling	Handling charges. Not quantity-specific, this handling cost is charged regardless of the number of items purchased.	Optional	
invoice	Pass-through variable you can use to identify your invoice number for this purchase.	Optional	127
redirect_cmd	Used only in conjunction with cmd="_ext-enter" for prepopulating a PayPal form during payment. Only valid value is _xclick.	Optional	40
shipping	Cost of shipping if you have enabled item-specific shipping costs. If shipping is used and shipping2 is not defined, this flat amount is charged regardless of the quantity of items purchased. Takes effect only if the override check box is checked in your Profile.	Optional	
shipping2	Cost of shipping each additional item.	Optional	
tax	Flat tax amount regardless of the buyer's location. Overrides tax settings set in your Profile.	Optional	

Cart Upload Variables

Variables for all cart upload transactions are shown in Table A-6. *Cart upload* means passing the total contents of the shopping cart to PayPal in a single form at the end of the transaction.

Table A-6. *Cart Upload Variables*

Variable	Description	Required?	Allowable Values
amount	Price of the item or the total price of all items in the shopping cart.	Required	Any valid currency amount
business	Email address for your PayPal account.	Required	An email address
handling_cart	Single handling fee to be charged cartwide.	Optional	Any valid currency amount
item_name	Name of the item or a name for the entire cart.	Required	
paymentaction	Type of transaction.	Optional	Sale, order, authorization
tax_cart	Total tax on entire cart. Overrides any individual tax_x values.	Optional	
upload	Indicates the use of third-party shopping cart.	Required	1

Cart Upload Variables for Individual Cart Items

Variables for including individual item details for a third-party shopping cart are shown in Table A-7.

Table A-7. *Cart Upload Variables for Individual Cart Items*

Variable	Description	Required?	Character Length
amount_x	Price of item x. *	Required	
handling_x	The cost of handling for item x.	Optional	
item_name_x	Alphanumeric name of item x in the cart.	Required	127
item_number_x	Variable for you to track order or other purchase.	Optional	127
on0_x	First optional field name for item x.	Optional	64
on1_x	Second optional field name for item x.	Optional	64
os0_x	First set of optional value(s) for item x. Requires that on0_x also be set.	Optional	200
os1_x	Second set of optional value(s) for item x. Requires that on1_x also be set.	Optional	200
quantity_x	Quantity of the item x. Must be a positive integer.	Optional	

Continued

Table A-7. *Continued*

Variable	Description	Required?	Character Length
shipping_x	Cost of shipping the first piece (quantity of 1) of item x.	Optional	
shipping2_x	Cost of shipping each additional piece (quantity of two or more) of item x.	Optional	
tax_x	Tax amount for item x.	Optional	

*x *must start with 1 and increment by 1 for each cart item.*

Address Override Variables

If you include address override variables, shown in Table A-8, the values will override those stored in the buyer's PayPal account. All variables are optional. These variables can also be passed in with a cmd=_ext_enter transaction when you want to send the buyer to an account creation page with certain variable prefilled.

Table A-8. *Address Override Variables*

Variable	Description	Format	Character Length
address1	Street address, line 1	Alphanumeric	100
address2	Street address, line 2	Alphanumeric	100
city	City	Alphanumeric	40
country	Country	Alphabetic	2
email	Customer's email address	Alphanumeric	127
first_name	First name	Alphabetic	32
last_name	Last name	Alphabetic	32
lc	Locale (language) of the PayPal login page	Alphabetic	2
night_phone_a	Area code for U.S. phone numbers; country code for phone numbers outside the U.S.	Numeric	3
night_phone_b	Three-digit prefix for U.S. phone numbers; entire phone number for phone numbers outside the U.S., excluding country code	Numeric	
night_phone_c	Four-digit phone number for U.S. phone numbers	Numeric	4
state	State	Two-character U.S. or Canadian abbreviation	2
zip	Postal code	Numeric	32

Prepopulating Business Account Signup Variables

If you include the variables shown in Table A-9 in a form to register a user for a PayPal account, the corresponding fields will be prefilled to speed up the registration process. All variables are optional.

Table A-9. *Prepopulating Business Account Signup Variables*

Variable	Description	Format	Character Length
business_address1	Business street address, line 1	Alphanumeric	128
business_address2	Business street address, line 2	Alphanumeric	128
business_city	Business city	Alphanumeric	128
business_state	Business state	Two-character official U.S. or Canadian abbreviation	2
business_country	Business country	Alphabetic	2
business_cs_email	Customer service email address	Alphanumeric	128
business_cs_phone_a	Customer service phone number area code for U.S. phone numbers; country code for phone numbers outside the U.S.	Numeric	3
business_cs_phone_b	Customer service three-digit prefix for U.S. phone numbers; entire number for phone numbers outside the U.S., excluding country code	Numeric	3
business_cs_phone_c	Customer service four-digit phone number for U.S. phone numbers	Numeric	4
business_url	URL of the business's website	Alphanumeric; must be URL-encoded	128
business_night_phone_a	Area code for U.S. phone numbers; country code for phone numbers outside the U.S.	Numeric	3
business_night_phone_b	Three-digit prefix for U.S. phone numbers, or the entire phone number for phone numbers outside the U.S., excluding country code	Numeric	
business_night_phone_c	Four-digit phone number for U.S. phone numbers	Numeric	4

PayPal Subscription Variables

Variables specific to using PayPal Subscriptions are shown in Table A-10.

Table A-10. *PayPal Subscription Variables*

Variable	Description	Required?
cmd	Must be set to _xclick-subscriptions.	Required
business	Email address of your PayPal account.	Required
item_name	Description of subscription (maximum 127 characters).	Optional
a1	Price of the first trial period.	Optional
p1	Length of the first trial period. This number is modified by the units variable t1.	Optional
t1	Units of first trial period. Acceptable values are D (days), W (weeks), M (months), and Y (years).	Optional
a2	Price of the second trial period.	Optional
p2	Length of the second trial period. This number is modified by the units variable t2.	Optional
t2	Units of the second trial period. Acceptable values are D (days), W (weeks), M (months), and Y (years).	Optional
a3	Regular price of the subscription.	Required
p3	Length of the regular billing cycle. This number is modified by the units variable t3.	Required
t3	Units of the regular billing cycle. Acceptable values are: D (days), W (weeks), M (months), Y (years).	Required
src	Recurring payments. If set to 1, payment will recur unless customer cancels. Default: Subscription will not recur.	Optional
sra	Reattempt on failure. If set to 1, a failed payment will be reattempted twice. Default: Payment is not reattempted.	Optional
srt	Number of payments that will occur at the regular rate. Default: Payment will continue to recur at the regular rate until the subscription is canceled.	Optional
no_note	Must be set to 1. This ensures that subscriber is not prompted to include a note with the subscription, a function that PayPal Subscriptions does not support.	Required
custom	User-defined field (maximum 255 characters) returned to you in payment notification emails. This field is not shown to subscribers.	Optional
invoice	User-defined field (maximum 127 characters) that must be unique with each subscription. Shown to subscribers.	Optional
usr_manage	Username and password generation field. If set to 1, PayPal generates a username and password for your subscriber. For use with Subscription Password Management.	Optional
modify	Subscription modification behavior. Default: Buyers can only create new subscriptions. 1: Buyers can modify current subscriptions and sign up for new subscriptions. 2: Buyers can only modify existing subscriptions.	Optional

IPN and PDT Variable Reference

This is a list of variables that can be included in the Instant Payment Notification (IPN) or Payment Data Transfer (PDT) post that PayPal sends to you. For more details on IPN and PDT, see Chapter 5.

In the Sandbox testing environment, IPN posts include an additional variable called test_ipn that will have a value of 1.

Buyer Information Variables

Buyer information variables are shown in Table A-11.

Table A-11. *Buyer Information Variables*

Variable	Description	Maximum Length
address_city	City of buyer's address.	40
address_country	Country of buyer's address.	64
address_country_code	Two-character ISO 3166 country code.	2
address_name	Name used with address.	128
address_state	State of customer's address.	40
address_status	Confirmed: Buyer provided a confirmed address. Unconfirmed: Buyer provided a unconfirmed address.	
address_street	Buyer's street address.	200
address_zip	ZIP code of buyer's address.	20
first_name	Buyer's first name.	64
last_name	Buyer's last name.	64
payer_business_name	Buyer's company name.	127
payer_email	Buyer's primary email address.	127
payer_id	Unique customer ID.	13
payer_status	verified: Customer has a verified PayPal account. unverified: Customer has a unverified PayPal account.	
residence_country	Two-character ISO 3166 country code.	2
test_ipn	This variable will be included with a value of 1 if it is a Sandbox IPN.	1

Transaction Variables

Variables specific to the transaction are listed in Table A-12.

Table A-12. *Transaction Variables*

Variable	Description	Maximum Length
business	Email address of the recipient.	127
custom	Custom value; never presented to the buyer.	255
invoice	Variable to identify the purchase. Must be unique.	127
item_name	Item name.	127
item_number	Item number.	127
memo	Memo as entered by the buyer during checkout.	255
option_name1	Option 1 name.	64
option_name2	Option 2 name.	64
option_selection1	Option 1 choice as selected by the buyer.	200
option_selection2	Option 2 choice as selected by the buyer.	200
quantity	Quantity of purchase.	
receiver_email	Primary email address of the recipient's PayPal account.	127
receiver_id	Unique account ID of recipient.	13
tax	Amount of tax charged on payment.	2 decimal places

Payment Variables

Variables used with Website Payments Standard and Website Payments Pro are shown in Table A-13.

Table A-13. *Payment Variables*

Variable	Description
auth_id	Authorization identification number.
auth_exp	Authorization expiration date and time.
auth_status	Status of authorization. Possible values: Completed Pending Voided
mc_gross_x	Amount in the currency of mc_currency, where x is the shopping cart detail item number.
mc_handling_x	Combined total of shipping and shipping2 variables. Only used when shipping amount for a specific item is submitted.
num_cart_items	If this is a PayPal Shopping Cart transaction, number of items in cart.
option_name1	Name of optional field 1.
option_name2	Name of optional field 2.

Variable	Description
`option_selection1_x`	Value of optional field 1.
`option_selection2_x`	Value of optional field 2.
`parent_txn_id`	In the case of a refund, reversal, or canceled reversal, this variable contains the `txn_id` of the original transaction.
`payment_date`	Timestamp generated by PayPal. Format: 18:30:30 Jan 1, 2000 PST.
`payment_status`	`Canceled-Reversal`: A reversal has been canceled. `Completed`: The payment has been completed. `Denied`: You denied the payment. `Expired`: This authorization has expired and cannot be captured. `Failed`: The payment has failed. `In-Progress`: The transaction is in progress (e.g., an authorization waiting for a capture or void). `Partially-Refunded`: The transaction has been partially refunded. `Pending`: The payment is pending (see `pending_reason` for why). `Processed`: All payments from the Mass Payment have been completed. `Refunded`: You refunded the payment. `Reversed`: A payment was reversed due to a chargeback or other type of reversal. `Processed`: A payment has been accepted. `Voided`: This authorization has been voided.
`payment_type`	`echeck`: Payment is funded via an eCheck. `instant`: Payment is funded with PayPal balance, credit card, or instant transfer.
`pending_reason`	Included only if `payment_status` is `Pending`. `address`: The payment is pending because your customer did not include a confirmed shipping address and your Payment Receiving Preferences is set to allow you to manually accept or deny each of these payments. `authorization`: You have not yet captured funds for an authorization. `echeck`: Payment was made by an eCheck that has not yet cleared. `intl`: Payment is pending because you hold a non-U.S. account and do not have a withdrawal mechanism. `multi-currency`: You do not have a balance in the currency sent, and you do not have your Payment Receiving Preferences set to automatically convert and accept this payment. `unilateral`: Payment is pending because it was made to an email address that is not yet registered or confirmed. `upgrade`: Payment is pending because it was made via credit card and you must upgrade to a Business or Premier account to receive the funds. `upgrade` can also mean that you have reached the monthly limit for transactions on your account. `verify`: Payment is pending because you are not yet verified. `other`: Payment is pending for a reason other than those previously listed.
`reason_code`	Included if `payment_status` is `Reversed` or `Refunded`. `chargeback`: A reversal has occurred on this transaction due to a chargeback by your customer. `guarantee`: A reversal has occurred on this transaction due to your customer triggering a money-back guarantee. `buyer-complaint`: A reversal has occurred on this transaction due to a complaint about the transaction from your customer. `refund`: A reversal has occurred on this transaction because you have given the customer a refund. `other`: A reversal has occurred on this transaction due to a reason not previously listed.

Continued

Table A-13. *Continued*

Variable	Description
remaining_settle	Amount that can be captured on the authorization this IPN references.
tax	Total tax.
transaction_entity	Type of transaction this IPN references. Possible values: auth reauth order payment
txn_id	Unique transaction ID.
txn_type	Transaction type. Possible values: cart: PayPal Shopping Cart transaction or Express Checkout with multiple items. express_checkout: Express Checkout with a single item. merch_pmt: Website Payments Pro monthly billing fee. masspay: Payment was sent via Mass Payment. send_money: Transaction originated via Send Money feature on PayPal website. virtual_terminal: Transaction originated via PayPal Virtual Terminal. web_accept: Transaction originated via Buy Now or Donation button.

Currency and Currency Exchange Variables

Variables dealing with currency exchange, if the transaction involved multiple currencies, are listed in Table A-14.

Table A-14. *Currency and Currency Exchange Variables*

Variable	Description
exchange_rate	Exchange rate used if a currency conversion occurred
mc_currency	Currency of the payment
mc_fee	Transaction fee associated with the payment
mc_gross	Amount of payment, before transaction fee is subtracted
mc_gross_x	Amount of item number x, if individual cart item details are available
mc_handling	Handling cost associated with the transaction
mc_handling_x	Handling cost of item number x, if individual cart item details are available
mc_shipping	Shipping cost associated with the transaction
settle_amount	Amount deposited into seller's primary balance after currency conversion
settle_currency	Currency of settle_amount

Auction Variables

Variables specific to an auction-based transaction, such as those originating on eBay, are listed in Table A-15.

Table A-15. *Auction Variables*

Variable	Description
auction_buyer_id	Buyer's auction ID. Maximum is 64 characters.
auction_closing_date	Auction's close date.
auction_multi_item	Number of items purchased in multi-item auction payments. Allows you to count the mc_gross for the first IPN you receive, since each item from the auction generates an IPN showing the amount for all auction items.
for_auction	Will be set to true for auction payments.

Mass Payment Variables

Variables included with IPNs associated with the MassPay API call or the file-based Mass Payment option are shown in Table A-16. For more information on Mass Payment, see Chapter 6.

Table A-16. *Mass Payment Variables*

Variable	Description
masspay_txn_id_x	Transaction ID, where x is the record number of the Mass Payment item.
mc_currency_x	Currency of the payment amount and fee, where x is the record number of the Mass Payment item.
mc_fee_x	Transaction fee, where x is the record number of the Mass Payment item.
mc_gross_x	Gross amount of the payment, where x is the record number of the Mass Payment item.
payment_date	First IPN is the timestamp when the Mass Payment started. Second IPN is the timestamp when all payments are completed or returned.
reason_code	Included if status is Failed. Possible values: 1001: Invalid User ID. 1003: Country of residence check failed. 1004: Country of funding source check failed.
receiver_email_x	Primary email address of payment recipient, where x is the record number of the Mass Payment item.
status_x	Status of the payment, where x is the record number of the Mass Payment item. Possible values: Completed: Payment has been processed. Failed: Payment failed because of insufficient PayPal balance. Reversed: Payment was not claimed after 30 days and has been returned to the sender, or the receiver's account was locked. Unclaimed: Payment remains unclaimed. Recipient has 30 days to claim Mass Payment payments.
unique_id_x	Unique ID from the input source.

Subscription Variables

Variables included with IPNs associated with subscription payments are shown in Table A-17. For more information on subscriptions, see Chapter 3.

Table A-17. *Subscription Variables*

Variable	Description
txn_type	Transaction type. Possible values: subscr_signup: New subscription. subscr_cancel: Canceled subscription. subscr_failed: Failed subscription payment. subscr_payment: Successful subscription payment. subscr_eot: End of term for a subscription. subscr_modify: Subscription has been modified.
subscr_date	Subscription start date or end date, depending on value of txn_type.
subscr_effective	Date when modified subscription will become effective, if txn_type is subscr_modify.
period1	Trial subscription first interval time period (e.g., six weeks would be 6 W).
period2	Trial subscription second interval time period.
period3	Regular subscription billing interval.
mc_amount1	Billing amount for the first trial period.
mc_amount2	Billing amount for the second trial period.
mc_amount3	Billing amount for the regular billing interval.
mc_currency	Currency for billing amounts.
recurring	If set to 1, the subscription is recurring.
reattempt	If set to 1, failed subscription payments will be reattempted up to two additional times.
retry_at	Date when PayPal will reattempt the failed subscription payment.
recur_times	Number of payment installments that will occur at the regular rate.
username	If Subscription Password Management is used, this is the PayPal-generated username.
password	If Subscription Password Management is used, this is the PayPal-generated password.
subscr_id	PayPal-generated unique identifier for the subscriber.

Dispute Notification Variables

Variables included with IPNs associated with dispute notifications are shown in Table A-18. For more information on PayPal's dispute resolution process, see Chapter 9.

Table A-18. *Dispute Notification Variables*

Variable	Description
txn_type	Will be set to new_case for the new case IPN.
txn_id	Seller's original transaction ID for which the dispute has been filed.
case_id	Case identification number. Format: PP-nnn-nnn-nnn, where n is a digit.
case_type	Case type. Possible values: complaint: Buyer filed a complaint via the Resolution Center chargeback: Buyer filed a complaint with his or her bank, which has then notified PayPal.
case_creation_date	Timestamp when case was created. Format: HH:mm:ss mon DD, YYYY TZ, where TZ is the three-character time zone.
reason_code	Reason for the case. Possible values: non_receipt: Buyer claims he or she did not receive goods or services paid for. not_as_described: Buyer claims goods and services received differ significantly from description. unauthorized: Buyer claims he or she did not authorize transaction. duplicate: Buyer claims a duplicate payment was made. merchandise: Buyer claims merchandise is damaged or unsatisfactory. special: Some other reason.

API Error Codes

This section contains PayPal API error codes and their corresponding messages. Each API error returns a short message and a long message. If you want to display an error code to a customer, such as on a failed credit card transaction, use the long message.

General API Errors

The error codes shown in Table A-19 can occur with any API call.

Table A-19. *General API Error Codes*

Variable	Short Message	Long Message
10001	Internal Error	Internal Error
10002	Authentication/Authorization Failed	Client certificate is disabled
10002	Authentication/Authorization Failed	You do not have permissions to make this API call
10006	Version error	Version is not supported
10008	Security error	Security header is not valid
10101	This API Temporarily Unavailable	This API is temporarily unavailable. Please try later.

Authorization & Capture API Error Codes

The error codes shown in Table A-20 can occur when using any of the APIs related to authorizations, captures, orders, and voids.

Table A-20. *Authorization & Capture API Error Codes*

Variable	Short Message	Long Message
10004	Internal Error	Invalid argument
10004	Transaction refused because of an invalid argument	Currency is not supported
10009	Transaction refused	Account is locked or inactive
10009	Transaction refused	Account is restricted
10010	Invalid Invoice	Non-ASCII invoice id is not supported
10011	Invalid transaction id value	Transaction refused because of an invalid transaction id value
10600	Authorization voided	Authorization is voided
10601	Authorization expired	Authorization has expired
10602	Authorization completed	Authorization has already been completed
10603	The buyer is restricted	The buyer account is restricted
10604	Authorization must include both buyer and seller	Authorization transaction cannot be unilateral. It must include both buyer and seller to make an auth
10605	Unsupported currency	Currency is not supported
10606	Buyer cannot pay	Transaction rejected, please contact the buyer
10607	Auth&Capture unavailable	Authorization & Capture feature unavailable
10608	Funding source missing	The funding source is missing
10609	Invalid TransactionID	Transaction id is invalid
10610	Amount limit exceeded	Amount specified exceeds allowable limit
10611	Not enabled	Authorization & Capture feature is not enabled for the merchant
10612	No more settlement	Maximum number of allowable settlements has been reached for the authorization
10613	Currency mismatch	Currency of capture must be the same as currency of authorization
10614	Cannot void reauth	You can void only the original authorization, not a reauthorization
10615	Cannot reauth reauth	You can reauthorize only the original authorization, not a reauthorization
10616	Maximum number of reauthorization allowed for the auth is reached	Maximum number of reauthorization allowed for the auth is reached
10617	Reauthorization not allowed	Reauthorization is not allowed inside honor period
10618	Transaction already voided or expired	Transaction has already been voided or expired

Variable	Short Message	Long Message
10619	Invoice ID value exceeds maximum allowable length	Invoice ID value exceeds maximum allowable length
10620	Order has already been voided or expired	Order has already been voided or expired
10621	Order has expired	Order has expired
10622	Order is voided	Order is voided
10623	Maximum number of authorization allowed for the order is reached	Maximum number of authorization allowed for the order is reached
10624	Duplicate invoice	Payment has already been made for this InvoiceID
10625	Transaction refused because of an invalid argument	The amount exceeds the maximum amount for a single transaction
10626	Risk	Transaction refused due to risk model
10627	Transaction refused because of an invalid argument	The invoice ID field is not supported for basic authorizations
10628	This transaction cannot be processed at this time	This transaction cannot be processed at this time
10630	Item amount is invalid	Item amount is invalid

Direct Payment API Error Codes

The error codes shown in Table A-21 can occur when using the DoDirectPayment API. If you choose to display an error code to a customer for a failed transaction, use the long message, not the short message.

Table A-21. *Direct Payment API Error Codes*

Variable	Short Message	Long Message
10004	Transaction refused because of an invalid argument	Handling total is invalid
10004	Transaction refused because of an invalid argument	Item total is invalid
10004	Transaction refused because of an invalid argument	Shipping total is invalid
10004	Transaction refused because of an invalid argument	Tax total is invalid
10102	PaymentAction of Order Temporarily Unavailable	PaymentAction of Order is temporarily unavailable
10400	Transaction refused because of an invalid argument	Order total is missing
10418	Transaction refused because of an invalid argument	The currencies of the shopping cart amounts must be the same

Continued

Table A-21. *Continued*

Variable	Short Message	Long Message
10500	Invalid Configuration	This transaction cannot be processed due to an invalid merchant configuration
10501	Invalid Configuration	This transaction cannot be processed due to an invalid merchant configuration
10502	Invalid Data	This transaction cannot be processed. Please use a valid credit card.
10503	Credit Limit Exceeded	The transaction failed as a result of the card exceeding the credit limit
10504	Invalid Data	This transaction cannot be processed. Please enter a valid Credit Card Verification Number.
10505	Gateway Decline	This transaction cannot be processed
10506	Transaction Declined	The transaction was declined
10507	Invalid Configuration	This transaction cannot be processed
10508	Invalid Data	Please enter a valid credit card expiration date. The expiration date must be a two-digit month and four-digit year.
10509	Invalid Data	This transaction cannot be processed
10510	Invalid Data	The credit card type is not supported
10511	Invalid Data	This transaction cannot be processed
10512	Invalid Data	This transaction cannot be processed. Please enter a first name.
10513	Invalid Data	This transaction cannot be processed. Please enter a last name.
10514	Street address 1 in the billing address is missing	Street address 1 in the billing address is missing
10515	The city in the billing address is missing	The city in the billing address is missing
10516	The state in the billing address is missing	The state in the billing address is missing
10517	The country in the billing address is missing	The country in the billing address is missing
10518	The zip code in the billing address is missing	The zip code in the billing address is missing
10519	Invalid Data	Please enter a credit card
10520	Invalid Data	This transaction cannot be processed
10521	Invalid Data	This transaction cannot be processed. Please enter a valid credit card.
10522	Invalid credit card number	Please check to make sure that the credit card number is valid
10523	Internal Error	This transaction cannot be processed

Variable	Short Message	Long Message
10524	Missing Shipping Address Name	You have passed shipping address without a name
10525	Invalid Data	This transaction cannot be processed. The amount to be charged is zero.
10526	Invalid Data	This transaction cannot be processed. The currency is not supported at this time.
10527	Invalid Data	This transaction cannot be processed. Please enter a valid credit card number and type.
10528	Unable to make this transaction	Unable to make this transaction. It is possible that the amount would exceed the spending limit of the payer.
10529	Street address 1 in the shipping address is missing	Street address 1 in the shipping address is missing
10530	The city in the shipping address is missing	The city in the shipping address is missing
10531	The state in the shipping address is missing	The state in the shipping address is missing
10532	The country in the shipping address is missing	The country in the shipping address is missing
10533	The zip code in the shipping address is missing	The zip code in the shipping address is missing
10534	Gateway Decline	This transaction cannot be processed. Please enter a valid credit card number and type.
10535	Gateway Decline	This transaction cannot be processed. Please enter a valid credit card number and type.
10536	Invalid Data	The transaction was refused as a result of a duplicate invoice ID supplied.
10537	Filter Decline	This transaction cannot be processed. The transaction was declined by the country filter managed by the merchant.
10538	Filter Decline	This transaction cannot be processed
10539	Filter Decline	This transaction cannot be processed
10540	Invalid Data	The transaction cannot be processed due to an invalid address
10541	Gateway Decline	This transaction cannot be processed. Please enter a valid credit card number and type.
10542	Invalid Data	This transaction cannot be processed. Please enter a valid email address.
10543	Credit Card Authorization Failed	We failed to authorize the credit card

Continued

Table A-21. *Continued*

Variable	Short Message	Long Message
10544	Gateway Decline	This transaction cannot be processed
10545	Gateway Decline	The transaction was refused
10546	Gateway Decline	This transaction cannot be processed
10547	Internal Error	This transaction cannot be processed
10548	Invalid Configuration	This transaction cannot be processed. The merchant's account is not able to process transactions.
10549	Invalid Configuration	This transaction cannot be processed. The merchant's account is not able to process transactions.
10550	Invalid Configuration	This transaction cannot be processed. Access to Direct Payment was disabled for your account.
10552	Invalid Configuration	This transaction cannot be processed. The merchant account attempting the transaction does not have a confirmed email address with PayPal.
10553	Gateway Decline	This transaction cannot be processed. The merchant attempted a transaction where the amount exceeded the upper limit for that merchant.
10554	Filter Decline	This transaction cannot be processed because of a merchant risk filter for AVS
10555	Filter Decline	This transaction cannot be processed because of a merchant risk filter for AVS
10556	Filter Decline	This transaction cannot be processed because of a merchant risk filter for AVS
10701	Invalid Data	There's an error with this transaction. Please enter a valid billing address.
10702	Invalid Data	There's an error with this transaction. Please enter a valid address1 in the billing address.
10703	Invalid Data	There's an error with this transaction. Please enter a valid address2 in the billing address.
10704	Invalid Data	There's an error with this transaction. Please enter a valid city in the billing address.
10705	Invalid Data	There's an error with this transaction. Please enter a valid two-character state in the billing address.
10706	Invalid Data	There's an error with this transaction. Please enter your five digit postal code in the billing address.
10707	Invalid Data	There's an error with this transaction. Please enter a valid country in the billing address.
10708	Invalid Data	There's an error with this transaction. Please enter a complete billing address.
10709	Invalid Data	There's an error with this transaction. Please enter an address1 in the billing address.
10710	Invalid Data	There's an error with this transaction. Please enter a city in the billing address.
10711	Invalid Data	There's an error with this transaction. Please enter your state in the billing address.

Variable	Short Message	Long Message
10712	Invalid Data	There's an error with this transaction. Please enter your five digit postal code in the billing address.
10713	Invalid Data	There's an error with this transaction. Please enter a country in the billing address.
10713	Invalid Data	There's an error with this transaction. Please enter a country in the billing address.
10714	Invalid Data	There's an error with this transaction. Please enter a valid billing address.
10715	Invalid Data	There's an error with this transaction. Please enter a valid state in the billing address.
10716	Invalid Data	There's an error with this transaction. Please enter your five digit postal code in the billing address.
10717	Invalid Data	There's an error with this transaction. Please enter your five digit postal code in the billing address.
10718	Invalid Data	There's an error with this transaction. Please enter a valid city and state in the billing address.
10719	Invalid Data	There's an error with this transaction. Please enter a valid shipping address.
10720	Invalid Data	There's an error with this transaction. Please enter a valid address1 in the shipping address.
10721	Invalid Data	There's an error with this transaction. Please enter a valid address2 in the shipping address.
10722	Invalid Data	There's an error with this transaction. Please enter a valid city in the shipping address.
10723	Invalid Data	There's an error with this transaction. Please enter a valid state in the shipping address.
10724	Invalid Data	There's an error with this transaction. Please enter your five digit postal code in the shipping address.
10725	Invalid Data	There's an error with this transaction. Please enter a valid country in the shipping address.
10726	Invalid Data	There's an error with this transaction. Please enter a complete shipping address.
10727	Invalid Data	There's an error with this transaction. Please enter an address1 in the shipping address.
10728	Invalid Data	There's an error with this transaction. Please enter a city in the shipping address.
10729	Invalid Data	There's an error with this transaction. Please enter your state in the shipping address.
10730	Invalid Data	There's an error with this transaction. Please enter your five digit postal code in the shipping address.
10731	Invalid Data	There's an error with this transaction. Please enter a country in the shipping address.
10732	Invalid Data	There's an error with this transaction. Please enter a valid shipping address.

Continued

Table A-21. *Continued*

Variable	Short Message	Long Message
10733	Invalid Data	There's an error with this transaction. Please enter a valid state in the shipping address.
10734	Invalid Data	There's an error with this transaction. Please enter your five digit postal code in the shipping address.
10735	Invalid Data	There's an error with this transaction. Please enter your five digit postal code in the shipping address.
10736	Invalid Data	There's an error with this transaction. Please enter a valid city and state in the shipping address.
10744	Invalid Data	This transaction cannot be processed. Please enter a valid country code in the billing address.
10745	Invalid Data	This transaction cannot be processed. Please enter a valid country code in the shipping address.
10746	Invalid Data	This transaction cannot be processed. Please use a valid country on the billing address.
10747	Invalid Data	This transaction cannot be processed
10748	Invalid Data	This transaction cannot be processed without a Credit Card Verification number
10750	Invalid Data	This transaction cannot be processed without a Credit Card Verification number
10751	Invalid Data	There's an error with this transaction. Please enter a valid state in the billing address.
10752	Gateway Decline	This transaction cannot be processed. (Usually CVV or AVS check)
10754	Gateway Decline	This transaction cannot be processed
10755	Invalid Data	This transaction cannot be processed due to an unsupported currency
10756	Gateway Decline	The transaction cannot be processed. The country and billing address associated with this credit card do not match.
10758	Invalid Configuration	There's been an error due to invalid API username and/or password
10759	Gateway Decline	This transaction cannot be processed. Please enter a valid credit card number and type.
10760	Invalid Configuration	This transaction cannot be processed. The country listed for your business address is not currently supported.
10761	Gateway Decline	This transaction cannot be processed. Please check the status of your first transaction before placing another order.
10762	Gateway Decline	This transaction cannot be processed. Check CVV code with card type.
10763	Invalid Data	This transaction cannot be processed.
15001	Gateway Decline	The transaction was rejected by PayPal because of excessive failures over a short period of time for this credit card
15002	Gateway Decline	The transaction was declined by PayPal

Variable	Short Message	Long Message
15003	Invalid Configuration	The transaction was declined because the merchant does not have a valid commercial entity agreement on file with PayPal
15004	Gateway Decline	This transaction cannot be processed. Please enter a valid Credit Card Verification Number
15005	Processor Decline	The transaction was declined by the issuing bank, not PayPal
15006	Processor Decline	Please enter a valid credit card number and type. The transaction was declined by the issuing bank, not PayPal.
15007	Processor Decline	This transaction cannot be processed. Please use a valid credit card.

Express Checkout API Error Codes

The error codes shown in Table A-22 can occur when using PayPal's Express Checkout APIs. If you choose to display an error code to a customer for a failed transaction, use the long message, not the short message.

Table A-22. *Express Checkout API Error Codes*

Variable	Short Message	Long Message
10004	Transaction refused because of an invalid argument	Handling total is invalid
10004	Transaction refused because of an invalid argument	Item total is invalid
10004	Transaction refused because of an invalid argument	Shipping total is invalid
10004	Transaction refused because of an invalid argument	Tax total is invalid
10004	Transaction refused because of an invalid argument	Maximum amount is invalid
10400	Transaction refused because of an invalid argument	Order total is missing
10401	Transaction refused because of an invalid argument	Currency is not supported
10401	Transaction refused because of an invalid argument	Order total is invalid
10402	Authorization only is not allowed for merchant	This merchant account is not permitted to set PaymentAction to Authorization
10403	Transaction refused because of an invalid argument	Currency is not supported
10403	Transaction refused because of an invalid argument	Maximum amount is invalid
10404	Invalid argument	ReturnURL is missing

Continued

Table A-22. *Continued*

Variable	Short Message	Long Message
10405	Invalid argument	CancelURL is missing
10406	Invalid argument	PayerID value is invalid
10407	Invalid argument	Invalid buyer email address
10408	Express Checkout token is missing	Express Checkout token is missing
10409	You are not authorized to access this info	Express Checkout token was issued for a merchant account other than yours
10410	Invalid token	Invalid token
10411	Express Checkout session has expired	Express Checkout session has expired. Token value is no longer valid.
10412	Duplicate invoice	Payment has already been made for this InvoiceID
10413	Invalid argument	The totals of the cart item amounts do not match order amounts
10414	Invalid argument	The amount exceeds the maximum amount for a single transaction
10415	Invalid argument	A successful transaction has already been completed for this token
10416	Invalid argument	You have exceeded the maximum number of payment attempts for this token
10417	Transaction cannot complete	The transaction cannot complete successfully
10418	Invalid argument	The currencies of the shopping cart amounts must be the same
10419	Express checkout PayerID is missing	Express Checkout PayerID is missing
10420	Invalid argument	Express Checkout PaymentAction is missing
10421	This Express Checkout session belongs to a different customer	This Express Checkout session belongs to a different customer. Token value mismatch.
10422	Customer must choose new funding sources	The customer must return to PayPal to select new funding sources
10423	Invalid argument	This transaction cannot be completed with PaymentAction of Authorization
10424	Invalid argument	Shipping address is invalid
10425	Express Checkout has been disabled for this merchant	Express Checkout has been disabled for this merchant
10426	Invalid argument	Item total is invalid
10427	Invalid argument	Shipping total is invalid
10428	Invalid argument	Handling total is invalid
10429	Invalid argument	Tax total is invalid
10430	Invalid argument	Item amount is missing
10431	Invalid argument	Item amount is invalid

Variable	Short Message	Long Message
10432	Invalid argument	Invoice ID value exceeds maximum allowable length
10433	Invalid argument	Value of OrderDescription element has been truncated
10434	Invalid argument	Value of Custom element has been truncated
10435	Invalid argument	The customer has not yet confirmed payment for this Express Checkout session
10436	Invalid argument	PageStyle value exceeds maximum allowable length
10437	Invalid argument	cpp-header-image value exceeds maximum allowable length
10438	Invalid argument	cpp-header-border-color value exceeds maximum allowable length
10439	Invalid argument	cpp-header-back-color value exceeds maximum allowable length
10440	Invalid argument	cpp-payflow-color value exceeds maximum allowable length
10441	Transaction refused because of an invalid argument	The NotifyURL element value exceeds maximum allowable length
10442	Button Source value truncated	The ButtonSource element value exceeds maximum allowable length
10443	This transaction cannot be completed with PaymentAction of Order	This transaction cannot be completed with PaymentAction of Order
10445	This transaction cannot be processed at this time	This transaction cannot be processed at this time. Please try again later
10446	Unconfirmed email	A confirmed email is required to make this API call
10727	Shipping Address1 Empty	The field Shipping Address1 is required
10728	Shipping Address City Empty	The field Shipping Address City is required
10729	Shipping Address State Empty	The field Shipping Address State is required
10730	Shipping Address Postal Code Empty	The field Shipping Address Postal Code is required
10731	Shipping Address Country Empty	
10736	Shipping Address Invalid City State Postal Code	A match of the Shipping Address City, State, and Postal Code failed

GetTransactionDetails API Error Codes

The error codes shown in Table A-23 can occur when using PayPal's GetTransactionDetails API.

Table A-23. *GetTransactionDetails API Error Codes*

Variable	Short Message	Long Message
10004	Invalid transaction type	You can not get the details for this type of transaction
10007	Permission denied	You do not have permission to get the details of this transaction

MassPay API Error Codes

The error codes shown in Table A-24 can occur when using PayPal's MassPay API.

Table A-24. *MassPay API Error Codes*

Variable	Short Message	Long Message
10003	Missing argument	The amount is missing
10003	Missing argument	The currency is missing
10004	Transaction refused because of an invalid argument	The amount is less than or equal to zero
10004	Transaction refused because of an invalid argument	The amount is missing
10004	Transaction refused because of an invalid argument	The amount is not a valid number
10004	Transaction refused because of an invalid argument	The currency is missing
10004	Transaction refused because of an invalid argument	The masspay receiver_type is not a recognizable type
10004	Transaction refused because of an invalid argument	The note string length exceeds the maximum limit of 4000 characters
10004	Transaction refused because of an invalid argument	The number of input records is greater than maximum allowed
10004	Transaction refused because of an invalid argument	The number of input records is less than or equal to zero
10004	Transaction refused because of an invalid argument	The recipient's email and UserID should not be specified simultaneously
10004	Transaction refused because of an invalid argument	The recipient's email is missing
10004	Transaction refused because of an invalid argument	The recipient's UserID is missing
10004	Transaction refused because of an invalid argument	The unique id string contains a space as a character
10004	Transaction refused because of an invalid argument	The unique id string length exceeds the maximum limit of 30 characters

Variable	Short Message	Long Message
10301	User not allowed	The user is not allowed to send money through Mass Pay
10302	Account locked	The user account is locked
10303	Restricted account	Account is restricted
10304	Unconfirmed email	The user account has unconfirmed email
10305	Limit Exceeded	The user account needs to have its sending limit removed in order to make a mass payment
10306	Limit Exceeded	The user's international account needs to have its sending limit removed in order to make a mass payment
10307	Receive only account	The user account is receive only and therefore cannot send payments out
10308	MassPay server configuration error	There is some configuration error
10309	MassPay server unavailable	The mass pay server is unavailable
10310	Unable to create payment	Unable to create payments for MassPay
10311	Unable to submit payment	Unable to submit payments for MassPay
10312	MassPay server error	The MassPay server has reported errors
10313	MassPay Invalid Data	The MassPay input file includes invalid data
10314	MassPay input parse error	The input to the MassPay server is incorrect. Please make sure that you are using a correctly formatted input.
10317	MassPay Invalid Email	The MassPay input file includes invalid email
10320	Transaction limit exceeded	The amount exceeds the max limit of a single MassPay item
10321	Insufficient funds	The account does not have sufficient funds to do this MassPay
10327	MassPay Invalid UserID	The MassPay input file includes invalid UserID
10360	Unable to find the user with the email address	Unable to find the user with the email address
10361	The user account not available	The user account not available

RefundTransaction API Error Codes

The error codes shown in Table A-25 can occur when using PayPal's RefundTransaction API.

Table A-25. *RefundTransaction API Error Codes*

Variable	Short Message	Long Message
10004	Transaction refused because of an invalid argument	A transaction id is required
10004	Transaction refused because of an invalid argument	The Memo field contains invalid characters
10004	Transaction refused because of an invalid argument	The partial refund amount is not valid
10004	Transaction refused because of an invalid argument	The partial refund amount must be a positive amount
10004	Transaction refused because of an invalid argument	You can not specify a partial amount with a full refund
10007	Permission denied	You do not have permission to refund this transaction
10009	Transaction refused	Can not do a full refund after a partial refund
10009	Transaction refused	The account for the counterparty is locked or inactive
10009	Transaction refused	The partial refund amount is not valid
10009	Transaction refused	The partial refund amount must be less than or equal to the original transaction amount
10009	Transaction refused	The partial refund amount must be less than or equal to the remaining amount
10009	Transaction refused	The partial refund must be the same currency as the original transaction
10009	Transaction refused	This transaction has already been fully refunded
10009	Transaction refused	You are over the time limit to perform a refund on this transaction
10009	Transaction refused	You can not do a partial refund on this transaction
10009	Transaction refused	You can not refund this type of transaction
10009	Transaction refused	You do not have a verified ACH

TransactionSearch API Error Codes

The error codes shown in Table A-26 can occur when using PayPal's TransactionSearch API.

Table A-26. *TransactionSearch API Error Codes*

Variable	Short Message	Long Message
10003	Transaction refused because of an invalid argument	Start date is a required parameter
10004	Transaction refused because of an invalid argument	Auction item id is not valid
10004	Transaction refused because of an invalid argument	Currency is not supported
10004	Transaction refused because of an invalid argument	End date is invalid
10004	Transaction refused because of an invalid argument	Payer email is invalid
10004	Transaction refused because of an invalid argument	Receipt id is not valid
10004	Transaction refused because of an invalid argument	Receiver can only be specified for payments you've received
10004	Transaction refused because of an invalid argument	Receiver email is invalid
10004	Transaction refused because of an invalid argument	Start date is invalid
10004	Transaction refused because of an invalid argument	Transaction class is not supported
10004	Transaction refused because of an invalid argument	You can not search for a transaction id and a receipt id
10007	Permission denied	You do not have permissions to make this API call
10007	Permission denied	You do not have permissions to search for this transaction
11002	Search warning	The number of results were truncated. Please change your search parameters if you wish to see all your results.

AddressVerify API Error Codes

The error codes shown in Table A-27 can occur when using PayPal's AddressVerify API. You must be granted authorization from PayPal to use the AddressVerify API.

Table A-27. *AddressVerify API Error Codes*

Variable	Short Message	Long Message
10004	Transaction refused because of an invalid argument	Invalid email format
10004	Transaction refused because of an invalid argument	Invalid street format
10004	Transaction refused because of an invalid argument	Invalid zip format
10009	The API is disabled	The AddressVerify API is currently disabled

BillUser API Error Codes

The error codes shown in Table A-28 can occur when using PayPal's BillUser API. You must be granted authorization from PayPal to use the BillUser API.

Table A-28. *BillUser API Error Codes*

Variable	Short Message	Long Message
10004	Transaction refused because of an invalid argument	Agreement id is not valid
10004	Transaction refused because of an invalid argument	Amount is not valid
10004	Transaction refused because of an invalid argument	Handling is not valid
10004	Transaction refused because of an invalid argument	Invoice is not valid
10004	Transaction refused because of an invalid argument	Shipping is not valid
10004	Transaction refused because of an invalid argument	Tax is not valid
10004	Transaction refused because of an invalid argument	The transaction could not be loaded
10004	Transaction refused because of an invalid argument	The transaction id is not valid
10004	Internal Error	Transaction refused because of an invalid argument
10009	The API is disabled	The API is disabled
10200	No instant	User does not have instant payment funding source
10201	Agreement canceled	Agreement was canceled

Variable	Short Message	Long Message
10202	Exceed max	Transaction would exceed user's monthly maximum
10203	Action required	Transaction failed action required by user
10204	Denied	User's account is closed or restricted
10205	Risk	Transaction refused due to risk model
10206	Duplicate	Transaction was already processed
10207	Retry	Retry
10207	Retry	Transaction failed but user has alternate funding source
10209	Disabled	Preapproved Payments not enabled
10210	No Funding	Transaction failed because buyer has no funding sources
10211	Invalid MP ID	Invalid MP ID
10212	Profile preference setting	A profile preference is set to automatically deny certain transactions
11001	Invalid argument	The button source field was truncated because it was too long
11001	Transaction refused because of an invalid argument	The custom field was truncated because it was too long
11001	Transaction refused because of an invalid argument	The item name field was truncated because it was too long
11001	Transaction refused because of an invalid argument	The item number field was truncated because it was too long
11001	Transaction refused because of an invalid argument	The memo field was truncated because it was too long
11001	Transaction refused because of an invalid argument	The subject field was truncated because it was too long

Payflow Pro RESULT Codes

This section contains the RESULT codes that can be returned from a Payflow Pro transaction. With Payflow Pro, RESULT is the first variable returned in the response string. A RESULT of 0 means the transaction was approved. A RESULT greater than 0 indicates a decline or error; a RESULT less than 0 indicates a communication error. Table A-29 lists RESULT values greater than 0; Table A-30 lists RESULT values less than 0.

RESULT Values for Declines and Errors

Table A-29 lists the possible RESULT values that can occur when a Payflow Pro transaction is declined.

Table A-29. RESULT *Values for Declines and Errors*

RESULT	Meaning
1	User authentication failed. Login information or processor information may be incorrect, the transaction may be coming from an unknown IP address, or you may be submitting a test transaction to the live servers.
2	Invalid tender type. Your Internet merchant account does not support the submitted credit card type.
3	Invalid transaction type. Transaction type is not appropriate for this transaction.
4	Invalid amount format. Use the format "#####.##". Do not include currency symbols or commas.
5	Invalid merchant information. Processor does not recognize your Internet merchant account.
6	Invalid or unsupported currency code.
7	Field format error. Invalid information entered.
8	Not a transaction server.
9	Too many parameters or invalid stream.
10	Too many line items.
11	Client timeout waiting for response.
12	Declined. Check the credit card number, expiration date, and transaction information.
13	Referral. Transaction cannot be approved electronically but can be approved with a verbal authorization. Contact your merchant bank to obtain an authorization and submit a manual Voice Authorization transaction.
14	Invalid Client Certification ID. Check the HTTP header. If the tag X-VPS-VIT-CLIENT-CERTIFICATION-ID is missing, RESULT code 14 is returned.
19	Original transaction ID not found.
20	Cannot find the customer reference number.
22	Invalid ABA number.
23	Invalid account number.
24	Invalid expiration date.
25	Invalid Host Mapping. You are not set up to accept this tender card type.
26	Invalid vendor account.
27	Insufficient partner permissions.
28	Insufficient user permissions.
29	Invalid XML document.
30	Duplicate transaction.
31	Error in adding the recurring profile.
32	Error in modifying the recurring profile.
33	Error in canceling the recurring profile.

RESULT	Meaning
34	Error in forcing the recurring profile.
35	Error in reactivating the recurring profile.
36	OLTP Transaction failed.
37	Invalid recurring profile ID.
50	Insufficient funds available in account.
99	General error. See RESPMSG.
100	Transaction type not supported by host.
101	Timeout value too small.
102	Processor not available.
103	Error reading response from host.
104	Timeout waiting for processor response. Try your transaction again.
105	Credit error. Make sure you have not already credited this transaction, or that this transaction ID is for a creditable transaction (e.g., you cannot credit an authorization).
106	Host not available.
107	Duplicate suppression timeout.
108	Void error.
109	Timeout waiting for host response.
111	Capture error. Either an attempt to capture a transaction that is not an authorization transaction type, or an attempt to capture an authorization transaction that has already been captured.
112	Failed AVS check. Address and ZIP code do not match.
113	Merchant sales total will exceed the sales cap with current transaction. ACH transactions only.
114	Card Security Code (CSC) mismatch. An authorization may still exist on the cardholder's account.
115	System busy; try again later.
116	VPS Internal error. Failed to lock terminal number.
117	Failed merchant rule check.
118	Invalid keywords found in string fields.
122	Merchant sale total will exceed the credit cap with current transaction. ACH transactions only.
125	Fraud Protection Services Filter—declined by filters.
126	Fraud Protection Services Filter—flagged for review by filters. The transaction flagged your account's fraud filters and needs to be manually reviewed to accept.
127	Fraud Protection Services Filter—not processed by filters.
128	Fraud Protection Services Filter—declined by merchant after being flagged for review by filters.
131	Version 1 Payflow Pro SDK client no longer supported.
150	Issuing bank timed out.
151	Issuing bank unavailable.

Continued

Table A-29. *Continued*

RESULT	Meaning
1000	Generic host error returned by your credit card processor.
1001	Buyer Authentication Service unavailable.
1002	Buyer Authentication Service—transaction timeout.
1003	Buyer Authentication Service—invalid client version.
1004	Buyer Authentication Service—invalid timeout value.
1011	Buyer Authentication Service unavailable.
1012	Buyer Authentication Service unavailable.
1013	Buyer Authentication Service unavailable.
1014	Buyer Authentication Service—merchant is not enrolled for Buyer Authentication Service (3-D Secure).
1016	Buyer Authentication Service—3-D Secure error response received. Instead of receiving a PARES response to a Validate Authentication transaction, an error response was received.
1017	Buyer Authentication Service—3-D Secure error response is invalid. An error response is received and the response is not well formed for a Validate Authentication transaction.
1021	Buyer Authentication Service—invalid card type.
1022	Buyer Authentication Service—invalid or missing currency code.
1023	Buyer Authentication Service—merchant status for 3D secure is invalid.
1041	Buyer Authentication Service—Validate Authentication failed: missing or invalid PARES.
1042	Buyer Authentication Service—Validate Authentication failed: PARES format is invalid.
1043	Buyer Authentication Service—Validate Authentication failed: cannot find successful Verify Enrollment.
1044	Buyer Authentication Service—Validate Authentication failed: signature validation failed for PARES.
1045	Buyer Authentication Service—Validate Authentication failed: mismatched or invalid amount in PARES.
1046	Buyer Authentication Service—Validate Authentication failed: mismatched or invalid acquirer in PARES.
1047	Buyer Authentication Service—Validate Authentication failed: mismatched or invalid Merchant ID in PARES.
1048	Buyer Authentication Service—Validate Authentication failed: mismatched or invalid card number in PARES.
1049	Buyer Authentication Service—Validate Authentication failed: mismatched or invalid currency code in PARES.
1050	Buyer Authentication Service—Validate Authentication failed: mismatched or invalid XID in PARES.
1051	Buyer Authentication Service—Validate Authentication failed: mismatched or invalid order date in PARES.
1052	Buyer Authentication Service—Validate Authentication failed: this PARES was already validated for a previous Validate Authentication transaction.

RESULT Values for Communication Errors

Table A-30 lists the possible RESULT values that can occur when the Payflow Pro transaction does not occur because of a communication error.

Table A-30. RESULT *Values for Communication Errors*

RESULT	Meaning
-1	Failed to connect to host
-2	Failed to resolve hostname
-5	Failed to initialize SSL context
-6	Parameter list format error: & in name
-7	Parameter list format error: invalid [ ] name length clause
-8	SSL failed to connect to host
-9	SSL read failed
-10	SSL write failed
-11	Proxy authorization failed
-12	Timeout waiting for response
-13	Select failure
-14	Too many connections
-15	Failed to set socket options
-20	Proxy read failed
-21	Proxy write failed
-22	Failed to initialize SSL certificate
-23	Host address not specified
-24	Invalid transaction type
-25	Failed to create a socket
-26	Failed to initialize socket layer
-27	Parameter list format error: invalid [ ] name length clause
-28	Parameter list format error: name
-29	Failed to initialize SSL connection
-30	Invalid timeout value
-31	The certificate chain did not validate, no local certificate found
-32	The certificate chain did not validate, common name did not match URL
-40	Unexpected Request ID found in request
-41	Required Request ID not found in request
-99	Out of memory
-100	Parameter list cannot be empty
-103	Context initialization failed
-104	Unexpected transaction state

Continued

Table A-30. *Continued*

RESULT	Meaning
-105	Invalid name/value pair request
-106	Invalid response format
-107	This XMLPay version is not supported
-108	The server certificate chain did not validate
-109	Unable to do logging
-111	The following error occurred while initializing from message file: . . .
-113	Unable to round and truncate the currency value simultaneously

Payflow Link Variable Reference

Table A-31 contains the variables that can be included in a Payflow Link HTML form transaction.

Table A-31. *Payflow Link Variable Reference*

Variable	Description	Maximum Length
ADDRESS	Billing address.	60
ADDRESSTOSHIP	Shipping address.	120
CARDNUM	Credit card number.	31
CITY	Billing city.	32
CITYTOSHIP	Shipping city.	32
COUNTRY	Billing country.	4
COUNTRYCODE	Shipping country.	4
COMMENT1	Custom value; information appears in Custom Report.	255
COMMENT2	Custom value; information appears in Custom Report.	255
CSC	Card Security Code.	4
CUSTID	Custom; value can be returned to your web server with the Post or Silent Post feature.	11
DESCRIPTION	Transaction description.	255
DLNUM	Driver's license number (TeleCheck transactions only).	33
ECHODATA	True/False: Return verbose amount of data when Payflow Link using the Post or Silent Post feature. Default: True.	5
EMAIL	Billing email address.	40
EMAILCUSTOMER	True/False: Whether or not to send the customer a notification email when a successful transaction occurs. Default: Set in PayPal Manager.	5
EMAILTOSHIP	Shipping email address.	40
EXPDATE	Card expiration date.	7
FAX	Billing fax number.	20

Variable	Description	Maximum Length
FAXTOSHIP	Shipping fax number.	20
INVOICE	Invoice number.	9
METHOD	Method of customer payment: C for credit card, ECHECK for electronic check.	
NAME	Billing name.	60
NAMETOSHIP	Shipping name.	60
ORDERFORM	True/False: Controls whether the customer's browser is redirected to the Payflow Link Order form, on which the customer enters transaction information. Default: True.	5
PHONE	Billing phone.	20
PHONETOSHIP	Shipping phone.	20
PONUM	Purchase order number.	25
SHIPAMOUNT	The cost of shipping. Decimal number with two decimal places.	
SHOWCONFIRM	True/False: Controls whether the Payflow Link Confirmation page is displayed to the customer before submitting the transaction. Default: True.	5
STATE	Billing state.	20
STATETOSHIP	Shipping state.	20
TAX	The amount of tax on a transaction.	12
USER1	Merchant-defined value; not shown to customer. Returned to merchant with the Post or Silent Post feature.	255
USER2	Merchant-defined value; not shown to customer. Returned to merchant with the Post or Silent Post feature.	255
USER3	Merchant-defined value; not shown to customer. Returned to merchant with the Post or Silent Post feature.	v
USER4	Merchant-defined value; not shown to customer. Returned to merchant with the Post or Silent Post feature.	255
USER5	Merchant-defined value; not shown to customer. Returned to merchant with the Post or Silent Post feature.	255
USER6	Merchant-defined value; not shown to customer. Returned to merchant with the Post or Silent Post feature.	255
USER7	Merchant-defined value; not shown to customer. Returned to merchant with the Post or Silent Post feature.	255
USER8	Merchant-defined value; not shown to customer. Returned to merchant with the Post or Silent Post feature.	255
USER9	Merchant-defined value; not shown to customer. Returned to merchant with the Post or Silent Post feature.	255
USER10	Merchant-defined value; not shown to customer. Returned to merchant with the Post or Silent Post feature.	255
ZIP	Billing ZIP code.	15
ZIPTOSHIP	Shipping ZIP code.	15

Index

forums.apress.com

FOR PROFESSIONALS BY PROFESSIONALS™

JOIN THE APRESS FORUMS AND BE PART OF OUR COMMUNITY. You'll find discussions that cover topics of interest to IT professionals, programmers, and enthusiasts just like you. If you post a query to one of our forums, you can expect that some of the best minds in the business—especially Apress authors, who all write with *The Expert's Voice*™—will chime in to help you. Why not aim to become one of our most valuable participants (MVPs) and win cool stuff? Here's a sampling of what you'll find:

DATABASES

Data drives everything.

Share information, exchange ideas, and discuss any database programming or administration issues.

PROGRAMMING/BUSINESS

Unfortunately, it is.

Talk about the Apress line of books that cover software methodology, best practices, and how programmers interact with the "suits."

INTERNET TECHNOLOGIES AND NETWORKING

Try living without plumbing (and eventually IPv6).

Talk about networking topics including protocols, design, administration, wireless, wired, storage, backup, certifications, trends, and new technologies.

WEB DEVELOPMENT/DESIGN

Ugly doesn't cut it anymore, and CGI is absurd.

Help is in sight for your site. Find design solutions for your projects and get ideas for building an interactive Web site.

JAVA

We've come a long way from the old Oak tree.

Hang out and discuss Java in whatever flavor you choose: J2SE, J2EE, J2ME, Jakarta, and so on.

SECURITY

Lots of bad guys out there—the good guys need help.

Discuss computer and network security issues here. Just don't let anyone else know the answers!

MAC OS X

All about the Zen of OS X.

OS X is both the present and the future for Mac apps. Make suggestions, offer up ideas, or boast about your new hardware.

TECHNOLOGY IN ACTION

Cool things. Fun things.

It's after hours. It's time to play. Whether you're into LEGO® MINDSTORMS™ or turning an old PC into a DVR, this is where technology turns into fun.

OPEN SOURCE

Source code is good; understanding (open) source is better.

Discuss open source technologies and related topics such as PHP, MySQL, Linux, Perl, Apache, Python, and more.

WINDOWS

No defenestration here.

Ask questions about all aspects of Windows programming, get help on Microsoft technologies covered in Apress books, or provide feedback on any Apress Windows book.

HOW TO PARTICIPATE:

Go to the Apress Forums site at **http://forums.apress.com/**.

Click the New User link.

You Need the Companion eBook

Your purchase of this book entitles you to buy the companion PDF-version eBook for only $10. Take the weightless companion with you anywhere.

We believe this Apress title will prove so indispensable that you'll want to carry it with you everywhere, which is why we are offering the companion eBook (in PDF format) for $10 to customers who purchase this book now. Convenient and fully searchable, the PDF version of any content-rich, page-heavy Apress book makes a valuable addition to your programming library. You can easily find and copy code—or perform examples by quickly toggling between instructions and the application. Even simultaneously tackling a donut, diet soda, and complex code becomes simplified with hands-free eBooks!

Once you purchase your book, getting the $10 companion eBook is simple:

❶ Visit **www.apress.com/promo/tendollars/**.

❷ Complete a basic registration form to receive a randomly generated question about this title.

❸ Answer the question correctly in 60 seconds, and you will receive a promotional code to redeem for the $10.00 eBook.

2560 Ninth Street • Suite 219 • Berkeley, CA 94710

eBookshop

Offer valid through 9/12/07.